When the Comm
they drove the m
largest mission fie
lost. This forceful .... minister of
the United Church of Canada who has
seen at first hand the problems confronting
Chinese Christians sets out to explain this
situation — no new story in Christian
history. Five times in 1,300 years great
waves of missionary activity succeeded
in planting Christianity in China, only to
lose out every time. Dr. Outerbridge be-
lieves that these losses in China were not
accidental, but were caused by glaring mistakes repeatedly made. Through a study
of both ancient and modern history, Dr.
Outerbridge tells why the Western world
lost both religious and political opportunities in China, and points the way to cor-
recting past mistakes and recapturing lost
ground in China.

First he discusses China's own religious
heritage, pointing out that the ancient religious concepts of China were higher than
those of Europeans in the same period, and
that China's moral background kept a
light of truth burning in Asia for 4,000
years. He shows, however, that missionaries very often ignored the values in this
heritage of China and purposefully broke
down Confucian ethics.

He tells the story of the Nestorians,
twice suppressed in China, the Jesuits, and
the Protestants, and how each group lost

out through political disfavor, competition with other orders, or mistaken methods of achieving its goal. In the twentieth century a long series of irritants to the Chinese people culminated in complete devastation and disillusionment after the secret deal at Yalta was made known. Missionaries were handicapped by the people's resentment of powers that had betrayed them, and finally the Communists won out in China by default. The Churches then faced their most overwhelming losses, as an agnostic generation arose in China, to which the missionaries themselves had unwittingly contributed by helping to undercut the traditional Confucianism without filling the void.

However, according to Dr. Outerbridge, Christians may hope and expect that after the Communists have suppressed the rights of individuals long enough, the people will again assert themselves. He concludes that, judging by the records of history, Christianity has lost out in China whenever it has allied itself with a political power, when it has failed to appreciate the Chinese religious heritage, when it has dissipated its influence through divisions and competitions, and when it has concentrated on a social message and program to the neglect of its basic spiritual message.

Today Christians of the West must recognize the mistakes that have been made in China; see Communism as a rival religion which is filling a void in Chinese life and subverting Christianity; and prepare missionaries through careful study of China's history and heritage, to go back and recoup losses when doors open again.

This thoughtful and readable book will be of especial interest not only to lay people, ministers, and mission-minded persons of many denominations, but also to non-Church people concerned with China and the Far East.

THE LOST CHURCHES OF CHINA

THE *Lost* *Churches* OF *China*

LEONARD M. OUTERBRIDGE

Philadelphia
THE WESTMINSTER PRESS

COPYRIGHT, MCMLII, BY W. L. JENKINS

Library of Congress Catalogue Card Number: 52–8859

Distributed in the Dominion of Canada exclusively by
The Ryerson Press, Toronto

PRINTED IN THE UNITED STATES OF AMERICA

PREFACE

M Y OBLIGATION to others for suggestions, encouragement, and criticisms is very great. I am especially grateful to Dr. Lorne A. Pierce, of Toronto, for the challenge to survey the problem of the lost Churches of China, and for his continued counsel throughout this undertaking. My thanks are expressed to Dr. Arthur W. Hummel, of the Library of Congress, for his gift, during my first years in China, of opening the window through which I began to discern the hand of the Eternal in China's historic past. I would also especially thank His Holiness Mar Eshai Shimun XXIII, Catholicos Patriarch of the East; and the Rev. Irwin St. John Tucker, St. Stephen's Episcopal Church, Chicago, who have given invaluable data on the history of the Nestorians.

I have leaned heavily on many friends, particularly Dean Bernard M. Loomer, and Professors Joachim Wach and Wilhelm Pauck, of the Federated Theological Faculty of the University of Chicago. Professor E. A. Kracke, of the Oriental Institute of the University of Chicago, has given valued help on the period of the Nestorians. Grateful acknowledgment is also made of the suggestions and encouragement received from Dean James S. Thomson, of the Faculty of Divinity of McGill University; Professor Hugh S. G. Garven, of Glasgow University; and Dr. Paul L. Meacham, of Philadelphia. My indebtedness to colleagues and friends is extensive. I am glad to express a deep sense of obligation.

2593

The greatest assistance has been given by my wife, who has been my companion and colleague in all the experiences and study involved in this work. The responsibilities for the inadequacies herein rest alone upon the author. These pages are not exhaustive. The subject is vast. The nature is complex. The defense must be a frank confession like that ascribed by Confucius to the man "who wished to make his faults few, but had not yet succeeded."

LEONARD M. OUTERBRIDGE.

CONTENTS

CONTENTS

INTRODUCTION

CHINA, with nearly one fourth of the human race, has long been the largest foreign mission field of the Christian Churches. The impact of Christianity has extended over thirteen hundred years, from the arrival of the first band of Nestorian missionaries in A.D. 635 at the ancient capital of Sian-fu. China is where we have attempted to win the world for Christ by the greatest investment in institutions and missionary personnel that the Church has ever made in any mission field. Today, China creates in our minds disappointment and disillusionment. It would be unfair to allow this mood to vitiate our sense of responsibility or to dull the vision of the missionary task of the Church, even though in the middle of the twentieth century we are witnessing the fifth expulsion of missionaries from China. Each of these upheavals has resulted in the massacre and persecution of Christians. Never before has the missionary enterprise faced such colossal losses as currently experienced in China. It has been a sobering experience to watch the rising tide of Communism engulfing this greatest field of missionary endeavor.

Missionaries in China often have set up for themselves and their supporting Churches great expectations. At times enthusiasm has substituted hopes and idealism for reality. We have dreamed of a world so far saved that it could not be lost again, such as the twentieth century slogan, " The evangelization of the world in this generation." [1] There is, however, no warrant for any such expectation, either in the Gospels or in the history of mankind. History has a faculty for repeating itself. The Church of this age is confronted with psychological conflicts that challenge Christians to discover a new point of departure from which they must seek in new ways to find again the abiding essence of Christianity. Lost Churches are in need of new truth; at least they need the rediscovery of ancient truths which are often new to present-day experience. Whenever one speaks of new truth, there is distress in some quarters, and an arousing of the protective spirit to former loyalties. Nevertheless, there exists today the most urgent need for a clarification of the essential issues that are involved in Christian missions in China. At the same time guard should be taken against two extreme views lest we fail to see the panorama of the Church because of its varied forms.

" A caution must be held against the radically exclusive position which sees all truth and all good and the beautiful in one, usually in his own community, treating the rest unqualifiedly with contempt or neglect.
" The other is an equally radical relativism, for which all the historical, sociological formations of Christianity are equally good or equally bad, and which in consequence is too timid or skeptical to commit itself to any one form or ideal." [2]

Toynbee holds that human societies are merely " the common ground between the respective fields of activity of a number of individual human beings." [3] Thus, we will proceed to treat the five periods of missionary work in China as a " common ground." Only in this way is it possible to discern that no one sector of the Church has ever held a mortgage on truth, nor has any part of the movement been free from human errors. The witness of the Christian gospel in China is a matchless story, as Browning puts it, " all with a touch of nobleness upward tending." The witness has never failed. Repeatedly the light has shone forth in the darkness, held aloft by hands that perished in the destruction of the institution that failed. Christians tend to defend the institutions of their own creation with tenacity. It is institutional Christianity that repeatedly shackles the Church. The Church again and again has to lose itself in order to find itself. It falls to rise; it fails in order to fight better. Many of the missionary institutions of the Church are expendable. They all should always be treated as expendable. The Churches of the West must be prepared to forget their material investment in institutional Christianity. Too often it has given an erroneous impression.

The panorama of thirteen centuries of Christian effort in China has its weird events, such as the banishment of missionaries who unwittingly founded academies of anarchy, and the plowing of fields that were dormant for centuries only to discover that an enemy came by night and sowed tares among the wheat. Nevertheless, there is real cause for hope in the realization of having lost the way. This is the first step toward finding it. Certainly the Church in China will never again be controlled by missionaries of the West. A few of the more progressive Mission Boards have already recognized this, and their missionaries have worked under the direction of the Chinese Church in recent years. The future will require that this policy be uniformly followed.

The present attempt of the Communist Government to control the Churches of China confronts every Chinese Christian with decisions that often hold life in the balance. Many have already given their lives for their faith. One thing can be certain: the Church that emerges from this hour of testing will not be a dependency. Chinese Christians dislike the irresponsibility of many of their Christian leaders who have attempted to reconcile the Churches of China with Communism. Similarly the Churches of the West find it impossible to understand the brutality of many trained in Christian schools and the treachery and heresy of cherished leaders. These will have their day and become a byword. They have not been without their counterparts among the few missionaries who loved the limelight and felt called to make themselves protagonists of Chinese political parties.

The Christian Church has always been a minority religion. The martyrs of China have kept faith with the catacombs. Crisis has been the meat and drink of the Church. Out of one came the cross. Only in this faith can the Church be conscious and confident that what came out of Nazareth goes marching on.

Thus it becomes an issue of immediate importance that the Church recognize its blunders, abandon its errors, and prepare itself to grasp the opportunity in the present crisis to seek and save that which is lost. This is a God-given opportunity for Christians to gain a new perspective, and from such vantage point to formulate new techniques. The Christian Church must not be content with mere changes in missionary methods. There is no inherent value in " newness " per se. It is supremely important that the " new " approach be a more faithful adherence to Jesus than many of the portrayals of Christianity evidenced in China in the past.

The Chinese language contains many word combinations that hold profound psychological import. The English word " crisis " presented a problem in translation. It required the creation of a new idea, given expression by combining the characters for " danger " and " opportunity." Where these two factors coexist, the condition is a crisis. The Chinese are thus unable to think in terms of a crisis without immediately seeking for the opportunity that is hidden in the danger. It is of paramount importance that in facing this danger Christians do not overlook the opportunity within the crisis. We can think of the present losses in China as the will of God or as the work of the devil. Many people have permitted themselves to make an oversimplification of the problem, in which the Communists are the scapegoat and the modern devil. It is easy to dismiss the present crisis as a result of uncontrollable political factors, but more sober reflection discerns the tragedy as a painful but necessary medicine and a judgment of the God of history. Those of us who have been missionaries in China must think of this hour as a judgment upon our work and upon ourselves.

It must be realized that the end, when it came, was a dramatic demonstration of many weaknesses. If Communism had not arisen to cast the Christian missionaries out of China, some other movement would have done it. What has already occurred in China could happen in other mission fields of Asia and Africa. This situation demands searching examination, with a quality of humility that will enable a recognition by Christians of their responsibility in these losses and the unwitting contribution of Christendom to the rise of Communism. The present crisis is, for the Christian, an agency in the deepening of his religious respiration. If it be regarded as the work of the Holy Spirit in leading the Church into further regions of truth, then there is reason to believe that this tragedy can lead to triumph. To believe otherwise would be to deny the most profound utterance in the Gospels: "For the Son of man is come to save that which was lost."

The essence of Christianity is contained in the four words that were so frequently used by Jesus: "Repent," "Believe," "Love," "Enter." The first step in the discovery of the ways of God is repentance. This does not occur until there is a recognition of the sense of being "lost." There should be no suggestion of irrecoverable loss in the Churches of China, nor should there be any thought of irrevocable lostness. There is, however, the humble and searching suggestion of our having lost "the way." This may be likened to the state of mind of one who begins to feel that he has been worshiping a false god, placing some creature of his own creation in the place of the Creator. This sense of lostness is but the yearning for a better vision of the truth. It is important that precise definitions be set down for clarification. For our purpose the idea "lost" in reference to the Churches of China means: (1) no longer possessed or retained, (2) no longer to be found, (3) bewildered as to place or direction, (4) destroyed or ruined. Courage should be taken, however, in the fact that the phenomenon of being lost has a function to perform in the growth of faith. Not until the Church humbly recognizes that it has lost its way will it be capable of the repentance that alone can enable it to rediscover the ways of God. " The perception and knowledge of the ways of God imply that we have a criterion by which to ascertain the work of God and to distinguish this work from all other happenings." [4] It is thus important to define what may be employed as a criterion in determining what right a given happening or experience may have to the claim of being Christian or a work of God.

Modern Christians are compelled by the facts of their physical environment to be concerned in the welfare of a world family of peoples. Although confronted by this demand for ecumenicity, the Christian Church is at the same time faced with the gamut of varying customs and conflicting conscience codes that emerge in a world clash of cultures. Whenever there is concern for the development of a world ethic, or " common ethical frame of reference," [5] there must be a recognition that a common foundation of moral principles and practice is the criterion by which Christians may be known throughout the world. Comparative study is valueless without a valid criterion. When the disciples requested Jesus to teach them how to pray, it was not that they were unfamiliar with the form of prayer, but that they had discerned in the life and manner of Jesus an entirely new quality of prayer, which was a complete communion with God. In his answer, Jesus taught the Lord's Prayer. To this model prayer were added the reasons: " For thine is the kingdom, and the power, and the glory " (Matt. 6:13). These eleven words constitute the criterion by which it may be determined whether a Church has a valid claim to being called Christian or whether it is " lost." History reveals that whenever the Church becomes unmindful of its divine origin and dreams of things as " ours " instead of " Thine," it is lost and disaster overwhelms it. Our frail humanity admires the manifestations of power. Even churchmen succumb to its attractions — that is, when the Church is not a victim of power. Whenever Christianity seeks to accelerate the coming of the Kingdom of God by political action through the exercise of power or influence of the organized Church, it needs to heed the caution given Zerubbabel: "Not by might, nor by power, but by my Spirit, saith the Lord of hosts (Zech. 4:6).

It must be admitted that contemporary Christianity plainly envies social and national movements their patriotic fervor and prestige and power.[6] This envy is a confession that Christianity has lost its grip upon its own sources of spiritual vitality.

" As Christianity is the best organized of all religions, and in its catholic (or world-wide forms) most adequate to the idea of the Church, so it is most of all in danger of the corruptions attending organizations. . . . If it cannot clean the stables of priestly greeds, political venalities in high places, connivance in the ambitions of states, and the silent suave corporate purchasing of mentality and conscience by posts and preferments, it not only surrenders much of its ascendancy over the human spirit, but ripens for such days of wrath as overtook the Church of Russia."[7]

The question arises as to what were the chief factors in each of these disasters that have brought recurring losses to the Churches of China, and whether there is any similarity or repetition in these occurrences. A search of the historical record reveals an amazing similarity in some of the chief causes of friction, so glaring that they issue an imperative to all Christians to face causal factors.

In this book the historical record is traced to discover why the Christian Church has again suffered catastrophic loss in China, and to ascertain what are the recurring factors that contribute to these recurring losses. The value of such a quest is important to those who are still interested in the continuity of the Christian Church in China. Our concern in the present work is only with those pertinent events that are here recorded, in order to exhibit their significance and not merely their occurrence. This analysis attempts to evaluate these historical events in order to ascertain the truth that lies in the cause, but that has too often been obscured in the results.

I

CHINA'S RELIGIOUS HERITAGE

MUCH of the misunderstanding in Occidental minds regarding China arises from Western insistence for immediate decisions in the light of current situations. Such decisions have repeatedly violated the most cherished traditions of China, where all thought is saturated with reverence for the past. It is, therefore, of first importance that those who would understand the problems confronting Christianity in China should pause sufficiently to gain some appreciation of those forces which, for many centuries, have been continually present in Chinese thought. One of the most recurring causes of loss to the Christian Church is that the expression of Christianity most frequently manifested to the Chinese has been so utterly foreign to them. In periods of antiforeign sentiment the Church that has not demonstrated any appreciation of the truths and values of China's own religious and cultural past inevitably suffers loss. It is not merely to avoid further losses, but because of the conviction that the Church cannot be Christian otherwise, that this chapter sets forth the reasons why Christianity must develop a full cultural appreciation of the values in China's religious heritage, in order that the Christian Church in China may be truly indigenous. China's moral background has given her people a stability that has enabled them to survive when surrounding cultures have tumbled into ruin. The author recalls entering the capital, Kwei-hua-t'ing, of Sui-yuan province. The majestic walls of the city rise above the sandy stretches of the Gobi desert that reach northward toward Inner Mongolia. Carved over the North Gate are the impressive characters giving the name of the city, " Entrance to Civilization! " To the ancient Chinese, outside the borders of China all were barbarians. China was paternally tolerant of the outer world. When the first Christian missionaries arrived in China, they found a highly developed and organized political entity, living a completely self-contained existence behind a wall of isolationism. China was more than a nation. It was a closed world.

It may be said with some justice that Chinese religious concepts begin in antiquity with animism, develop into ancestor worship and the worship of heaven and earth and spirits, and culminate in what may be called nature theism. The early ancestors found the animus in nature which in time became the basis of ancestor worship. The Chinese have sometimes been described as irreligious, since they do not care about particularities of doctrine and form. To them theological controversies and denominations cannot have at any time any very deep meaning. The mass of the people are grossly commercial and calculating in their religious life, since they often trade their gods for prosperity, posterity, and long life by means of meager sacrificial offerings. The religious conceptions of the Chinese have undergone many changes from time to time, but throughout all the changes the spirit of reverence for the past remains. We may criticize Chinese society as having failed through the centuries to practice the ethical teaching of its great sages, Lao Tzu, Kung Fu-tzu (Confucius), Meng Tzu (Mencius), and Moh Tzu, in any degree approaching the concepts originally held by these great thinkers. But it is equally true that the Jews often failed to observe the exhortations of their prophets, Isaiah, Micah, and Amos, who urged their people to abandon idolatrous practices and return to the observance of the law given by Moses. The fact that the Jews in the days of Christ had failed to keep the teachings of their sages as a vital quality in daily life, even to the degree that blinded them to the mes-

sage of Jesus, does not deter us from cherishing, to this day, the
ethical teachings of the Old Testament. Christian concepts of
God are not originally Anglo-Saxon. Indeed they are a synthe-
sis, principally of Hebrew, Syrian, Roman, Greek, and Anglo-
Saxon experience. In marked contrast, the Chinese ideas of the
Supreme Being, as found in their classics, are the indigenous
product of China's own experience.

The emphasis of China's wisdom literature tends to be more
humanistic than theistic, but there are sections of the Bible, in
the Old Testament, that are not so theistic as others. Truth,
whether found in the Analects of Confucius or in the sayings
of Lao Tzu, must be acclaimed by Christians as imperishable.
To do less contradicts the stand taken by Jesus, who declared
that he had not come to destroy but only to fulfill. The attitude
of many missionaries toward the ethical teachings of China is
an exceedingly difficult one to interpret without danger of
misunderstanding. One would prefer to avoid it, because to
many Christians in the West the cause of the evangelization
of the "heathen" is so important that it is placed at the
pinnacle to which the energies of Christendom should be consecrated. But the Christian missionary movement has contributed so great a force in undermining the prestige of Confucius
in China that this disturbing fact simply cannot be ignored.
There are notable instances of Roman Catholic and Protestant
missionaries who have taken the necessary time to understand
the Chinese classics and who have entered into an appreciation of their values. But the number of such objective minds
is too few. Most missionaries have been primarily evangelists,
educators, physicians, nurses, or scientists. The pressure of
their assigned duties left little, if any, time for sympathetic
study of Chinese culture. Missionaries have been far from
unanimous in their estimates of China's religious heritage;
they have differed among themselves regarding the teachings
of Confucius. Many have felt it was a serious obstacle to the
spread of the Christian faith. Buddhism and Taoism were de-
caying forces in China which Christianity has largely disre-

garded, but Confucian ethics, with a lofty code of morals and a high prestige among all classes, presented grave problems. "Pioneer missionaries came to China more or less with the attitude that whatever of religion was already here was the work of the Evil One."[1]

However varied and delicate the fabric of Confucian thought, it was originally expressed very simply. Confucius' writings are acknowledged to be compilations and editing of the wisdom of the past which reached back to the Golden Age of Yao and Shun.[2] If his teachings have been hidden by embellishments and additions which at times distorted their truth or if his teachings have not been fully followed in every generation, this does not detract from the truth or value of his original principles. For instance: "The master said, there are three things of which the superior man stands in awe. He stands in awe of the ordinances of Heaven. He stands in awe of great men. He stands in awe of the words of the sages. The mean man does not know the ordinances of Heaven, and consequently does not stand in awe of them."[3]

According to W. Morgan's definition of religion, Confucius should be given a high rating as a religious thinker:

"To love and possess God is to love and possess truth, beauty and goodness, and to know and feel that on these realities the universe is founded, is to have religion. . . . Religious faith can be described as a trust in the rational, the beautiful, and above all, the good, as the ultimate in the universe."[4]

Even though Confucius be recognized as a profoundly religious man, yet he did not found a religion. The ceremonies in honor of Confucius which were developed several centuries after his death would have shocked him. However, most writers in the field of comparative religions have considered Confucianism as one of the religions of China. It would be more nearly correct to say that the animism that existed in China as a religion at the time of Confucius, and for centuries before him, continued to be practiced by both the illiterate peasants and the literati for centuries after him. His own

attitude regarding the nature of God is perhaps best (
by employing a saying of Saint Augustine: "We (
what God is not; we cannot know what He is." [5]

Hocking rightly says, "Confucianism is a minimal theism,
leaving in its wake the hunger of unanswered questioning." [6]
Matteo Ricci, of the seventeenth century, grasped this truth
and courageously blazed a trail of cultural appreciation that
the Roman Church was not prepared to follow. In the nineteenth and twentieth centuries it fell to Protestant missionaries to pick up the torch held aloft by the great Jesuit scholar
and employ the noblest ideas of Confucius as the Christian conception of God in the Chinese language. Ricci was the first
to advocate this but had been overruled by Rome. Where else
would one go to find an adequate vehicle to transmit the idea
of God except to search the wisdom literature of China for its
loftiest concept? It was thus that "Shang Ti" was taken from
the Confucian classics, meaning the "Spirit above all Spirits."
Likewise, Christians have taken the ancient term of Confucius
for Supreme Being, "T'ien," which was so frequently used
interchangeably with "Heaven," and coupled with the word
"Fu," Father. This combination, "T'ien Fu," is used in the
Lord's Prayer. In the use of the term "Shang Ti," did Confucius mean a personal God, or a mere force, or an anthropomorphic ancestor? What did he mean in the use of "T'ien"?
Was it just the material sky or did it refer to the Lord of heaven
and earth? When Confucius said, "*T'ien hsia shih i chia,*" did
he mean the literal translation that all under the panoply of
heaven are one family, or did he conceive the loftier idea that
all men are the children of one Heavenly Father? Religious
thought to the Chinese has been so overshadowed with animism
and anthropomorphic ideas, rather than speculative and theo-
centric ideas, that it was natural for those missionaries who re-
sponded to their first impressions of China to dismiss all its
religious practices as incompatible with Christianity. On questioning friendly Chinese regarding the meaning of these terms,
they were amazed that the Chinese held no precise or fixed

opinions on these subjects. China has not produced any great theologian who set his heart on trying to understand the attributes of Deity or the genesis of the universe.

Confucius stands in the midst of bewildering gropings of the common people and gives utterance to moral and ethical teachings that have endeared him to countless millions across twenty-five hundred years.

" Those who criticize Confucius because he made no implicit or precise statement regarding the nature of God forget that *un Dieu défini* no longer intrigues the human mind and soon becomes in danger of being treated by men as *un Dieu fini.*" [7]

The secret of Confucius lies in the strength and power of the highest type of true greatness, namely, in the moral sphere. Faithfulness and truthfulness were the groundwork of all his teachings. Legge affirms that the status of Confucius is of a sage, of the same order as the simplest and least advanced of mankind, and that the ordinary man is the potential equal of Confucius.[8]

" Regarding his belief in a Supreme Being . . . he felt from the perfect wisdom which he saw everywhere manifest throughout the universe that there must be a supreme overruling power governing in all things, which power he styled ' The Will of Heaven.' To this Power he felt ' profoundly reverent and humbly submissive.' " [9]

Because Confucius had very little to say about the future life and refrained from discussing supernatural things, and because many forms of animistic worship still prevail, there is a popular misconception that the Chinese are atheistic. " Confucius was not at all atheistic. Not only did he recognize the existence of a Supreme Being of the universe, whom he sometimes referred to as ' Heaven ' (T'ien) and sometimes as the ' Supreme Ruler ' (Shang Ti), but he took it for granted that everybody would agree with him on this point." [10] There are many pages in the Confucian classics that illustrate deep religious feeling. One of the most striking is that which records Confucius' answer to someone who asked him to explain the meaning of a certain popular saying: " To propitiate the divinity of the cooking stove is more effective than to propitiate the divinity of the inner rooms." Confucius replied: "It is useless to pray to such as these. . . . Address your prayers to God alone. If he rejects them there is no other deity to whom you may pray." [11]

Tradition has set Confucius upon a pedestal and has employed his name to lay down rules for men to follow, but the classics reveal that he studiously refrained from imposing any rules because he believed that every man should think for himself. The whole genius of his philosophy was that every man could and should become a superior man through the process of self-discipline. To him, what a man was like at birth was an accident over which he had no control, but if by sheer determination and self-discipline he should die a scholar, it was a mark of human achievement excelling all else in man's experience.

Historically, it should be noted that Confucius failed to restore order in his time. His ideas were not popular in his own day. The Chou dynasty continued to decline, and chaos prevailed until the ascendancy of the Chin dynasty. It was not until the Han dynasty that the teachings of Confucius obtained a hold on the Chinese which continued to very recent times. By millions in China, he has been looked upon for many centuries as the greatest man that ever lived. "His philosophy had a potent force in the development of some of the basic social and political conceptions of both East and West. He is described as being completely unoriginal but rather a transmitter of the values of antiquity which he had both appreciated, assimilated and collated in the classics, which are attributed to his editorship and thus are transmitted in a cohesive form to posterity." [12] A duke who sought advice from Confucius asked, "Is there a single sentence that can ruin the country?" Confucius replied: "If a ruler's words be good, is it not also good that no one oppose them? But if they are not good and no one oppose them, may there not be expected from this one sentence the ruin of his country?" [13] The Chinese have always cited this admonition of Confucius to justify an uprising of the people against a corrupt government. The emperor reigned as the "Son of Heaven" so long as he ruled in accord with the principles of virtue and benevolence. He forfeited his right to the throne and ceased to be considered the Son of Heaven whenever he was guilty of unseemly conduct and the aggrieved people could find a leader to organize them for victory. The voice of the people was construed to be the indisputable will of heaven.[14] There are those who erroneously accuse Confucius of seeking to bolster the authority of the hereditary aristocracy, yet he advocated such social and political reforms that he must be counted among the greatest revolutionary leaders of the world:

"If a superior man love propriety, the people will not dare not to be reverent. If he love righteousness, the people will not dare not to submit to his example. If he love good faith, the people will not dare not to be sincere. Now, when these things obtain, the people from all quarters will come to him, bearing their children on their backs."[15]

Within a few centuries after Confucius' death the hereditary aristocracy had ceased to exist in China. He more than anyone else had contributed the psychological changes that brought about its destruction. He created in its stead an aristocracy of achievement, particularly in the realm of letters.

The teachings of Lao Tzu, born a half century before Confucius, contain even loftier and more spiritual values than any found in the writings of Confucius. The tragedy is that Confucius was so eminently practical that the more spiritual thoughts of Lao Tzu were submerged and to a large degree lost for many centuries. Taoism was never founded by Lao Tzu. The chief effect of Taoism, with its multiplicity of deities and vain attempt to compete with Buddhism, was to obscure the true teachings of Lao Tzu, who was the "least racial and most universal writer China has ever produced."[16]

"No one who is interested in religion can afford to leave

unread Lao Tzu's *Tao Teh King*." [17] Lao Tzu's most beautiful thought is found in his conception of the " Tao " (the Way). He mentioned the three distinguishing qualities of the possessor: " I have three precious things which I prize and hold fast. The first is gentleness; the second is economy; the third is shrinking from taking precedence of others. With that gentleness I can be bold; with that economy I can be liberal; shrinking from taking precedence of others, I can become a vessel of the highest honor." [18] Those who rejoice with the writer to the Hebrews that God has spoken to different races and ages " at sundry times and in divers manners " (Heb. 1:1) expect to meet earnest and courageous seekers of God in all lands and among all peoples, and that he is being found by them (Amos 9:7). The idea of " Logos " as identified with the Supreme Being was familiar to the Greeks. The Stoics identified it with the cosmos. Plato at times agrees with this idea of a cosmic ruler. Philo used it as expressive of God. But in none of these instances was it clearly conceived of as personal. It was the writer of the Fourth Gospel who gave the full meaning to " Logos " by affirming that it had appeared in the flesh. In a similar way the translators of the Fourth Gospel into Chinese have affirmed that Jesus Christ has come as the fulfillment of the Chinese religious yearning embodied in Lao Tzu's " Tao."

The widespread influence of Lao Tzu's philosophy thirteen hundred years after his death is seen in a poem, " Peaceful Old Age," by Po Chü-i, A.D. 772–846, from which the following lines are taken:

> " Swiftly and soon the golden sun goes down,
> The blue sky wells afar into the night.
> ' Tao ' is the changeful world's environment;
> Happy are they that in its laws delight.
> ' Tao ' gives me toil, youth's passion to achieve,
> And leisure in life's autumn and decay.
> I follow ' Tao ' — the seasons are my friends;
> Opposing it misfortunes come my way.
> If I depart I cast no look behind:
> Still wed to life, I still am free from care
> Since life and death in cycles come and go,

> Of little moment are the days to spare.
> Thus strong in faith I wait, and long to be
> One with the pulsings of Eternity." [19]

Lao Tzu preaches the necessity of becoming like unto a little child, of returning to primitive simplicity and purity, of non-assertion and nonresistance, and promises that the deficient will be made entire, the crooked will be straightened, the empty will be filled, the worn will be renewed, those who have too little will receive, while those who have too much will be bewildered. Lao Tzu's *Tao Teh King* contains so many surprising analogies with Christian thought and sentiment that were its authenticity in doubt, one would be inclined to look for evidences of a later authorship and Christian influence. But it undeniably belongs to the sixth century before Christ. [20]

Whatever may be the origin of such an exalted and noble idea, the fact is undeniable that as far back as we can go the Chinese believed in a Supreme Being, a God, who stood out as a clear and vivid personality separated from the rest of spiritual beings by the uniqueness of his character and power.

Confucius spoke of "Shang Ti." Lao Tzu spoke of "Tao." This fact made it easier for the translators of the Bible into Chinese to do much as was done in ancient Greece and Rome, namely, to take the noblest concepts of God that existed and give them Christian significance. This was not plagiarism but consistent with the Christian faith that there is only one God, by whatsoever name he may be known. But acceptance of this truth must logically be accompanied by respect for the Chinese sages who also apprehended it. The non-Christian Chinese upon seeing a copy of the Chinese Bible is arrested by the discovery in the first chapter of Genesis that "in the beginning Shang Ti made the world." As the pages are turned to the New Testament, in the opening of the Fourth Gospel the reader is again held by the affirmation that the "Tao" of which Lao Tzu wrote six hundred years before Christ has indeed walked in the flesh, and men have beheld his glory, full of grace and truth.

It is a sorry commentary on Christianity that although it produced scholars who translated the Bible faithfully by adapting the idea of "Shang Ti" from Confucius and the idea of "Tao" from Lao Tzu, yet the use of these terms by the Church has not been accompanied by the same degree of appreciation that the translators had for the teachings of the great sages who first conceived them. The missionaries were dependent on these terms to make real their message. The Church must face the glaring fact that Chinese students are quick to discern the incredible incongruity in this situation. The terms used for God in the Chinese version of the Bible are not the terms used by Abraham, Moses, Isaiah, Jeremiah, Micah, or Jesus. They are the thoughts of Confucius and Lao Tzu, woven into the Chinese Bible to give meaning to God and Jesus.

Every missionary is indebted to Legge's translation of the Chinese classics.[21] But a caution was given by Sir Reginald Johnston, when professor of Chinese in the University of London, who noted that Legge wrote wistfully, expressing the hope that a Christian scholar someday would produce a commentary, for the benefit of Chinese, which would "clearly and minutely" uncover the errors in the Chinese ideas of the constitution of nature and providence. Legge hoped that "from this ground we might go on to shake the stronghold of their confidence in all the ancient teachings and the wisdom of their so-called sages." [22] In such effort to shake the confidence of the Chinese in their cultural past, missionaries were only faithful to the convictions of the supporting Churches in the West which had sent them to China. But unless the Christian Church humbly and loyally acknowledges its debt to China's sages for the terms used for God and the Son Incarnate, found in the Chinese translation of the Bible, it is guilty of theft of the noblest ideas of Lao Tzu and Confucius while attempting to supplant them in their own land.

"The strategy of the apostle Paul in his first missionary journeys is the supreme example that should have been followed by the Church in its modern missionary endeavour. If the Church of the first five centuries had followed the methods often employed in the earlier part of the twentieth century, it would be reasonable to expect that small and feeble communities of Christians might indeed have established themselves on the fringes of Roman society but they would have remained as foreign to the life of that society as the Jewish communities of the Diaspora." [23]

The ancient religious concepts of China are considerably higher than those of our own forefathers before Roman civilization and Christianity made their contribution in the countries of Europe and the British Isles. The Romans found it necessary to prohibit by law the widespread sacrifice of human beings that they found to be prevalent in Europe and Wales.[24] Cicero claimed that "Socrates was the first to fetch philosophy from heaven and bring it down into the cities and houses of men, compelling them to inquire about life, and morality, and good and evil." But no one in Europe, including Cicero, had heard of Confucius or Lao Tzu, both of whom had lived and died before Socrates was born. Lao Tzu preceded Confucius. Confucius died in 479 B.C. Socrates was born about 470 B.C.

Very little reference is made in this chapter to Buddhism because it does not rightly belong to China's religious heritage. It came to China nearly nineteen hundred years ago from India, at a time when Chinese life presented an aching void in religious things. The people had suffered greatly from the suppression of the teachings of Confucius, the destruction of the classics, and persecution of the scholars under the Chin dynasty. The Chinese turned to Buddhism to satisfy their religious aspirations. The people were hungry for religion, and Buddhism was the best religion that they found. And yet Buddhism does not seem to be inherently adapted to the practical Chinese; it is too otherworldly. It renounces this world and seeks satisfaction in the ideal realm — quite the opposite from Confucius. Christianity and Confucius have much more in common than Confucianism and Buddhism. The development of Neo-Confucianism in the Sung dynasty was an attempt to nationalize Buddhism by assimilating into the Confucian system the elements in Buddhism that appealed to the Chinese. "Buddhism alone could never be sufficient religion for China, because it lacks moral and particular relation to Chinese culture." [25]

Christianity must not take false comfort from the disintegration of China's religious past.[26] Instead the Church should be alarmed by it. There are those who have erroneously thought that this development indicated a day of opportunity for the Christian Church to supplant the former religions. Christians are duty bound to apply the attitude of Jesus to the truths in China's religious heritage. When this is done, the Church will become what Jesus proclaimed, namely, not the means of destruction, but the fulfillment of the noblest aspirations of the oldest civilization in existence. A great deal has been written regarding the importance of establishing an indigenous Church in China. In some cases this seems to mean a Church managed or directed by Chinese, but if the Chinese who are given the responsibility of this direction have first been divorced from an adequate appreciation of their own religious heritage, how can they help to build an indigenous Church? The Chinese equivalent of indigenous means literally "local grass roots." This implies much more than a Western form of Christianity, led by Chinese with a Western message. The indigenous Church must grow upon the roots that God alone has planted in human hearts. This makes it imperative that the Church enter into an appreciation of China's religious heritage.[27]

Modern Christians need to take their stand beside Clement of Alexandria, who believed that God had one great plan for saving the world in which Christianity was the final fulfillment, but he refused to believe that Judaism was the only divine preparation for it.

China stands at this hour in crucial need of a champion of its ancient truths. The Christian Church can claim this privilege with justice in that Christianity is a religion born in Asia and already rooted upon China's historic past by those early missionaries who pioneered in cultural adaptation. If organized Christianity is unable to manifest sufficient humility to set

Christ free in China, free from the restrictive theological controls placed upon missionary work for many years by supporting agencies, then the hour has come for Christians in China to declare boldly that the Christian faith for them is indissolubly joined with China's religious heritage, and defend their action by the words of Christ: " I am not come to destroy, but to fulfil."

The future of missionary work in China will belong to those missions and missionaries prepared to co-operate with Chinese Christians in this great venture of faith " to seek and to save that which was lost." In the succeeding chapters the successive periods in which Christianity has been active in Chinese history are examined, setting forth the reasons for its recurring losses, and finally lifting into prominence the crisis that confronts the Christian Church in the middle of the twentieth century.

II

THE FIRST CHRISTIANS IN CHINA

CHRISTIANS of the Eastern or Syriac Church, known as Nestorians, were living in China as early as the sixth century.[1] They gained such an extensive place under the T'ang emperors in the seventh to ninth centuries that it becomes important to trace their historical connection, which stems from the apostles. Timothy I, patriarch of the Nestorians (A.D. 777–820), wrote that the Magi had introduced the Christian religion among them after their return from their discovery of the infant Jesus at Bethlehem. Christianity was well established in the East within twenty years after the ascension of our Lord.[2] A tradition of the Nestorians is that Christianity was founded among them at Edessa in the first century by Saint Thaddeus and Saint Mari, of the " seventy," who had been commissioned to go to Asia by Jesus in response to a letter from King Abgar. This legend is well recorded by Eusebius and other authors.[3] Edessa was the capital of a small kingdom east of the Euphrates and the starting point of early Christian life and literature of the Nestorians. From the end of the second century it was the center of active missionary work in Persia and Armenia. It is important to remember that the Church of the West, dominated by Rome, was predominantly Gentile in the fifth century, while the Church of the East was predominantly of Hebrew extraction and Syriac-speaking. At the time of Christ most of the Jews lived east of the Euphrates in Parthia. Ancient Assyria, which had carried the Ten Tribes into captivity, had been conquered by Parthia. Likewise Parthia had conquered Babylonia, whither Nebuchadnezzar had taken the two tribes of Judah. It is a historical fact that only a small fraction of the Jews had returned to Jerusalem at the time of Cyrus. To Jews of the first century there were no " lost tribes." At least the apostle Paul did not think of them as lost but only as dispersed. In his defense before King Agrippa, Paul referred to " the promise made of God unto our fathers: unto which promise our twelve tribes, instantly serving God day and night, hope to come " (Acts 26:6, 7). The visitors to Jerusalem at the time of Pentecost included " Parthians, and Medes, and Elamites, and the dwellers in Mesopotamia " (Acts 2:9). These pilgrims to the Feast of Pentecost undoubtedly carried home the news of the crucifixion and resurrection, and recounted the great experience that came upon the apostles and the sermon of Peter. The Church of the East also holds the belief that Peter wrote his First Epistle from Babylon (I Peter 5:13). This Church grew to maturity in the now forgotten kingdom of Parthia, which in its zenith was able to keep Rome at a respectful distance for four hundred years. " From the end of the second century to the beginning of the fourteenth it was marked by a flaming 'missionary zeal.' Through the whole of Central Asia, Turkestan, Mongolia, China, and Japan its messengers wended their way." [4]

The Eastern Church was not the creation of Nestorius. It would be more accurate to say that Nestorius was a disciple of the Eastern Church. Eastern Christians felt that he was misrepresented and persecuted unjustly by the Western Church. They approved the opposition of Nestorius to the doctrine of purgatory and his fight against the adoption of the title " Mother of God " for Mary, the Mother of Christ.

We first hear of Nestorius as a member of the monastery of Euprepius near Antioch. Of his early life we know nothing except that he was a native of Germanica, in the Euphrates district, within the patriarchate of Antioch. To Antioch evidently he belonged by theological lineage and point of view.

The graduates of the Antioch school could admit no doctrine
of the Deity of Christ that would in any way obscure the fact
that he lived upon earth the life of man. They started from the
one quite certain fact that he lived as a man among men. They
reasoned from the known to the unknown. They tried to find
some means of reconciling the traditional faith in the Godhead
of Jesus with their conviction that God was one. Nestorius was
selected by the emperor Theodosius for the patriarchate of
Constantinople (A.D. 428–431). He was a great scholar, lec-
turer, and eloquent speaker. Controversy arose soon after he
was consecrated patriarch of Constantinople, when he raised
serious objections to the emerging cult of Mariolatry, which
was advocated by Cyril, bishop of Alexandria. Nestorius
appealed to the Church of the East and to its doctrinal faith
received from the apostles as defense for his stand. The
Council of Ephesus, which deposed and excommunicated him,
was improperly constituted.[5] There are indications that the
Council of Ephesus was " rigged " against Nestorius. " Every
avenue of the throne was assaulted with gold." [6] Cyril rendered
a constructive or peaceful settlement impossible by insisting,
against the expressed wish of Count Candidian, who represented the emperor, on holding the Council without waiting
for the arrival of John, bishop of Antioch, and the Eastern
bishops, who had been delayed by bad roads and inclement
weather. The sentence of the Council was that Nestorius
should be excluded from the episcopal office; it was proclaimed in the streets of Ephesus, and the members of the
Council, as they issued from " the church of the Mother of
God," were saluted as her champions and their victory was
celebrated by torches during the night. Nestorius was condemned in an edict that proscribed his opinions and his followers, condemned his writings to the flames, and banished
his person to Petra in Arabia, and afterward to an oasis in the
Libyan desert. This was done, so far as history records, without any trial and without giving the accused any opportunity
of making his defense.[7]

Exiled to the desert, Nestorius was dragged to and fro and subjected to continued persecution by his relentless enemies. Gibbon describes his exile as "devoutly tortured" by the magistrates, soldiers, and monks of Egypt. His death will be regarded by some as an ecclesiastical murder, but to his enemies it appeared an act of merit, while among his friends it was glorified as martyrdom. Edicts seemed powerless to crush his followers, who were generally known as Nestorians, though they spoke of themselves as Chaldean or Assyrian Christians. They spread his name and his teaching throughout the East, everywhere planting churches, in which the death of Nestorius was condemned and the Ephesine decrees rejected.

The Persian government relaxed its opposition to Christianity as soon as it discerned the rupture between the Eastern and Western Churches of Christendom. Cyril, bishop of Alexandria, was not content with the expulsion and death of his rival Nestorius, but led the persecution of all who supported Nestorius. In this movement the bishop of Alexandria was upheld by the bishop of Rome. Thus following the Council of Ephesus Christian refugees streamed from the West to the East of the Euphrates, where they found both religious freedom and protection. Gibbon records that "to this standard of natural and religious freedom myriads of fugitives resorted from all provinces." [8]

The Eastern Church accepted the first two ecumenical Councils of Christendom and subscribed to the Nicene Creed. Now having broken with Rome, it set itself to frame its own ritual and order. The rule of celibacy was set aside; a more liberal spirit of education was introduced into the schools; houses of charity were endowed for the education of orphans and foundlings. The Eastern Church at the height of its strength extended from the Euphrates to the Indus and from the Caspian Sea to the Indian Ocean. It was placed beyond the pale of Christendom by the Western Church through the interdiction of Rome which followed the Council of Ephesus.

Some feel that the first message about Jesus Christ was

brought to China by the followers of Mani. Latourette refers to Christianity's doubtful earliest attempts to enter China as about the year 300.[9] For the purpose of this study the Nestorians are the first clear beginning of the Christian Church in China. However, we need to remember the caution given by Jesus to his disciples, who were disturbed that a certain one was preaching in a manner different from the disciples (Mark 9:39). Mani and his followers carried word of Christ into the vast stretches of Asia, including China. Mani, born near Baghdad about A.D. 216, seems to have started from Persia with certain Christian ideas and to have absorbed as he traveled other ideas from every religion.[10] Following his journey to China, he returned to Persia in A.D. 273, only to be put to death through Zoroastrian intrigues in A.D. 275. Banned from Persia, Manichaeism was soon a very strong movement through Central Asia.[11] It survived among the nomadic tribes north of China for several centuries, until the coming of Nestorian Christians, when Manichaeism seems to have faded out with the rise of Nestorian Christianity among the Mongols. It is for this reason that it is just to recognize the Nestorians as contributing the first Christian missionary movement to China. The persecution of Christians in Europe had sent Christian scholars seeking freedom in the East.[12] This infusion of new blood strengthened the Church in Persia.[13] By the opening of the seventh century this Church was well organized, with provinces corresponding to the territorial divisions of the Persian Empire. In 624 the patriarch had been declared catholicos, with supreme authority within his own communion.[14] Eleven years later missionaries of this Church appeared at the court of the emperor of China, in the ninth year of the Chen-kuan period, A.D. 635.

The Nestorians were able to enter China because of the open trade routes; the first Christians to arrive in China were not missionaries but traders who brought their faith with them. Similarly the Europeans known to have arrived in China first were merchant adventurers and not missionaries. This contradicts the idea so often expressed that the missionary was the pioneer in causing whatever upset has resulted from the mixing of the civilizations and cultures of East and West.[15] "We must remember that this is the year in which the Nestorian Mission made a public and glorious entrance to the capital by the special favor of the reigning emperor, whilst the propagation of Nestorianism or the immigration of the Nestorians into China must naturally have preceded this public entrance of the missionaries in A.D. 635, since it is recorded in Chinese history that even in A.D. 578 already a great Nestorian family of Mar Sargis emigrated from the Western Lands to Lin-t'ao, Kan-su." [16]

The alliance between Persia and China in the seventh century and the suppression of Buddhism in China just a few years before the arrival of the Nestorian missionaries are two factors in the remarkable welcome they received at the court of China. " The T'ang dynasty (A.D. 618–907) has been called the Augustan age of Chinese literature, and under its sway China was governed by some of the best and most liberal-minded rulers that the Celestial Empire has ever known." [17] The emperor T'ai Tsung (A.D. 627–650) was a strong Confucianist and had no sympathy with either Buddhism or Taoism which had become so widespread during his father's reign. The Confucian scholars who had been successful in crushing Buddhism were " in the saddle." When the first Nestorian missionaries arrived in the ancient capital of Sian-fu,[18] the T'ang dynasty was centered in the mountainous provinces of Shan-si, Shen-si, and Ho-nan. This area is known as the cradle of Chinese civilization and culture. It was there that the Nestorians cradled the Christian Church. It was there they were known as the " Luminous Religion " [19] and flourished under this name for two hundred years, until they were persecuted and driven out in the ninth century, leaving only a number of stone monuments and relics to tell their story. These were obscured for many centuries until the epochal discovery of the Nestorian monument in Sian-fu, A.D. 1623. In this same area modern missionaries to China suffered the greatest martyrdom in the Boxer massacre of 1900, when more missionaries were killed in Shan-si than in any other province. The author worked for a number of years in Shan-si and Shen-si. One cannot escape from the feeling of the tremendous impact of Church history that pervades this area of China.

When the first Europeans arrived at the court of Pe-king in the seventeenth century, no trace was known to exist of the ancient Nestorian Church. Almost all our present knowledge of this Church in China begins with the discovery in the year 1623 near Sian-fu of a massive slab of stone, nine feet high and over three feet wide. The front and sides were beautifully carved, mostly in Chinese characters, but some in a strange language, which was later found to be Syriac. The Jesuit scholars in Pe-king at the time sent one of their number to investigate, and Chinese and Jesuit scholars soon began to decipher it. Thus was unfolded the first authentic story of the earliest Church in China.[20] Chinese scholars were quick to note the imperial inscription of the T'ang emperor on the monument. " The Emperor ordered Fang-li-wen-ling, first minister of the empire, to go with a great train of attendants to the Western suburbs to meet the strangers and bring them to the palace. He had the Holy Scriptures translated in the Imperial Library. The court listened to the doctrine, meditated on it profoundly and understood the great unity of truth." [21]

The exact date of the discovery of the Nestorian monument remains unsettled. It was found at Chou-chih, about forty miles southwest of Sian-fu, while workmen were making certain excavations.[22] It had first been erected in A.D. 781 and had been carefully buried, doubtless during the persecution of the ninth century. One of the early Jesuits, Etienne Faber, was told by an old native of the district that it was well known that snow would melt first on a small patch of ground, the spot under which the stone was found.[23] Whether out of curiosity or some other reason, the stone was discovered, carefully raised, and cleaned. It was found in a state of perfect preservation. Most likely it was discovered in 1623 and moved to Sian-fu in 1625.[24]

The important fact is that the discovery revealed for the first time that Christianity had entered China in the seventh century or earlier and had received the patronage of the T'ang emperors.[25] A friend of a Christian sent a copy of the inscription to Hang-chow to Li Chih-tsao, who lost no time in having it printed, with an explanatory note which bears the date of 12 June, 1625. Copies of this *editio princeps* are preserved in Paris.[26]

In the seventeenth century the news of the discovery was greeted with skepticism by Western critics. Voltaire poured scorn upon the story as an impossible fraud. La Craze joined his voice in France with Voltaire in scoffing at the very thought of Christianity in China at so early a date. In England, Bishop Horne and others contended that it simply could not have occurred, and they challenged the whole report as a Jesuit forgery. The cynics and skeptics prevailed over the factual evidence until the middle of the nineteenth century. This was undoubtedly due to the extreme distance of China from the Western world and the long overland journey involved in going to Sian-fu in the heart of China. Very few Westerners, even among the missionaries in China, had ever actually seen the monument. Thus for two hundred years after the discovery doubts still prevailed in Europe and America, as evidenced by Neumann of Munich, Stanislas Julien of Paris, and Salisbury of America, who as late as 1853 expressed their doubts.[27] The Protestant missionary movement of the nineteenth century came from Europe and America. It is not surprising that many missionaries of this period were sure that the story of the Nestorian monument was a fiction of Jesuit propaganda.[28] Certainly most of the Protestant missionaries of the nineteenth century were sent to China without any knowledge that Christian missionaries of the first Protestant Church in history had labored there before them. Fortunately, among the nineteenth century missionaries were scholars who later became the most renowned Sinologists, such as Alexander Wylie and James Legge of England. Wylie personally examined the monument in Sian-fu and published a translation of the inscription in Shang-hai in 1854. This included in detail the opinions of Chinese authorities, many historical notes and calligraphical records of the T'ang dynasty. Chinese and Japanese scholars from the outset held that the monument found at Sian-fu in 1623 was genuine. But doubts persisted in the West until removed by scholars in the nineteenth century. Unhappily this element of doubt prevented the Western world from appreciating the significance of the Nestorian monument and the invaluable lessons to be derived from it. The tardiness of the modern missionary movement to recognize this connecting link with historic Christianity is deplorable. So hard is it to accept truth rather than prejudice!

In 1883, James Legge published his translation of the inscription on the Sian-fu monument. Since then M. G. Pauthier and Paul Pelliot of France have also confirmed its genuineness from many sources until there is no longer any doubt whatever regarding the authenticity of the monument. P. Y. Saeki, of Tokyo, has gathered the contributions of many scholars, together with extensive research work on his own part, and presented an invaluable contribution regarding the Nestorians in the T'ang dynasty.[29] There are many translations of the text of the monument. One of the best is given by Moule, who acknowledges his debt to other eminent authorities as Wylie, Legge, Pelliot, and Saeki.[30] Since the recognition of the authentic character of the Nestorian monument, the zeal of scholars, both Western and Chinese, has been whetted to unravel the history of this lost Church of China. Many supporting evidences have been brought to light from the official Chinese records of the T'ang dynasty. The inscriptions and manuscripts found in China reveal that doctrinally the faith of the Nestorians was apostolic and essentially the same as the Nicene Creed.

The imperial edict recorded on the Sian-fu monument was issued by an emperor who was not a Christian, in a land long dominated by Buddhism and Taoism, in a period of reaction against those religions. It reveals the pronounced liberal spirit of the emperor and must have issued from a sincere conviction and appreciation of the gospel interpreted by the Nestorians. This official welcome suggests that there was a foreknowledge of the coming of the missionaries, who must have been encouraged by the earlier residence in China of Nestorian Christians.[31] There are those critics who feel that at best the inscription on the monument reveals an imperfect grasp of the Christian faith, but when one considers the stage of development in Europe at the same period, and that this stone was erected nearly three hundred years before the Battle of Hastings, the significance of it is tremendous. " The sixty-seven Nestorian missionaries whose names and labors are recorded on this tablet must have been residents in some portion of China at a much earlier date than that named upon the tablet, for the eggs of silkworms were brought from China to Constantinople in A.D. 551 by Nestorian monks." [32]

Timothy, patriarch of the Nestorian communion (A.D. 777–820), was a stanch supporter of the missionary movement and appointed to China the metropolitan David. " At a Synod in A.D. 850 called by the Patriarch Theodosius, it was announced that all metropolitan Bishops were to convene at Baghdad once in four years, with the exception of the metropolitans of India and China who were excused on account of the great distances. These were to communicate with the patriarch at least every six years." [33]

The Nestorians in China did not have a complete Bible as is known today. From the relics and documents that have been discovered it is possible to gain some idea of what was included in the Nestorian Scriptures. A beautifully printed edition in colors showing Bishop Alopen's Documents was published in 1931 in Japan by the Kyoto Institute of the Oriental Culture Academy. These reveal a distinct Christian message.[34] The success of the Nestorians under the T'ang dynasty is indicated in the official records dealing with the suppression of all foreign religions in the ninth century. At the pinnacle of their expansion there were from eleven hundred to two thousand religious workers, monks, and teachers, who were compelled to return to civilian life or leave the country.[35] That the Nestorian Church did not meet the conditions of this edict without protest is evidenced in the accounts of martyrdom.[36] These records suggest the extent of a church membership that had need of so many religious leaders. The Nestorians demonstrated a marked degree of cultural adaptation as evidenced by the translations of the Scriptures into Chinese. They had unusual capacities for building Christian communities as self-supporting, self-governing, and self-propagating entities, which must have something to teach modern highly and heavily subsidized organizations working toward the same objective.[37] " Their simplicity of faith and worship, their reverence for scriptures, their abhorrence of image and picture worship, of the confessional and of the doctrine of purgatory, and their not adoring the host in Communion, constitute them the Protestants of Asia." [38]

The tradition that the Magi returning from Bethlehem had so interpreted their discovery of the Messiah that the Syrian mind was prepared for the reception of the gospel persists as a cardinal strand. It is woven in Nestorian lore through many centuries. It appears on the Nestorian monument discovered in Sian-fu in the seventeenth century.[39] It is also found in the manuscripts discovered in North China by Pelliot in 1908.[40] In a small room cut out of the rock in the village of Ch'ien-fo-tung near Tun-huang on the northwest frontier of China, a treasure of manuscripts had lain for centuries, sealed and forgotten. Among the treasures found there by Pelliot was a small Christian scroll, torn in three pieces but yet complete. It was written approximately in A.D. 800. It contains a hymn to the Holy Trinity that has been identified with the Syriac form of " Gloria in Excelsis Deo." It is now preserved in the Bibliothèque Nationale in Paris. The name given to Jesus Christ in China in the ninth century is the one still used by Christians in China, " Mi Shih-he," the Messiah. The following translation

42   *The Lost Churches of China*

of the first and last stanzas of the " Gloria " shows the unquestionable Christian character:

" If the highest heavens with deep reverence adore,
If the great earth earnestly ponders general peace and harmony,
If man's first true nature receives confidence and rest,
It is due to A-lo-he, the merciful Father of the Universe.
Most holy, universally honoured Mi Shih-he,
We adore the merciful Father, ocean-treasure of mercy,
Most holy, humble, and the Holy Spirit nature.
Clear and strong is the law; beyond thought or dispute." [41]

Modern missionaries in Shan-si and Shen-si have found many evidences of the Nestorians, in monuments, carvings, manuscripts, ornaments, and jewels. Present-day Chinese distinguish between the descendants of Nestorians, Jews, and Mohammedans in an interesting manner. The Mohammedans are called " *Hui-hui*"; they are also spoken of as the " *San-chiao* " (three religions) because they have borrowed from the Jews, Christians, and Gentiles. The descendants of the Nestorians are called " *Shih-tzu Hui-hui*," which literally is "the Cross Moslems." This hints that many Nestorians were swallowed up in the Moslem victory in the fourteenth century, yet kept their identity through the sign of the cross. The Jesuit missionaries of the seventeenth century were delighted at this discovery, supposing that these descendants of Christians would easily rally to their ancestral faith. But the memory of massacre and persecution was still vivid, and the difficulties confronting the Jesuits during their first years in China were too numerous, to permit the Chinese with Christian traditions to show their sympathies. Following the discovery of the monument in 1623, when the Jesuit scholars had won the confidence and favor of the Ming emperors, they discovered a wave of support that had its strength in those areas of North China where the Nestorians had been strongly rooted centuries earlier. In 1886 two Nestorian cemeteries were located at Pish-pek and Tok-mak. Four more are now known in the area of Kuld-ja. The Tok-mak cemetery has over six hundred stones with Syriac inscriptions, with dates from 858 to the middle of the fourteenth century.[42] On each of the tombstones was a deeply cut cross. In 1890, Cesar de Brabander discovered the ruins of a cemetery halfway between Pe-king and Shang-tu.[43] Great interest was aroused in 1919 by the discovery of a Buddhist temple named "The Monastery of the Cross," forty miles southwest of Pe-king, in which were found carved stones with crosses surrounded by a quotation in Syriac from Ps. 34:5,6: "Look ye unto it and hope in it." The Syriac inscription clearly traces the stones to the Nestorians.[44] Over the entrance gate is an inscription in Chinese, *Shih Tzu Ssu,* "The Monastery of the Cross." By the end of the eighth century the cross was called by the purely Chinese term *Shih Tzu,* "Symbol of Ten." Because this character was in fact a cross, it was used as a seal by Christians, and in usage the cross came to be called *Shih Tzu.*[45]

Unfortunately, after two hundred years Nestorian Christianity does not seem to have made much adaption of the Chinese terms for God or Christ as postulated by Confucius or Lao Tzu. Instead it remained a foreign religion in China, using wholly Syriac terms for God and Christ.[46] Whether they wore Chinese dress or Persian attire, we do not know. Whether the missionaries shaved to appear more like the Chinese or wore beards like the Syrians, we do not know. We know that in the hour of antiforeign uprising in the ninth century the Nestorians were linked with the Indian and Persian religions.

The loss of the Nestorian Church in the T'ang dynasty is due to its precarious position of being dependent on political favor. The Nestorians were welcomed by a Confucian emperor who had just suppressed Buddhism. The Confucian scholars had examined the new doctrine and reported favorably on it to the court. The intrigue which brought about this disastrous loss to the Church was deep-rooted and stemmed from the jealousies that had long existed between the Confucian scholars and Buddhism. The Confucian school first became a state cult under the Han dynasty.[47] The Confucian manuscripts were made the basis of civil service examinations, which gave the scholars a political influence that rose and fell throughout Chinese history. The phenomenal expansion of Buddhism during the first six centuries was an alarming development to the Confucian scholars. By the end of the sixth century Buddhism rivaled the state in its power and wealth. The suppression of Buddhism in the seventh century restored power and wealth to the state. This just preceded the Nestorians, who found on their arrival an atmosphere of diligent seeking for truth in religion as against a riot of superstition.[48]

The abhorrence of Emperor T'ai Tsung for superstitions was strengthened by the empress Ch'ang Sun. The Nestorians reached the court just one year before her death. Her dying words to her son reveal a freedom from superstition and a confidence in God:

" Our life is in the hands of Heaven, and when it decides that we shall die, there is no mortal power that can prolong it. As for the Taoist and Buddhist faiths, they are heresies, and have been the cause of injury to both the people and the state. Your father has a great aversion to them, and therefore you must not displease him by appealing to them on my behalf." [49]

In A.D. 650 the great T'ai Tsung died and was succeeded by his son Kao Tsung (650–684), a feeble man. He was completely under the control of one of his wives, the unprincipled Wu Hou. Still he, like his parents, favored the Christian religion. Wu Hou did not oppose her husband's favor toward the Christians. She had deeper designs of restoring Buddhism. In her early life she had been a Buddhist nun. From the convent she entered the palace as a concubine of T'ai Tsung and later became the wife of Kao Tsung. Was this a deep plot of Buddhists to gain favor at court, and for this purpose was an attractive nun offered to the emperor? We shall see in the seventeenth century that when a later emperor was almost persuaded to accept Christianity Buddhist intrigue provided him with a nun as concubine who undermined the influence of the Jesuit missionaries.

Following the death of Kao Tsung, Wu Hou was lavish in her favors to the religion of which she had once been a nun. Concubine to one emperor and wife of the next, she now, as a widowed empress, became the lover of a Buddhist monk, Hwai Yi. She built a vast monastery for him, where he was to become abbot. Under her patronage Buddhist art reached the zenith of its glory in China. The Nestorian monument records that in the year 698 " the Buddhists took advantage of their strength " to oppose the Christians.[50]

The Sian-fu monument does not refer to this persecution of the Buddhists in 698 other than "controversy-derision-slander." But there must have been more than mere words. A later footnote carved at the base of the stone refers to the fact that when the storm was over, fallen roofs and ruined walls had to be raised, desecrated altars and sanctuaries were restored.

It was toward the close of the T'ang dynasty that the Confucian scholars found their first opportunity in two centuries of again challenging Buddhism. The upsurge given Buddhism by Wu Hou in the eighth century continued until Buddhism had usurped the prerogatives of the State. The Confucian opposition was led by Han Yu, the author of the famous caustic "Memorial on a Bone of the Buddha," which was largely responsible for the imperial edict of A.D. 845 proscribing all religions of foreign origin.[51] The strength of the Confucian scholars lay in the Han Lin Academy of letters which was founded in the Han dynasty. "This Academy, at which were assembled some of the most competent scholars of the day, had charge of all the court's literary activity. . . . Still functioning well ten centuries later, it was held up as an example to the much newer academies in Europe."[52] The Confucian scholars in the ninth century succeeded in striking a blow at Buddhism from which it has never recovered. However, one of the major weapons employed was national and cultural pride, fanned into a fire against the foreign religious invasion from India. In the holocaust that destroyed Buddhism, it was unavoidable that Christianity should also suffer because it too fell under the stigma of being "foreign." Confucian scholars were able to counsel the court to institute wide "reforms," which included the persecution of foreign religions whereby the State gained control of vast amounts of land and monasteries belonging to the religious orders. The extensive character of the property held by the "foreign" religions which was expropriated by the State in the persecution of A.D. 845 is fully described in the new T'ang records. "When Wu Tsung was on the throne he destroyed Buddhism. Throughout the empire he demolished four thousand six hundred monasteries, and settled as secular subjects two hundred and sixty-five thousand nuns and monks, and one hundred and fifty thousand male and female serfs; while of land he resumed some tens of millions of Ch'ing." [53]

In this condition of affairs of rising tension against Buddhism as a foreign religion it was impossible to confine the conflagration. The official decree against Christians followed:

"As to monks and nuns who are aliens and who teach the religions of foreign countries, we command that these over three thousand people of Nestorians, Moslems, and Zoroastrians return to the secular life and cease to confuse our national customs and manners." [54]

The Moslems were not numerous. They had to come to China as envoys and merchants or mercenaries.[55] The Zoroastrians were also numerically small. Thus most of this number of three thousand religious workers must be presumed to be Nestorians.[56]

The T'ang dynasty records reveal how the Confucian scholars had conspired to replenish the wealth of the state.[57] All religions were supervised by a single board at the T'ang court. The Nestorians suffered with all foreign religions in the efforts of the State to wrest from Buddhism the power which it had usurped.[58]

Thus Nestorian Christianity was erased, leaving only its monuments in stone. If Buddhists were to be cast out, by Confucian rivalries, on the grounds of being a foreign religion, it is unthinkable that Christianity should have escaped without loss.[59] And although remnants survived the persecution for a time, ultimately the Nestorians disappeared from China and found their means of survival among the northern tribes of Turks and Mongols.[60] There were small groups who survived in North China for almost a century, but most of those who did not escape were put to death. Refugees of the Nestorians found a welcome north of China in the territory of the Uigurs. That Manichaeism was not truly a heresy but a partial expression of Christianity is suggested by the fact that the Uigurs, who were Manichaeans when they welcomed the Nestorian refugees, abandoned Manichaeism. According to Bar Hebraeus, the tribes south of Lake Baikal adopted the Christian faith of the Nestorians in A.D. 1007.[61]

After the suppression of all foreign religions, Confucian temples appeared for the first time in China. The T'ang emperors recognized that Confucian ethics provided a sound foundation for the unification of society and the establishment of orderly government. Thus they gave the movement support for political reasons.[62]

In A.D. 987 a Christian monk, returning from China, reported in Constantinople that "the Christians of China had disappeared and perished for various reasons and that in the whole country only one was left." [63]

When history records the Nestorians in strength again, they are moving from the land of the Uigurs back to China as advisers to the Mongol princes.

It is important to recognize that the loss of the Nestorians in the T'ang dynasty was due to three major factors:

1. Their dependence upon the political favor of the court placed them in a vulnerable position in an hour when influences at the court conspired against them.

2. Although they had, at first, received a cordial welcome

from the Confucian court, and while they prospered for two hundred years, they continued as a foreign religion with little attempt to relate the Christian message with the legitimate truths found in China's religious heritage.

3. A third reason is not quite so apparent, but it is clearly suggested in the downfall of the Buddhists. The Nestorians were engulfed in the holocaust that crushed Buddhism, and it is to be inferred that in a proportionate degree they shared in the mistake made by the Buddhists of amassing wealth and power for support of their monasteries by landholdings. The wrath of the Confucian scholars, which transmitted itself into the wrath of the court, was rooted in economic considerations. Buddhism had become immensely wealthy through tax exemptions on its landholdings surrounding monasteries. Moreover the thousands entering the monasteries were thus able to avoid their economic responsibilities and political obligations. In effect Buddhism had become a state within a state. Even if the Nestorians were guiltless in this regard, nevertheless the lessons from the holocaust that crushed Buddhism and engulfed the Nestorians should ever be borne in mind. In the twentieth century, as we shall later note, the wrath of the Communists is vented against the large property holdings of the Church and particularly against the landlord policy of Roman Catholic missions by which they financed their work through rentals.[64]

III

THE CHURCH OF THE EAST MEETS
THE CHURCH OF THE WEST

THE connecting link in the history of the Nestorians with the events in the preceding chapter is to be found in the Liao and Chin dynasties, which existed beyond the borders of North China, to which the Nestorian refugees fled in the ninth century. There they survived and prospered in the land of the Uigurs in Inner Mongolia. Manichaeism had been quite strong in Inner Mongolia until the arrival of the Nestorians. Christianity soon developed an extensive place among the Uigurs and Mongols, gradually displacing Manichaeism, which had taught only a partial reference to Jesus Christ in its eclectic system.

The Liao dynasty (907–1124) is generally classed in history with the Chin (1115–1234), the Yuan or Mongol (1260–1368), and the Ch'ing or Manchu (1644–1912) dynasties. These four dynasties share a fundamental feature: they were established by inner Asiatic peoples who invaded Chinese territory and ruled over a population that was mainly Chinese. When the Nestorians returned to China in the thirteenth century, it was under the patronage of the Mongols. Thus when we speak of Christians in China in the thirteenth and fourteenth centuries, it should be understood that most of them were of tribes from north of the border, who were looked upon by the Chinese as members of the conquering force that had occupied China. There is no evidence that Christianity gained its second foot-

hold in China in this period except in the areas of Mongol influence.

While Christianity was gaining ascendancy in Mongolia during the tenth to twelfth centuries there were important developments within China proper. During the tenth to twelfth centuries, the Sung dynasty, which held power from the downfall
of the T'ang until the Mongol conquest, had encouraged the
Confucian school and enabled art and literature to reach a
stage of development not later excelled. The Neo-Confucian
school, founded by Chu Hsi, flourished under the Sung dynasty
and borrowed greatly from Buddhism and Taoism. The insistence of Chu Hsi on " Infinite Love " as being the final explanation of the universe, and such phrases as, " Heaven is
a Father to man, and the feeling of man to Heaven should be
none other than the love and reverent service of a son," seem
to have a note not found in Chinese writings prior to the Nestorians. Buddhism had not been completely eradicated in the
ninth century, for the decree expropriating the lands and
closing thousands of monasteries had expressly permitted the
continuance of a very limited number.

These were the contemporary developments within China
proper under the Sung dynasty, while Nestorian Christianity
was gaining ascendancy and influence in Inner Mongolia.
When the Nestorians returned to China proper, they came as
the trusted advisers of the new rulers. By this time they evidenced pronounced political consciousness. When the Nestorians appeared in Pe-king, it was as priests of the religion in
favor with the Mongol court.

The influence of the Nestorians under the Mongols, first in
the Liao state of Inner Mongolia and later in China under the
Yuan dynasty, was one of ascending scale. In the twelfth century Europe was astonished by the renown of a Christian king
in the East, whose riches and power were reputed to be without limit.

In 1145, the bishop of Gaula, Syria, during a visit to Italy,
narrated that

" a few years ago a certain John, who dwells beyond Persia and Armenia, in the extreme Orient, a king and a priest and a Christian with his whole nation, though a Nestorian, conducted a war against the kings of the Persians and Medes. . . . They fought for three days. . . . Presbyter Johannes, for thus they used to call him, yet having routed the Persians emerged victorious from the most atrocious slaughter." [1]

Otto von Freisingen is the first to mention the " Presbyter " as the Eastern ruler who defeated the king of Persia, Samiardi, and his followers. All travelers of the eleventh and twelfth centuries speak of the existence of a great Christian ruler in the Far East during this period. Undoubtedly the name Presbyter or Prester John was handed down from father to son, and there was probably a succession of Mongol kings bearing this title, who were Nestorian Christians.

The Mongol Empire of Jenghis Khan, like the Khitan state of the Liao dynasty, started on the northern border of China. These states faced China aggressively and set up dynasties that derived their strength from the borders of China and yet were vulnerable to attack from the tribal world north and west of them.

Jenghis Khan, after taking Yen-ching (modern Pe-king) in 1215, returned to Turkestan. Defeating and then uniting the peoples of Mongolia and central Asia, Jenghis created as base, Ning-hsia, from which he could carry the Mongol attack in any direction: into Russia, Europe, the Near East, India, and China. He and his successors formed the greatest continental empire the world has seen. But they turned back from Europe and all but the northern part of India; so China became the most important part of their holdings.

Under Ogotai, Jenghis Khan's successor, Kai-feng, in Ho-nan, was captured in 1233. Mongol assaults upon Europe and disputes about the succession delayed their attack upon the southern Sung empire. This was begun by Kublai Khan in 1251 and completed in 1276. . . . Kublai Khan made Pe-king his capital in 1263 and established the Yuan dynasty in 1264.

The reign of Kublai saw the Mongol Empire at its apex. In

political administration, Kublai enlisted Chinese scholars and
gave them minor offices. Relatively few were in high positions.
Foreign contingents were in the Mongol armies. The administrative posts were filled with aliens, among whom many were
Nestorian Christians.

Nestorian Christianity was at that time widely spread in
central Asia and on the borders of China proper, and numbers
of the foreigners who came from these regions into China
under the Yuan dynasty were Christians.

The influence of the Nestorians on the court during the Mongol Empire is evidenced in " Collection of Inscriptions on
Metals and Stones," by Wang Ch'ang, in which the phrase,
" Being the Emperor by the Power of the Eternal God and by
the Protection of the Great Felicity," is found on at least ten
inscriptions that also carry references to Nestorian Christians.
An imperial rescript in 1272 ordered: " By the command of
Genghis, Ogdai, Satchen, Olshaitu and Guluk Khans . . .
the priests, Erkehuns (Nestorians) and teachers shall be exempt from all official service and shall give themselves entirely
to the duties of supplicating the blessings of God." [2] More than
one hundred bronze crosses have been discovered in recent
years in the Ordos country and in Sui-yuan province, which was
a stronghold of Nestorian Christianity in this period.[3] Father
Mostaert has found in the Ordos country the Erkut tribe, de-
scended from the Christian Onguts.[4] The records left by William of Rubruck and Marco Polo show that Nestorian Uigurs
almost monopolized the secretariat offices throughout the Yuan
dynasty.[5] Moule has found that there were Christians under
the Mongols in the provinces of Chiang-cho, Chiang-hai,
Chiang-nan, Han-erh (North China), Ho-hai, Ho-nan, Shang-
hai, Tibet, Uiguria, Yu-nan, and that they were very strong in
fourteen major cities.[6]

There are many evidences that under the Mongol Empire
the Nestorians gained widespread footholds throughout North
China and were able to penetrate south to the Yang-tze Valley,
and even as far south on the coast as Fu-kien. In the historical

records of this period there are many references in Chinese official documents to the Nestorians. The province of Shan-si became a stronghold of Christians as it was nearest to the headquarters of the Mongol King George. It also was the area where Christianity had been the strongest in the T'ang dynasty. In the *Yuan Shih,* March, 1267, it is decreed that Christians in P'ing-yang and T'ai-yuan-fu were exempted from military service. In *Yuan Shih I Wen,* 1287, it is noted that when Christian monks of Chiang-nan travel they ride in sedan chairs. This denoted great respect. But, as often revealed in history, privilege and power corrupts even monks and priests. Thus in 1293 an edict was published in *Yuan T'ung Chih* restraining Christian and other monks from illegally evading taxes. In the year 1300 an order was issued in *Yuan T'ung Chih T'iao-ko* requiring Christian monks in the provinces of Ho-nan, Che-chiang, and Shan-si who trade to pay taxes. In the *Yuan T'ung Chih* supplement of July, 1320, it was decreed that Moslems, Christians, and Jews in Chiang-hai, except those in actual temples, were to pay taxes. Moule observes that it was the official protection given to the Nestorians by the Mongol court which exposed them to the difficulties revolving around these special regulations that had to be issued to control them. It would seem that either through their vested privileges they had claimed exemptions or avoided taxes and thus incurred the jealousy of the populace, or else they were falsely accused, with the result that it was deemed necessary to issue these increasingly stringent regulations.[7]

There are references to a Nestorian under Kublai Khan being placed in charge of the astronomical bureau, who later became a member of the Han Lin Academy and a minister of state; to a Nestorian physician from Samarkand who was governor of Ching-kiang, and to an archbishopric of the Nestorian Church established at Pe-king. Kublai Khan also established an office to supervise the Christians. Marco Polo described the northern provinces of China through which he traveled as composed of three kinds of people: idolaters, those who worship

Mahomet, and Nestorian Christians. Polo was not in China in any religious capacity. Therefore, his observations stand out because of his surprise at finding Christians there.

He mentions a Nestorian church in Hang-chow, and two Nestorian churches were in Ching-kiang-fu when he visited it. Those, he tells us, were built in A.D. 1278 by a baron named Mar Sarghis, a Nestorian Christian, who was sent by the great khan as governor of the city.

According to Bar Hebraeus, in A.D. 1265, the Nestorians inhabited twenty-five Asiatic provinces and administered over seventy dioceses.[8] References to Christians in China in the thirteenth and fourteenth centuries are found in many contemporary Chinese texts.[9]

It is important to recount briefly what happened between the seventh century when the first Nestorians came to China, and the thirteenth century in western Asia and Europe. At the time Christianity was expanding eastward into China, the Moslems of Arabia advanced northward and westward in military conquests. When the Arabs invaded Persia, they found the Nestorians already a power in the East. The Nestorians observed a neutrality that was favorable to the invaders; they did not assist the Persians against the foe, but welcomed the Arabs as liberators. The Arabs soon discovered that the learning of the East was chiefly nurtured among the Nestorians and entrusted them with prominent positions, as treasurers, physicians, and scribes. They translated for the Arabs the works of the Greek philosophers and physicians. Caliph al-Mamum sent learned Nestorians to Syria and Egypt to collect manuscripts and translate them. He replied to a critic who asked how the translation could be entrusted to a Christian: "If I confide to him the care of my body in which dwell my soul and spirit, wherefore should I not intrust him with the things which do not concern our faith or his faith? He has eaten my bread and salt." [10]

This amicable relationship between the Nestorians and the Moslems continued for centuries until the rise of the Mongols.

The elementary beginnings of our knowledge of chemistry, gunpowder, the compass, medicine, philosophy, and even in some measure theology, are due in large measure to the combined labors of the Nestorians and the Arabs.[11] The Nestorians gained their knowledge of making paper, the secret of making gunpowder, the art of making porcelain, and printing by stone lithography, in China. From the Nestorians the Arabs derived this knowledge. The Arabs also borrowed the mariner's compass from the Chinese. Paper was used in China as early as A.D. 105. The secret of its manufacture was known in Mecca in 707, in Egypt in 800, in Spain in 950, in Constantinople in 1100, in Sicily in 1102, in Italy in 1154, in Germany in 1228, in England in 1309. Paper made possible the making of books wherever it went.

Behind this cultural borrowing smoldered fires. In the seventh to ninth centuries, during the period of missionary success in China, Christian scholars had retreated out of Europe as far west as Ireland. Islam was on the march and western Europe was a chaos of conquest and disintegration of both morals and government. What classic culture survived was silent and hidden.[12] For three centuries Christianity in the West had trembled before the advance of the Moslem invasion of North Africa and into Europe. This was the crisis that produced the Crusades, which served to unite a divided Europe. They were the culminating act of the medieval drama, and the most picturesque event in the history of Europe and the Near East. The Crusades demonstrated that mankind's deepest hatred is fanned into flame by those who challenge his sustenance and creed.

In the East the rising tide of the Mongols took advantage of the preoccupation of the Moslem world in the Crusades; and the Nestorians, feeling the animosity of the Moslems toward Christians that had been engendered by the Crusades, sought their security in the Mongol Empire. The middle of the thirteenth century witnessed the final bankruptcy of the Crusades after Saladin's capture of Jerusalem in 1187.[13] Europe was exhausted from their failure. Pope Innocent IV (1243–1254) conceived the plan of converting the Mongols to Christianity in order to get at the Moslem world from the East through an alliance with the Mongols. There does not appear to be any thought that an extensive Christian Church then existed in the lands of the Mongols. These pious and political schemes of Western Christendom in the hour of extremity cannot be called missionary. To be sure of securing political alliances, even in the name of the Church, is not the missionary task of the Church. A recent Catholic scholar admits that the first missionaries were sent to the Mongols because of the threat of the Moslems.[14] The most famous of these were John de Piano Carpini and Benedict the Pole, who were commissioned by Pope Innocent IV in 1245 with a letter to the king of the People of the Tartars.[15] In 1253, Louis IX of France sent William of Rubruck to the Mongols from the Holy Land. Another mission of Dominicans was sent by the pope to the Mongols who controlled Persia, but the demands of the Dominicans were too arrogant.[16] The information secured by these missions evoked an interest in the Orient. In 1250 a General Chapter issued by the Vatican decreed that Arabic should be taught in addition to Greek and Hebrew. In 1311, Pope Clement V founded colleges of Oriental languages at Rome, Paris, Oxford, Bologna, and Salamanca.[17]

If the overtures from Europe to the Mongols had given any recognition to the Nestorian Christians, or manifested any degree of tolerance, or sought a reconciliation between the two historic Churches, there might have been hope of success. In the *Annals of China* references to Nestorians serving in the armies of the Mongols mention them as the " God Grant Stratagem Army."[18]

When the Mongols captured Baghdad, it was not unnatural that the Nestorians there in the western parts of Asia should hail the Mongols of the East as their deliverers. Abaqu Khan (1265–1282), the son of Khulaqu Khan, was most favorable to Christianity. He presented Patriarch Denkha, after his con-

secration, with magnificent gifts of a diploma, staff, and umbrella. The silk umbrella was the emblem of royalty so universally adopted by the Eastern nations.[19]

In the defeat of the Moslems, and the massacre of their caliph
at Baghdad by the Mongols in the thirteenth century, the Nestorians abandoned the political neutrality they had maintained
for nearly eight hundred years during which they had lived
among the Moslems. During the period Europe was involved
in the Crusades, the Nestorians had become an influential
Church throughout Asia. They had developed a keen political
sensitivity evidenced in the election, at Baghdad, in A.D. 1281,
of the metropolitan of Pe-king to be Patriarch Yahballaha III.
Since a great majority of the electors were not Chinese, this
must be interpreted as a political attempt to win the favor of
the Mongols.

At the close of the thirteenth century the Church of the East
and the Church of the West met in the most dramatic exchanges
which precipitated the downfall and eclipse of the Nestorians
in China. The Mongol court was sensitive to Moslem pressure.
The court besought the Nestorian patriarch, Yahballaha III, to
nominate a churchman to serve as ambassador to the European
courts, in the hope of establishing an alliance against the Moslems. Rabban Sauma, visitor-general of the Nestorian Churches,
born in Pe-king, was chosen by the patriarch for this mission.
This appointment caused great satisfaction to the Mongol
princes, who realized the favorable impression likely to be created by a Christian envoy at the courts of Europe. Rabban
Sauma carried letters from the Mongol court and gifts for each
of the European kings, also letters and gifts from the patriarch
of the Nestorian Church to the pope at Rome, who was considered the patriarch of the West.[20] Sauma arrived in Rome in
A.D. 1288. His was a twofold mission, seeking reconciliation
with the Western Church, and a political alliance with European states against the Moslem world. But the Nestorians in
seeking rapport with the Western Church of Europe were not
prepared to be subordinated to the papacy. The extensive in-

fluence of the Nestorians under the Mongol Empire reveals the significance of the mission to Europe.

" At the opening of the fourteenth century, the Patriarch Yahballaha III (1281–1317), who was himself of Chinese origin, ruled over a hierarchy of twenty-five metropolitans, which would mean some two hundred to two hundred and fifty bishops; and we may gain a vivid impression of the vitality of the Church of the East and of the interest it excited in Europe from the account written by Rabban Sauma who was recommended to Khan Argon, prince of the Mongols, as envoy to the West in order to concert an alliance for the taking of Jerusalem. He was received by the Emperor Adronicus II, 1282–1328, at Constantinople, and then went on to Rome. The pope, Honorius IV, 1285–1287, was just dead so Sauma continued his journey to Paris, where he was received by Philip IV of France, 1285–1314, and to Gascony, where he had an audience of Edward I of England, 1272–1307. On his return, he passed through Rome, where he was not only entertained by Pope Nicholas IV, 1288–1292, but allowed to make his communion at the papal Mass on Palm Sunday and given permission to celebrate his own." [21]

That this embassy headed by Rabban Sauma was seeking a political and military alliance between the forces of Western Christendom and the Mongol Empire is clearly established. It also sought friendly relations between the Church of the East and the Church of the West. This overture, instead of developing Christian unity, produced only suspicion, which led to intrigue by the papacy, with renewal of antagonisms rooted in the fifth century. The political purpose of Rabban Sauma's mission doubtless became known to the Moslem world. The European courts that had followed the leadership of the pope during the Crusades against the Moslems naturally looked to the papacy for a clue in regard to what response they should make to the Mongol court.

The visit of the Nestorian-Mongolian mission to Europe aroused the papacy. The very next year Pope Nicholas IV sent John of Monte Corvino as a missionary to the Orient on July 15, 1289. In 1307 seven more Franciscans were sent to act as suffragans after they had consecrated Monte Corvino to be archbishop of Pe-king, then known as Khan-baliq. The letters of the pope to heads of the Mongol states express joy at the news of their sympathy with Christianity and seek the continuance of this favor to the Order of Friars Minor. These letters carefully draw the attention of the Mongol princes to the assertion of the papacy regarding its supremacy over all Christians: "We who though unworthy are the vicar of Christ and successor of St. Peter the chief of the apostles," [22] etc.

"The letters which Rabban Sauma took to Europe are not known to exist, but copies of Pope Nicholas' reply have been preserved. It greets the patriarch as 'Bishop in the lands of the East' and while it professes Christian good will and blessing, it did not recognize the patriarch's supremacy in the East and ends with an unbending claim of universal supremacy for Rome." [23]

The Nestorians had been the only Christian Church in China for almost seven hundred years until, after several unsuccessful attempts, the Roman Catholics established the Franciscan mission beside them in Khan-baliq (Pe-king). The leader of this mission, John of Monte Corvino, spent four years in travel through Persia, India, and Mongolia en route to the Mongol capital. He reached the capital in A.D. 1293 shortly before the death of Kublai Khan. The Mongol court looked upon his coming as a response to the earlier overture sent to Europe by the hand of the Nestorian visitor-general, Rabban Sauma. When the court discovered the conditions upon which further help from Europe depended, the Mongols requested the pope to send a larger number of missionaries. This message was carried to Europe by Marco Polo.[24] The second band of Franciscans arrived at the capital in 1307. Had these two groups, Nestorians and Roman Catholics, found a way to work together, the whole of world history might have been changed. "Unfortunately from the very outset they worked in opposition to one another, and apparently made no effort to understand each other or to see whether some agreement or division of labor was not possible." [25]

That the Church of Rome was determined to permit on reconciliation with the Nestorians, and that the antipathy of the Franciscans was officially inspired is evidenced in the letters of license sent by Pope Clement V to John of Monte Corvino, appointing and ordaining him to be archbishop of Khan-baliq. This license of authority praises Monte Corvino for his success in reaching the capital of the Mongol Empire, and his securing leave of the Mongol court to build a church " to the honor of God and of the Catholic faith, after many and varied persecutions and intrigues and injuries brought upon you by the Nestorian heretics." The pope's document also contained very adroit suggestions of the advantages to be gained by the Mongols by their transfer of allegiance from the Nestorian faith to the pope. " When pernicious errors have been wholly removed, heresies in those regions will be taken out, schisms uprooted, and great — nay even the very greatest — good will come to the said great king and to his kingdom and very many desirable things will follow." [26]

The Franciscans not only lacked any tolerance for the Nestorian Christians, but they also lacked any cultural appreciation of the Chinese, evidenced by the fact that they conducted their services in Latin and trained their converts in Latin. However, in their letters back to Rome, they sensed their cultural barrier:

" We truly believe that if we had their tongues wonderful works of God would be seen. The harvest is great but the laborers are few, and with no sickle. For we are but a few brothers, and very old, and unable to learn languages. May God forgive those who hindered brothers from coming." [27]

The Franciscans were conditioned in their approach to the Orient and also in their attitude toward the Nestorians by the school of thought in which they had been nurtured. The license of authority from Pope Clement V left the Franciscans in China with no freedom to meet the Nestorians in Christian fellowship but to require of them capitulation.

John of Monte Corvino lays the blame of the misunderstanding on the Nestorians.[28] Up to now no record has been found in Chinese manuscripts of this period that could even suggest that the Nestorians were guilty of all calumny of which the

Franciscans accuse them. Naturally the Nestorians objected to the establishment of another Church, which brought no fraternal greetings from the pope to the Nestorians, but rather deliberately sought to supplant them in the favor of the Mongol court. The crisis that confronted the Nestorian bishops and monks in China must have been a difficult one. The Mongol court was known to be seeking an alliance with European states against the Moslems whose enmity had been incurred by the massacre of Baghdad.

In the year A.D. 1333 a Franciscan monk from Florence, John de' Marignolli, wrote a glowing picture of his cordial welcome: " The Friars Minor of Cambulac (Pe-king) have a cathedral church immediately adjoining the palace, with a proper residence for the archbishop, and other churches in the city besides, and they have bells, too, and all the clergy have their subsistence from the emperor's table in the most honorable manner." [29]

Thus the Mongol court went out of its way to win the favor of the papacy. Certain Roman Catholic authors carry this idea of favorable support of the Mongols beyond factual evidence. One of the most damaging rumors, repudiated by the Church of the East, is the disputed account that affirms that the Nestorian patriarch, Yahballaha III, sent his acceptance of the pope in a profession of faith that was received, and blessed, by Pope Benedict XI, A.D. 1304.[30] If this were true, it is inconceivable that Pope Clement V, when creating John of Monte Corvino archbishop of Khan-baliq, should have execrated the Nestorians as heretics in his letter of license to the new archbishop. Under the conditions of travel in the fourteenth century communications were difficult, involving considerable time. When the Nestorians discovered that the Franciscans had been sent with deliberate instructions to undermine them, it is understandable that consternation and confusion were created.

From the outset the Franciscans played on the political hopes of the Mongols for an alliance with the European states. The Mongol princes were mindful of the strategic political in-

fluence of the pope in Europe. This intrigue was fraught with
the greatest peril. Thus the result of the joint Nestorian-Mon-
gol overture to Europe was abortive. The pope had deferred
an alliance until the Mongols should abandon what Rome denounced as the Nestorian heresy. The Nestorians who had
shared with the Mongol court in the overture to Europe had
not only been betrayed but they had, thereby, forfeited their
position of neutrality in the eyes of the Moslems, thus losing a relationship they had maintained for nearly eight centuries.

It is one of the stark tragedies of Christendom that the Franciscans were incapable, either by training or because of precise
directions to the contrary from their superiors, of showing any
appreciation of the Nestorians, whom they sought to supplant. What might have become a source of strength and confidence resulting from love and tolerance became instead a
divisive and destructive force within the ranks of Christendom.
In the meantime intrigue was rife in both Europe and Asia.
At the very time Pope Clement V was sending missionaries to
China to undermine the Nestorians, he was entering into a
dark conspiracy with King Philip IV of France to destroy what
had been the life-giving sinews of the Church during the Crusades, namely, the Religious and Military Orders of the Knights
Templars. The pope was jealous of the power that lay in the
hands of the Order, which the papacy had sanctioned for the
prosecution of the Crusades. Now its spiritual independence
from the hierarchy of the Church was irksome to the pope.
Thus he conspired to seize control over the Order. Philip IV
was heavily in debt to the Knights Templars and was a willing
tool of the pope in suppressing the Order and confiscating
their properties. In this unholy alliance the Templar Order,
which was the military strength of Europe, was destroyed;
while in the heart of western Asia the leader of the Moslems,
Tamerlane, watched for his opportunity. With the martyrdom
of the leaders of the Knights Templars, Europe was thrown
into confusion. The news of the sabotage of the Knights Tem-

plars was not long in reaching the ears of Tamerlane. The Moslems also learned from China that the machinations of the Franciscans at the Mongol court destroyed hope of co-operation between the Church of the West and the Church of the East. It was the Moslem's hour to strike. The hour was already later than many dreamed. Thus, when Europe was shorn of its military strength by the suppression of the Religious and Military Orders, and while the Nestorians were being undermined in China, Tamerlane led his Moslem hordes in a scourge of fire and sword that swept Christianity out of Asia from the Caspian Sea to the Yellow Sea. The Black Death, which scourged Europe in the Middle Ages, was unleashed by this holocaust and prevented any further missionary endeavor from Europe for two centuries.[31]

The only relic of the Franciscan mission is a Latin Bible of the thirteenth century which was obtained at Ch'ang-chou by P. Philip Couplet of the Society of Jesus, toward the end of the seventeenth century. This Bible was in a stage of irreparable decay, but still wrapped in Chinese yellow silk. It is preserved in the Laurentian Library in Florence. In marked contrast is the cultural adaptation of the Nestorians, who definitely used hymns, liturgies, and Scriptures in the native language.

In the scourge of Tamerlane no mercy was shown to the Nestorians. On the ruins of Isfahan, seventy thousand human heads were piled, and at Baghdad, the heap of Nestorian heads numbered ninety thousand.[32] It is said of Tamerlane that his mere nod caused multitudes to abandon Christianity. He pursued the Christians with relentless fury, destroying churches, forcing them to accept Islam or death. Those who escaped took refuge in the almost inaccessible fastnesses of the Kurdistan mountains.

The news of Tamerlane's scourge was not long in reaching China, where it gave courage to forces waiting for an opportunity to overthrow the Mongols. In the area of China that had formerly been the center of the Sung dynasty, uprisings under Chu Yuan-chang followed. Thus the Nestorians were caught between pincers. They were the privileged class whose favor was derived from the Mongol court. The Chinese who sought to overthrow the Mongols also cast out the Nestorians, identified with them. Between the Moslems of Tamerlane, driving relentlessly toward China from the west, and the upsurge of Chinese in rebellion against the Mongols, pushing north from the Yang-tze Valley, the Nestorians had nowhere to flee.[33] It was impossible that all perished under the Moslem fury; part of the explanation may be found in the large number of Mohammedans found in China at the present time, over twenty million in the northwest, a number that cannot be accounted for by the usual laws of natural increase.

Thus in 1368 the Mongol dynasty, which had been so friendly to the Nestorians, came to an end. The Moslems also blotted out the great Church of the East throughout China and much of Asia, and at the same time obliterated their young and vigorous Franciscan rival. The last authentic fact known about the Franciscans is the martyrdom of James of Florence, Roman Catholic bishop of Hang-chow, A.D. 1362.[34] No one has yet found any Chinese manuscripts or inscriptions that mention the Franciscans, although there is much documentary evidence in Chinese sources of the activities of the Nestorians in this period.

The small number of Nestorians who survived in Kurdistan were able to send missionaries to China again in the succeeding century. In 1490, Patriarch Shimun sent a metropolitan to China.[35]

There is no record found in China up to the present that reveals any success in re-establishment of the Nestorian Church as a result of this appointment of a metropolitan to China in A.D. 1490. There are suggestions that many Nestorians joined secret societies, particularly the Chin-tan-chiao, and that in this manner Nestorian Christianity went "underground." [36] The curtain that fell with the collapse of the Yuan dynasty was one that so completely shut off all communications between China and the West that it was to be reopened again only with the greatest difficulty.[37]

The scholar-official in China had waged a struggle for supremacy that had continued for many centuries, in the course
of which the scholars suffered many reverses, but in the ascendancy of the Ming dynasty they triumphed. In the hour of their
victory the Confucian school hadn't any mind to tolerate new
ideas.

Orthodoxy became synonymous with truth, and fidelity to
the interpretations of the Confucian school became synonymous
with any hope of advancement. China turned its back squarely
upon both the future and the outside world. The problem of
introducing and finding a sympathetic hearing for the doctrine
of the Christian faith seemed hopeless.[38]

The eclipse of the great Church of the East in the fourteenth
century is not without lessons that should be remembered by
Christians through all time. The tragedy that befell the Nestorians in the Yuan dynasty has often led to the question arising
out of bewilderment: " Where was God that he would allow
Christianity to be persecuted almost to extinction? " This questioning reveals that mankind needs to rediscover anew the confidence that history is in God's hands and that it has a goal, sur-
passing human understanding.[39] The revelation of God is not
finished — it continues. The Church must open its eyes, more
than it does, to see how God is perpetually revealing himself.[40]
The late archbishop of Upsala reminded us that " God reveals
himself in history, outside the Church as well as in it. . . .
God reveals himself as much in the vicissitudes of nations as
in the institutions of religion." [41]

Failure to discern the reasons for the lost Churches of China
under the Yuan dynasty has prevented Christendom from de-
riving help from the lessons imparted out of this tragedy.
That God moved in this crisis there can be no doubt. The Nestorians in this period had become a privileged and powerful
group that held positions of political preferment under the
Mongol court. The Franciscans sought the same. They both
vitiated their witness by their rivalries and contradicted their
message by their hatreds. In the end Christians of both Europe

and Asia were caught in the conflagration of their political schemes.

The scourge of the Moslems under Tamerlane, followed by the Black Death which it unleashed, must be faced by Christians as a judgment of the God of history against those Churches which willfully attempted to strengthen their position by placing their trust in political alliances with the kingdoms of this world, ignoring the words of their Lord: " The kingdom of God is within you " (Luke 17:21). The Nestorians and Roman Catholics in China were lost in the fourteenth century when they forgot the significance of the last phrase of the Lord's Prayer (Matt. 6:13).

IV

MISSIONARY MANDARINS

THIS chapter begins with the
failure of sixteenth century
Christians, because of their intolerant attitude, to make any
headway in China. For fifty years the Society of Jésus kept
knocking in vain at the gate of Can-ton, until a little group of
Jesuit scholars were given special permission to make a radically different approach. In their remarkable successes, in the
seventeenth century, they so far outran the parent Church by
their fearless and progressive methods of cultural adaptation
that they were enjoined by the pope as a result of the rites
controversy. The outstanding mind of this group was Matteo
Ricci, who adopted the terms used by Confucius to denote the
Supreme Being in order to make real to the Chinese the Christian idea of God. However, Ricci's own associates were not prepared fully to accept his views. Without his scholarly research
the Jesuits would have been utterly unaware that there was
any knowledge of God in China before their arrival. The Jesuits
were products of their own day and imbued with the strong
conviction that political means should be employed to obtain
protection and support for their work. The historical records
show that their political schemes nullified most of the good
they rendered through their cultural contributions. They were
continually running into difficulty because of their connection
with the colonial and imperialistic designs of Portugal, which
had pledged its support to the pope.[1] In the end they were
suppressed because of their political involvements both abroad

and in China. But this fact must not unduly prejudice one against them, lest the creative contributions they have given Christian missions be overlooked and lost.

In fairness to the Jesuits it should be said that when the Spanish missionaries arrived at a later date, they were just as politically minded. The age was one of intense identification of Christianity with Western culture, empire, trade, and power, which unfortunately characterizes many aspects of Christianity down to the twentieth century. Clashes among missionaries were inevitable because of the intransigent position which was characteristic of the Spanish Franciscans, Dominicans, and Augustinians, who lacked any capacity for cultural appreciation of the Chinese, and envied the successes of the Jesuits. Jealousy blinded them and was responsible for the acrimonious " Rites Controversy " which raged for a hundred years and seriously handicapped all missionary work in China. The Jesuits tolerated certain Chinese rites, such as veneration of ancestors. These rites were denounced by rival groups and the Jesuits were accused of attaining their great successes by compromising the Christian faith. But it was the political intrigues of the missionaries that were ultimately responsible for the suppression of the faith and the banishment of missionaries by imperial edict in 1724. The lost Churches of this period, which suffered destruction and martyrdom, cry out to heaven that the Church come to its senses and " render therefore unto Cæsar the things which are Cæsar's; and unto God the things that are God's " (Matt. 22:21).

In the famous papal bulls of May 3 and 4, 1493, Pope Alexander VI drew a line of demarcation between the colonial dreams of Spain and Portugal.[2] The Treaty of Tordesillas, which was concluded in 1494, moved the dividing line between the projected colonial empires of Spain and Portugal 370 leagues west of the Azores. This was ratified in 1506 by Pope Julius II.[3] Thus in their expansion to the East the Portuguese were motivated, as were the Spaniards to the West, not only by economic aims but by a fanatical zeal to spread Christianity and to turn back the pagan world. The identity of Christianity and European cultural forms and customs was so much believed that even slight concessions to non-European usages or attitudes ran the risk of being regarded as a betrayal of the faith. It was the age of the Inquisition. Pope Nicholas V, on January 8, 1455, had enlarged the privileges of the Portuguese. Pope Leo X further extended these privileges over all lands discovered or conquered, " from the Capes of Bojador and Neon to the Indies, wherever situated and even though in our day unknown." [4]

Thus the missionary movement became entwined with the political dreams of conquest. The clergy or laity were forbidden to trade, or to fish or to sail the seas, in these remote regions of the Orient without the permission of the king of Portugal. In return for these privileges the king was obligated to promote, as far as possible, the spread of Christianity in the sphere of influence assigned to him by the pope. The king was to send, and support, missionaries into these regions, and not only provide for their maintenance but establish churches, chapels, cloisters, and other mission foundations. Thus emerged the worst expression of Europeanism, the union of the missionary task with the colonial imperialism that has prevailed to a greater or less extent in connection with Roman Catholic missions until modern times. The Portuguese explorers of the fifteenth century were soon followed by Portuguese conquerors in the sixteenth century.

" In the first ten years of the sixteenth century, the naval victories of the Portuguese Albuquerque imprisoned Islam in the Red Sea and established in Asiatic waters the supremacy of the Christian flag. The papacy saw opening before its apostles the great maritime routes leading to China, Japan and the Philippines, the Moluccas." [5]

Europe of the sixteenth century was ill prepared for the missionary task. Courage, zeal, heroic self-sacrifice abounded with bigotry and intolerance. To uproot the non-Christian violently and to plant instead a Christian culture, which to the Roman world of the Middle Ages meant a European culture, was considered to be the work of God. Tolerance for the ideas of others could only be evidence of the betrayal of the eternal King. This was the spirit that engendered the Inquisition. It had departed from the Christian tolerance of the first centuries, when Saint Augustine could speak with respect of the natural virtues of non-Christians.[6] As a slowly growing awareness of other non-Christian peoples besides the Moslems dawned upon the consciousness of Europe, the papacy set itself to conquer the entire non-Christian world. The Crusades had developed this attitude of undertaking missions to the " heathen " with the cross and the sword.[7] To the Roman Church of the Middle Ages, all non-Christians were doomed to hell; the Roman Catholic missionaries of this period were sure of it. Moreover, the age was one of intense intolerance of all Christians who did not acknowledge the supremacy of the pope. Evidences of this mood are found in the massacre of the Nestorians, who had survived the Moslem scourge of the fourteenth century, on the Malabar coast of India. When the Portuguese reached there, they brought the Inquisition with them. The Jesuits gave the Nestorians the choice of death by the sword or submission. Thousands perished, while others preferred to live even though life meant acceptance of the supremacy of the pope. Roman authors admit this " clash and intrigue." [8] The Jesuits drew the membership of their Society from different countries. It was the good fortune of the China mission in the seventeenth century that men were assigned to China who manifested a more tolerant appreciation of non-Christian cultures. In this way they represented a complete break with the dominant spirit of the Society and of the age in which they moved. It was not, however, until the Society had experienced fifty years of failure in attempting to enter China that this new venture was permitted.[9]

The first Jesuit to set foot on the mainland of China was Melchior Baretto, who landed on the island of Shang-ch'uan in 1555 in July. By November he had reached Macao. Being unable to go beyond Macao, except for two brief excursions

with the Portuguese traders to Can-ton, where he was prevented from preaching, he departed for Japan the next year.[10]
Shortly afterward, a Dominican, Gaspar da Cruz, arrived at
Macao. His efforts met with no more success than was experienced by Baretto. His mission a failure, he returned to India.[11]
The Portuguese had been allowed to carry on a small amount
of trade with China through their settlement at Macao, but in
all other respects the Chinese were as firm as ever in their resolve to allow no foreigner to enter China.[12] All efforts to break
down this reserve met with disillusionment. In 1573 the Chinese erected a small wall between Macao and the mainland.
The guarded gate was opened once every fifteen days to allow
foodstuffs for the Macao market. Eight Jesuits had reached Macao by 1563. There they stayed, unable to enter China. They
devoted themselves to the five thousand inhabitants of the pen-
insula, of whom only nine hundred were Portuguese. In November, 1565, Francisco Peres determined to renew the efforts
to enter China. He accompanied Portuguese merchants on
their semiannual trading visit to Can-ton.[13] The magistrate was
courteous, but suggested that Peres should first endeavor to
learn the Chinese language. Three years later Joao Baptesta
Ribeira, a pioneer Jesuit, tried to force his way into China.
He arranged for a Chinese boatman to take him to the coast,
whence he hoped to set out on foot, unaided, unauthorized, un-
versed in the Chinese language, to evangelize China. This
failed and incurred the displeasure of his superiors and led
to his recall to Europe. Ribeira, upon his return to Europe,
wrote to the general of the Society of Jesus in 1575, "During
the three years I resided at Macao (1568–1570), I did everything possible to penetrate the continent, but nothing I could
think of was of any avail." [14] Jesuits of Ribeira's spirit believed
that the sword must be used to carve the way of the cross,[15] and
pleaded their cause with eloquence:

" If the princes of Europe, instead of quarrelling among themselves, would undertake to extend the Kingdom of Christ and force
the sovereign of China to grant to the missionaries the right to

preach and to the natives the right to hear the truth, the Chinese people would easily be converted, because our morals and our religion find favor with them." [16]

Meanwhile the flag of Spain appeared in the Far East and was planted on the island of Cebu in the Philippines in 1565. The missionaries accompanying the Spanish conquerors were Augustinians. To them the Philippines were but island steppingstones en route to China. Ten years later the first two Augustinians, de Rada and Marin, took advantage of a Chinese ship returning from the Philippines to Fu-kien. The viceroy of Fu-kien received them with courtesy, but when the Spaniards attempted to stroll around the city of Foo-chow, they were politely confined to guest quarters. The viceroy entertained his guests at a military review, and served them a feast, but gave no reply to their request that they be allowed to remain in China to preach the gospel. Instead, after presenting them with gifts, he sent them back to Manila in Chinese ships. Fortunately the gifts included about a hundred volumes of Chinese books in which they could have begun a study of Chinese culture.[17]

Four years later the Franciscans arrived at Manila to make their attempt to enter China. "There is nothing to indicate that the Franciscans of the sixteenth century were in any way aware that earlier Franciscans had successfully entered China and lived there two hundred and fifty years before them, notably John of Monte Corvino." [18] As soon as possible four Franciscans, Alfaro, Lucarelli, Tordesillas, and Beza, set sail for China with three soldiers, four native Filipinos, and a young Chinese as their interpreter. They landed near Can-ton, with the skill of their young guide escaped notice of all sentries on the coast, and were not detected until they had gained entry of the city of Can-ton. Once discovered, they were harshly treated, resulting in the death of Beza. Tordesillas returned to the Philippines. Lucarelli and Alfaro were permitted to remain at Macao.[19]

The presence of the Franciscans in Can-ton aroused the Portuguese merchants at Macao, who were always fearful of Spanish encroachments upon what the Portuguese claimed as their sphere of influence. The Portuguese bishop at Macao gave hospitality to the Franciscans, but the opposition of the Portuguese merchants did not abate. " All their fears come from the fact that they expect to be attacked by a squadron of Spaniards, and think that we have come to China as spies to do them harm and to interfere with their commerce." [20] In 1581 the Franciscans were forced to leave Macao. When Philip II of Spain became king of Portugal, the old argument which resulted in the division of the world of conquest between Spain and Portugal, and which had been used by Portuguese Jesuits to keep Spanish Franciscans and others out of China, was challenged. Those who think that the Chinese are without grounds for their suspicions of missionaries should note how diligently certain nationalistic minds wove the missionary task into the pattern of imperial and colonial conquests.

In 1583 the bishop of Manila, Domenico de Salazar, took up the fight and wrote to Philip:

" Granting as established the titles and rights which Your Majesty holds and possesses in all the Indies as king of Spain, and those which you have in China as king of Portugal . . . I maintain . . . that you can send an army so strong that the whole power of China will be helpless to injure it, and that this army has the right to enter and traverse the provinces of China; it can impose peace upon those who disturb order; it can oblige the king and the officials of this realm to allow the gospel to be preached and to protect its heralds. . . . If the king of China should be so perverse as to prohibit the preaching of the gospel, Your Majesty can even deprive him of his kingdom. . . . Let Your Majesty set everything else aside, even were it question of the conquest of a thousand Flanders or the recovery of the Holy Land. Neither Julius Caesar nor Alexander the Great was ever confronted with the challenge of so magnificent a military venture; and there has not been since apostolic times a spiritual undertaking of such high importance." [21]

On December 12, 1600, Pope Clement VIII removed the restriction that had barred all religious orders but the Jesuits from China, and permitted orders, regardless of nationality, to labor in China. However, Portugal " bullied out of the Curia " [22] a regulation that all non-Portuguese missionaries to southern and eastern Asia would be required to pass through Lisbon and Goa, by which process the Portuguese delayed their departure for as much as two years.[23]

The Church that embarked on these missionary adventures, financed by the colonial expansion of Spain and Portugal, was the Church that had just used the Inquisition to force Galileo to recant upon his knees and renounce his "dangerous doctrine." But the same Church had discovered that the earth moved just the same. The jolt to orthodoxy threw enough doubt upon the rigidity of that period to prompt younger scholars to launch out in independent thought. Such was Alessandro Valignano, the superior of the Society of Jesus. No one before him had revealed any respect for the Chinese and their historic past. When he visited Macao, Valignano realized that the Portuguese Jesuits there were imbued with a narrow and intense nationalism which identified Christianity with Portuguese culture.[24] In response to his request the Society of Jesus sent out Michele Ruggieri, an Italian, who arrived at Macao in 1579. On his arrival, Ruggieri found a letter awaiting him from Valignano, directing him to " read, write, and speak " the Chinese language. No one had yet begun this task. The Jesuits at Macao required their converts to learn the Portuguese language. Until this was accomplished, they conversed with the Chinese through interpreters. Valignano's perception of the problem and his proposed solution found no sympathy from the Portuguese. Ruggieri was confronted with two difficulties, first, an utter lack of sympathy for the work he had been given by the superior because he was not a Portuguese, and secondly, the position of superiority assumed by the Jesuits at Macao derived from their years of prior residence. They scoffed at the idea of wasting time and strength to learn the Chinese language. The superior at Macao continually assigned Ruggieri duties designed to interrupt his studies of the Chinese language. After eighteen months of this, Ruggieri was almost heartbroken. On November 8, 1580, he wrote to the general of the Society: " It would be wise for your paternity to recommend this enterprise to our superiors in India, because if Father Alessandro Valignano were not here, I do not know what would happen to this business of the conversion of China. I write this because I hear certain ones say: ' What is the sense of this father occupying himself with this sort of thing when he could be of service in the other ministries of the Society? It is a waste of time for him to learn the Chinese language and to consecrate himself to a hopeless enterprise.' " [25] Those Jesuits who shared Valignano's dream for China were soon convinced that the only hope of their success lay in keeping out of China the divisive and hostile influences within the Roman Church itself, until they had demonstrated the worth of the new policy they proposed to follow. The greatness of the Jesuits in China in the seventeenth century lies in their radical departure from the accepted pattern of missionary work as followed by their Society in Macao and other lands.

Ruggieri accompanied Portuguese merchants to Can-ton for the first time in November, 1580. En route up the Pearl River, he persuaded the merchants of the importance of paying respect to Chinese customs, to which they had never given a thought. For this reason the Chinese had insisted that the Portuguese were barbarians. The officials on this visit were surprised and pleased with Ruggieri. It was the first time they had before them a " barbarian " who spoke their language and who revealed a respect for Chinese customs.[26] When Ruggieri asked permission to remain on land instead of on board the ships, as the Portuguese traders were obliged to do, the officials granted his request and assigned him a small house and issued an order, forbidding, under pain of death, any injury to the foreign guest. It was thus that the unyielding door to China, so long closed to the repeated efforts of half a century, began to open with gracious welcome to the first foreigner who took the trouble to understand the language and customs of the Chinese.[27] When Ruggieri came the second time to Can-ton with the traders in 1581, he repeated his request to be allowed to remain on shore. He was assigned the residence set apart by the

government for official visitors. In the official audiences, when
the Portuguese traders were compelled to kneel, the officials
permitted Ruggieri to stand. On his third visit in November,
1581, the friendliness of the Chinese officials increased. The
welcome to Ruggieri did not please the Portuguese Jesuits at
Macao. Moreover he was rebuked by the Franciscan Montillas
for solemnizing the Mass in the presence of unbelievers.[28] It
was at this time that Ruggieri worked on his translation for the
Chinese, "An Exposition of Christian Doctrine." In 1583, Ruggieri could proceed with a freedom from control by Macao,
because Valignano, on discovering the friction, transferred the
superior of Macao to another assignment. He requested the
officials of Can-ton, in writing, to give a little piece of land
"on which we may build with our alms a small church and
house in order that we may there serve the King of heaven
whom we adore." [29] Within a week, an officer of the Chinese
government appeared at the Jesuit residence at Macao with
an official permission from the prefect of Chao-ch'ing, granting this request. Ruggieri, accompanied by Matteo Ricci,
reached Chao-ch'ing in September, 1583. There the two missionaries founded, on property given them by the viceroy, the
first Jesuit mission in the interior of China. These young men
spent their lives in China, far removed from Europe by both
distance and time. Thus they were relatively free to develop
their mission on original lines. This is the secret of their success.
Ricci's thinking was dominated by his project of a papal embassy in China, which he believed the essential step toward the
evangelization of the country.[30] He felt that this objective
called for the utilization of every agency the Society could
command. At the outset he felt that the first step to be taken
called for a deeper study and appreciation of Chinese culture,
language, history, philosophy, and religion. Therefore, after
gaining command of the language, he applied himself to a
serious study of the classics. In his *In senectute mea* he wrote:
"I return as a boy to school; it is not so great a thing inasmuch
as I have resolved to do it for love of Him who, though God,

became man for love of me." [31]

Evidence of the command of Chinese language acquired by Ricci is discernible in his early differentiation between the original teachings of Confucius and the interpretations given to these texts by the Neo-Confucian school of Chu Hsi in the Sung period. The latter were frankly and deeply materialistic. Ricci became convinced that the original works attributed to Confucius held a much loftier meaning. It was this fine sense of perception and accuracy that marked Ricci's scholarship. This discovery influenced his entire approach to the missionary task in China, and when it was brought to light by Ricci, it profoundly influenced Chinese thought. His research convinced him that this materialistic emphasis had been arbitrarily imposed, or it would be more correct to say that it had been superimposed, on the original teachings of Confucius, and the superstructure attributed as a whole to Confucius by the Neo-Confucian school. Once he discovered this, Ricci began to work with increased zeal to discover such truths in the ancient classics of China as would serve as cultural stocks upon which he could graft Christian teachings. In November, 1585, he wrote: "I have, therefore, noted many passages that favor the doctrines of our faith." [32] Searching for the Chinese words with which to express Christian concepts of God, and such theological terms as "salvation," was a radical innovation in a Church that had permitted only Latin terms. Ricci was opposed by Longobardo, who insisted that the Chinese had no notion of the spiritual substance of the true God, of angels, or of the soul. Ricci was supported by the Chinese scholars in his belief that "the ancients in China, by observing the natural law, were saved through the help which God gives to those who on their part do all they can to receive it." [33] His position seemed scandalous to many of his contemporaries, although it is given strong support in theology and is based on the utterances of Jesus. Although his discovery was based solely on the original Confucian documents, without any of the archaeological data now available, nevertheless Ricci's conceptions are essentially true.[34] Rising far above the Europeanism of his day, daring to disagree with the Jesuits at Macao, confronting the difficulties that had blocked every attempt to enter China for half a century, consumed with an utter devotion to his Lord and Saviour, whom he would make known to China, Ricci blazed a path conceived in his own mind and justified by the example of missionaries of the first centuries of the Christian Era. He simply adopted the same attitude toward Confucius as the Early Church had adopted toward the Greek philosophers. He held that the idea of God in the Confucian texts embodied a monotheistic concept of the highest order.

Söderblom has contributed a valuable chapter on the monotheistic concept embodied in the ancient Chinese use of Shang Ti. It transcends the impersonal idea in T'ien, which is so commonly used for heaven. The use of Shang Ti implies the presence of the numen, or soul, which is not found where T'ien is used. Söderblom finds importance in the fact that Shang Ti is used with the same meaning in different dynasties of Chinese history. Had it not this transcendent meaning and had it not always conveyed the idea of God to the Chinese, it would have had to change under the pressures exerted by the different trends in different dynasties.[35] Shang Ti is seldom used to mean " heaven " in the same sense as T'ien. Since the discovery of the royal tombs, from a Stone Age period to the middle of the millennium preceding the Christian Era, at An-yang in Ho-nan province in the twentieth century, scholars have confirmed the validity of Ricci's position. The royal tombs of An-yang revealed a treasure of carvings on bone which have added much light to an unknown period of Chinese history.[36] Modern scholars like Pelliot, Creel, and Menzies have had access to vastly greater and more accurate source materials than were available to Ricci. Their confirmation of the essential accuracy of Ricci's perceptions is a remarkable tribute to his scholarship and integrity. Although China possessed a hierarchy of gods, Shang Ti was unmistakably above this galaxy of deities which man had postulated to explain the various phenomena of his experience, and, as used in the earliest Chinese classics, it held the idea of " Creator " as a definite monotheistic conception. The term " Shang Ti " has been rejected by the Roman Catholic Church as an appropriate name for God, although Ricci and the early Jesuits used it most effectively for fifty years before the rites controversy. In the twentieth century it has been generally adopted by Protestant missionaries for the name of God, since for more than three thousand years it has stood for the chief deity of the Chinese, and thus Ricci's search for truth was not wasted.[37]

Critics at times have jumped to the conclusion that Ricci's appreciation of the values in the ancient classics was but part of a diabolical or Jesuitical plot to ally the Christian mission with Confucian ethics to oppose Buddhism and Taoism, and gain at the same time an advantage over rival missions of the Franciscans and the Dominicans. The Spanish missionaries most unjustly accused Ricci and his associates in their letters to Rome.[38] Ricci discovered that there did exist in the Chinese classics preambles of faith and reasoned conclusions that postulated the existence of God, of a spiritual soul, and of immortality. Ricci, in thus resolutely taking a stand on the terrain of Confucius' philosophy, seems to us simply to have renewed upon the shores of the Pacific Ocean what Justin Martyr, Athenagoras, and Clement of Alexandria had attempted in the Hellenic world.[39]

There still persists in the thought of many regarding this period that the Jesuits from the outset had determined upon a strategy of employing Confucian ethics to bolster their position in China. One Protestant author feels " the lines of strategy having been determined, it remained to carry them out, and this required an intelligence and a personality above the ordinary. These Ricci possessed." [40] This implies that the strategy was predetermined and Ricci chosen to implement it. The facts reveal that no strategy of this nature existed. What emerged was the discovery, by a diligent scholar, that God was in China before

the arrival of the Jesuits.[41] He attempted to win his colleagues
and his Church to see this, and urged them to employ the
Chinese terms for God. While Rome took fifty years to make up
its mind, Chinese scholars admitted the correctness of Ricci's
discovery. When Rome repudiated it, and forbade the use of
Shang Ti as a term for God, the confidence of the Chinese
scholars was shattered.

Ricci was equally alert in the realization that China needed
to adapt itself to the scientific truths that had been discovered
in Europe, particularly in mathematics and astronomy. He believed that it would be unnecessary to confute the Buddhist
doctrines, but would be sufficient to teach the sciences; the
Chinese upon learning the truths of nature, would of themselves recognize the falsity of the Buddhist teaching. The Buddhists in addition to their false theological speculations had
pronounced on questions of astrology and cosmography. Ricci
noted: "Many after learning our mathematical science make
sport of the laws and doctrines of the Buddhists. . . . Attempting to explain the recurrent cycle of day and night, they say
that during the night the sun hides behind the mountain called
Simui. . . . Attempting to explain the cause of solar and lunar
eclipses, they say that a genie, called Holchan, causes the
eclipse of the sun by covering the moon with his left hand."[42]
Ricci believed that the Chinese would rightly judge that it was
unreasonable to give credit in supernatural matters pertaining
to the next life to those who fall into so many errors in matters
pertaining to this life.[43] Because of these considerations the
Society of Jesus was asked to send to the China mission scholars
whose brilliant achievement in the field of astronomy would
confound the conceit and complacency in Chinese thought.[44]
Arthur W. Hummel, chief of the division of Orientalia at the
Library of Congress, who spent many years in China, feels
that "there is nothing more certain than that Ricci was in inti-
mate touch with and had a deep understanding of the various
currents of Chinese thought, whereas the contrary is true of
later critics of his methods." It was a Chinese scholar who

studied mathematics under Ricci's direction during his stay at Nan-king (1599–1600) who urged upon Ricci the instrumental efficacy of science in propagating Christianity. He believed science would arouse a questioning spirit that would not be content with tradition in the face of contradictory facts.

In the spring of 1600 a eunuch, who was in charge of a small flotilla of barges bearing silk to the court, agreed to take Ricci and his companion to Pe-king, on the Grand Canal. They had waited long years for this opportunity. After forty-five days they reached Lin-tsing in Shan-tung, where they were held awaiting an imperial order that arrived in January, 1601, permitting them to go on to Pe-king. On arrival they were examined by the Board of Ceremonies. On this first visit to Pe-king, Ricci carried letters of introduction in which he sought official permission to establish himself in the capital. From the outset he was a pawn in the machinations of the eunuchs attached to the court and was held in detention. Only after considerable delay were the two priests permitted to enter the forbidden city. Their gifts were presented to the emperor by the eunuchs. One of the gifts was a clock in which the emperor showed the keenest interest because it sounded the hours. But when the clock stopped, no one knew how to start it and the Jesuits had to be summoned again to start the clock. Thus they were held near the palace until they could teach the eunuchs how to operate the clock. In 1601 the two Jesuits were released from detention and allowed to rent a lodging of their own. According to Ricci's commentaries, he never once saw the emperor Wan Li.

"From 1601 until his death in 1610 he remained at the capital, arousing interest of the educated class in European science and technology, making converts, and reported to the Church in Rome." [45] Since 1588 there had been continual strife in the palace between the eunuchs and the scholar officials. The Jesuits began their work at a time when the intellectuals were organizing in groups to combat the machinations of the eunuchs. The patriotic intellectuals were almost in despair. It

was into this maelstrom that the Jesuits carried their intellectual approach.[46] Ricci set out to combat what he conceived to
be the two chief obstacles to the propagation of the Christian
faith. He found that the Jesuits were suspect because they were
supported by the Portuguese government. The Jesuits never
escaped from this handicap, that their support came from the
king of Portugal in exchange for the grant to him by the pope
of all the lands of the East. The second obstacle was the foreign
attributes of Christianity: it was a new doctrine in a land that
had turned its back on both the foreigner and the future. For
these reasons Ricci sought friends among the scholars in the
literary and philosophical societies. The most important of
these was the Tung Lin Society, which subsequently developed
a political significance as the Tung Lin Party. This was not
deemed a handicap by the Jesuits but rather their opportunity.
They hoped to make Christians of some of the scholars, and
that someday these men would be officials and that through
them there would be an increasingly favorable attitude toward
Christianity on the part of officials. It is not an accident that
during the last forty years of the Ming dynasty all the eminent
Christian converts of the scholar class and the many non-
Christian friends of the Jesuits emerged from these societies.
Ricci set out to convince the scholars of China that the sciences
of the West were soundly based and would confound superstitions, and that the materialism of Chu Hsi was not an integral
part of the original ethics of Confucius.

The Jesuits were repeatedly embarrassed by the highly ex-
aggerated reports that were circulated in Macao and the Philippines and from there to Europe regarding their amazing
successes in China.[47] Ricci's own records reveal only modest
reports. Writing to his brother in Macerata in 1608, he reported that there were in China at that time more than two
thousand Christians, among them many scholars. This represented the work of twenty-six years. Ricci constantly warned
against lowering the standards to seek a larger number of converts. In his last letter from Pe-king he stressed the urgency of

sending missionaries to China who are not only " good, but also men of talent, since we are dealing here with a people both intelligent and learned." [48]

In 1610, Matteo Ricci died, following a sudden illness in the month of May. The tribute to him from the imperial court is eloquent of its esteem for China's distinguished guest. The imperial rescript gave to the Jesuits the title to a plot of land situated near the gate of the western wall of Pe-king where Ricci was buried. During his life no formal reply had come from the court to his request for permission to remain in Pe-king. He had received only a verbal message assuring him that the emperor would be displeased if he should leave Pe-king. Now, upon his death, the imperial rescript was interpreted by the Jesuits at Pe-king as official recognition. Whether the emperor intended it to be so, or not, the rescript gave an implied protection to the Christian religion. At least it signified honor which led to encouraging developments.

In December, 1610, the astronomers of the Imperial College erred in predicting the solar eclipse. One of the Christian converts persuaded the Board of Ceremonies to petition the emperor to entrust the correction of the calendar to the Jesuits. The emperor gave his approval and de Ursis and de Pantoia accepted the assignment. The mathematicians attached to the imperial court soon vented their jealousy, and the opposition became so serious that the emperor ordered the project abandoned. It was at this point that serious trouble began for the Jesuits. Their superior scientific knowledge discredited the officials at the court, who " lost face." To them the Jesuit scholars were rivals who presaged their complete ruin. In May, 1616, a leader of the reactionary school memorialized the throne to have the Jesuits and their converts condemned to death, on the grounds that they acknowledged the Lord of Heaven and thus belittled the dignity of the emperor. The accusation to the emperor from the Confucian scholars claimed to have discovered a subversive plot designed to overthrow the empire. The memorial was secretly presented at Pe-king, but the two Jesuits who had aroused their ire learned of it through their friends. Chinese Christian scholars published an essay in defense of the new religion, but the opposition was renewed until finally the Board of Ceremonies dispatched couriers to the provinces with orders that all missionaries should be arrested and imprisoned. The courage of Chinese Christians in this crisis was superb, and their efforts to defend the foreigners to whom they felt so greatly indebted were not lacking, but the opposition prevailed. In 1617 the emperor signed the edict of expulsion.[49] This edict took the four Jesuits in Pe-king by surprise. Efforts to reach the ear of the emperor with an appeal were unavailing. Those named in Pe-king and Nan-king were deported. Although the edict was supposed to wipe out Christianity, there remained in China fourteen Jesuits, of whom eight were European and six were Chinese lay brothers. These went into hiding, most of them at Hang-chow, where they prepared themselves for a more opportune day by intensive study of Chinese.

In 1620 the chief eunuch at the court, Wei Chung-hsien, savagely attacked the Tung Lin scholars. All the Chinese Christian scholars were Tung Lin academicians. The fate of Christianity was thus related to the fate of the Tung Lin Party. The Tung Lin Academy in Pe-king had its own building, which Wei refused to regard as an Academy, insisting it was only a rendezvous of rebels. This crisis increased in intensity until 1624. An incident contributing to the climax arose from the rivalry connected with the lunar eclipse expected on October 8, 1623. The minister of finance was attracted by the scientific attainments of the German Jesuit, Adam Schall. At the request of the finance minister, Schall calculated the time with precision. The minister was anxious to have this gifted scholar in the government service and secured an appointment for Schall to make a revision of the calendar. This encouraged liberal scholars to think it opportune to protest to the emperor regarding the corruption of Wei Chung-hsien. In 1624, Yang Lien, who was senior vice-president of the bureau of censors, bitterly denounced Wei in a Memorial to the emperor. Unfortunately, this Memorial passed through the hands of the chief eunuch who controlled the court, and whose intrigues resulted in having Yang Lien and most of the leaders of the Tung Lin Party imprisoned on false charges. Yang died of continual floggings. Five others were executed. Others committed suicide. Over three hundred scholars were stripped of all office and rank. By 1626 the eunuch reached the peak of his power. He arranged for his political appointees to petition the emperor to exalt the chief eunuch, whereby he was soon created a duke. On the death of the emperor in 1627, the chief eunuch's political supporters turned against him. The young emperor had no use for one who had tried to supplant him, and soon made his displeasure known, ordering Wei to retire to his native village, declaring him guilty of treason, theft, and murder. Wei committed suicide. He remains in Chinese history as a byword of infamy.[50]

It was during these dark days that word reached the Jesuits in Pe-king, through Chinese friends, of the discovery of the Nestorian monument in Sian-fu in 1623. No one, not even the Jesuits, knew at the time that the monument recounted the work of the Nestorian Christians of the seventh century. In the same year the Jesuits formed new missions in Shan-si, Shensi, and Fu-kien, in addition to their former work at Nan-king and Pe-king. In the year of the discovery the chief eunuch was still in power and had his spies everywhere. Otherwise there would have been a greater outburst of enthusiasm.[51] The Jesuits were deeply sensitive to the importance of their discovery. In spite of the very cautious character of the official report to Rome, the event received extravagant publicity in Europe, where the Jesuits were falsely accused of having invented the story to create prestige.

One of the objections of the Chinese, often expressed to the Jesuits, was the newness of Christianity. In China, more than anywhere else in the world, objection was always raised to new ideas, and reverence was given to antiquity. This was particularly true in the seventeenth century. Now the basis for this skepticism was shattered. Nearly a thousand years before the Jesuits the Christian gospel had been preached in the ancient capital and had found favor with emperors. It was not long after the discovery that imperial favor began to shine again upon the Pe-king Jesuits. In 1629 an edict of the emperor approved employment of the Jesuits in the work of the calendar reform. This edict brought great attention to the Jesuits, since it was published in the official gazette that reached every part of the empire. That this should happen so soon after the discovery of the Sian-fu monument brought further attention to the Jesuits, who received the congratulations of the scholar-officials. Three Jesuits, Schall, Terrenz, and Longobardo, became employees of the imperial government. Under Schall's leadership they rose to positions of great influence and held a rank that no European had ever held before them. Others joined them, and in the course of the next forty years three Jesuits served as head of the bureau. In the scientific service of the court the Jesuits enjoyed a prestige that was not given to the missionaries in the provinces. In 1627, after nearly fifty years in China, and almost a century after the Society began to knock at the door of China from Macao, the Jesuits reported a total of 13,000 baptisms up to that date. Within ten years after the discovery of the historic monument, the number of baptisms increased to 40,000. By 1647 it had reached 150,000, and by 1667 the number recorded was 263,780.[52]

The successes attending the Jesuit labors soon were noised abroad and encouraged the Spanish missionaries to renew their attempts to open missions in China. In 1631 a Dominican landed in Fu-kien. Although ordered deported, a Japanese was substituted for him and Angelo Cocchi remained, disguised in Chinese clothes and shorn of his beard. He wrote back to his superior that missionaries should have a knowledge of the Chinese language, and warned that " simply to land on the coast as so many continued to advocate was only to incur the wrath of the Chinese and unfailingly be deported." In 1633, Pope Urban VIII extended permission to all orders to send missionaries to China. In that year three more Spanish missionaries reached Fu-kien in a small boat from Formosa. These included Juan Baptista de Morales, a Dominican, and two Franciscans, one of whom was Antonio Caballero a Santa Maria. The Spanish Franciscans journeyed to Nan-king, where they caused great anxiety to the Jesuits, who had just previously experienced the most severe persecutions. The Franciscans considered it their sacred duty to preach in city streets, aided by an interpreter, garbed in the Franciscan habit, with a crucifix in hand. The Jesuits endeavored to dissuade the newcomers, with an anxiety to prevent further official reprisals and persecutions. But the Franciscans stigmatized the Jesuit warnings as pretexts arising from jealousy. The difficulties between these religious orders in China had their roots far more in differences of national temperament than in differences of religious orders. It was not because they were Dominicans or Franciscans but because they were Spaniards. Nowhere in Europe had nationalism, in particular cultural forms, become so thoroughly identified with the Roman Catholic religion as in Spain. In marked contrast, the Jesuits in China had forsaken Europeanism and espoused the cause of cultural adaptation. This was radically different from the Jesuit policy elsewhere. The members of the China mission were chosen for their scholarship, and had come from those countries in Europe where the spirit of nationalism was not so dominant as in Spain and Portugal. Because of the Portuguese padroado, many writers have assumed erroneously that the Jesuits in China were predominantly Portuguese. Of the sixteen in China in the early years of the seventeenth century, only three were from Portugal, one was from France, one was from Germany, one was from Switzerland, and ten were from Italy. This fact is essential to the understanding of the bitter conflicts which arose between the religious orders within the Roman Catholic Church regarding missionary work in China.

The Franciscans, from the outset, sensed that the Jesuits were unhappy about their presence. They began to collect data based on interrogation of Chinese Christians and the observations of the four Spanish missionaries. They determined to carry their fight to Rome. In February, 1636, Antonio a Santa Maria, who was later to take so prominent a part in the rites controversy, started for Manila, armed with arguments against the Jesuit policy. In 1637 a Chinese author made an attack on Christianity which was published in Fu-kien. The two Franciscans, who remained in China, felt called to defend their faith against this attack, and left Fu-kien to follow him and " to defend our immaculate doctrine with argument and with our lives, and to preach Jesus Christ, our crucified Lord." [53] The Franciscans lacked any knowledge of Mandarin, which was the official language. Accompanied by three young interpreters, they arrived in Pe-king where they found hospitality from Adam Schall, but they found fault with everything Jesuits were doing. The thing that most deeply shocked the Franciscans was a painting of the twelve apostles which hung in the chapel at Pe-king. Out of regard for the Chinese feelings on the subject, the artist had endowed the apostles with shoes of cloth, like those worn by the Chinese. This " scandalous " thing was immediately noted by the Franciscans, who later included it among the list of errors reported to their superiors. To them this was almost a complete betrayal of the faith. The minds that could cry scandal at so minor a concession to the Chinese could never be expected to understand the Jesuits of Pe-king. The Jesuit chapel was a gift of Emperor Wan Li in honor of Matteo Ricci. In acknowledgment of this imperial favor the Jesuits had placed upon a table in the chapel a wooden plaque bearing the carved inscription in Chinese: " Long Live the Emperor." This was fraught with no more idolatrous significance than the customs observed in Protestant churches in our day in placing the national flag in a conspicuous part of the sanctuary, or of the counterpart in Europe in the seventeenth century of " *Vive le Roi* " in France, or " God Save the King " in England. But to the Spaniards, inclined to put the very worst interpretation upon Jesuit activities, which they always construed to be " schemes," the table with the plaque was interpreted as one of the idolatrous " rites." Their report of their discovery was later magnified in Europe through repetition, in the rites controversy, until the scandal of " Jesuit idolatries " in China rocked the Church! Did these seventeenth century Franciscans come to China unaware that three centuries earlier their famed predecessor, John of Monte Corvino, as archbishop of Pe-king, considered it his duty to go out and meet the great Kublai Khan in public ceremonies and bestow his blessing upon the emperor? It would appear that the Spaniards did not know that any Franciscan had been in China before them!

While they stayed with him in Pe-king, Schall endeavored to dissuade the Franciscans from their determination to present their case to the emperor. But they only imagined that Jesuit jealousy was seeking to thwart their aim. They expected Schall to obtain permission for them to establish themselves permanently in Pe-king, following the interview they expected him to arrange for them with the emperor. Their requests revealed a profound ignorance of the true situation. The Jesuits, who had been almost forty years in Pe-king, had never met the emperor. The Jesuits had labored patiently for twenty years before they had a residence, and had spent a generation winning friends and confidence. Yet the two Franciscans thought that all that stood between them and their objective was the opposition of the Jesuits. They were unconscious even of the first barrier of language.[54] After two weeks had elapsed, two officials from the Board of Ceremonies, accompanied by soldiers, appeared at the house to question the visitors. The Franciscans appeared before them with crucifix in hand " prepared to give their lives to preach Jesus Christ." " When the officials were told that unless they accepted Christianity they would be damned, their patience gave out and they ordered the soldiers to take away the crucifixes from the missionaries. The two priests were forbidden to leave the house and their interpreters were led away in chains." [55]

The Franciscans were deported in disgrace. It was an embarrassing day for the Jesuits to see Christian missionaries paraded through the streets of Pe-king in humiliating circumstances. Soon after, Schall wrote to a close friend:

> " There came to this capital two fathers of Saint Francis, determined to be martyrs or to convert the emperor and all of the Chinese. Neither of them knew how to speak Chinese. . . . Both of them wore their habits. Each of them carried his crucifix in his hand and wanted to begin preaching. . . . We received them into our house, our servants waited upon them, and despite this they spoke most unfavourably about our affairs, as if they alone had the apostolic spirit. For this we pardon them as our older brothers." [56]

Alvarez Semedo published a defense of the Jesuits in 1667.

> " The zeal and fervor of those who wish to convert the world in an instant is worthy of praise, and surely we hold it in esteem and veneration. But in these new missions, and especially those which are not capable of receiving so great a fire, which would quickly be extinguished because of the need for disposition of firmer consistency only developed over a period of time, we try to keep ourselves within the limits of prudence, always more sure, and of patience, more profitable for the end we have in view. The laborers of our Society who have too much fervor are not suitable for us. They should be employed in the pulpits of Europe, where their great fire can illuminate without burning." [57]

The controversy over the Chinese rites was started in 1638. It arose directly from jealousy of the great missionary achievements of the Jesuits and the inability of the Franciscans and Dominicans to compete. From 1649 to 1664 the Dominicans won slightly more than five thousand converts in fifteen years; the Franciscans had made less than four thousand in thirty-four years; while the Jesuits during the same period were bringing an average of five to six thousand converts into the Church annually. The Jesuits had laid a ground work, and they had not been discouraged with only two thousand converts in their first twenty years of endeavor. After fifty years of patient work they were reaping the rewards of their policy. They lived as scholars and received the honors accorded by the Chinese to scholars, but the record reveals that they lived often in pen-ury.[58] The controversy over whether to permit certain Chinese ancestral rites raged for a century, receiving the attention of nine popes, the repeated intervention of the Congregation for the Propagation of the Faith, and the Inquisition. It neces-sitated the dispatch of two apostolic legates to China, and the dispatch of a special representative of the Jesuits from China to Rome. It was finally closed by the Constitution *Ex quo singulari* of Benedict XIV forbidding the toleration of the Chi-nese ancestral rites and banning further debate.[59]

The overthrow of the Ming dynasty by the Manchus saw years of trouble and brought heavy losses as well as gains to the Jesuit mission. The losses were heavy in personnel and property. Six Jesuit missionaries lost their lives in the disorders attendant upon the upheaval. The mission lost many churches by fire and destruction. Thanks to the favor of the Ch'ing em-peror toward Adam Schall in Pe-king, the gains soon out-weighed the losses. Schall was the one Jesuit who had re-mained in Pe-king when the Ming dynasty collapsed. On the arrival of the Manchus, Schall petitioned for permission to re-main. His petition was investigated, and granted when they discovered that he had in his house a large store of printing blocks which had been prepared for a revision of the calendar. "A few weeks after he was secured in the possession of his property, he was summoned before the Council of State to ex-amine the calendar for the year 1645 which had been submitted by the Bureau of Astronomy. Schall pointed out seven major errors which the officials of the Bureau, present at the inter-view, were forced to acknowledge. The Council ordered Schall to prepare the calendar for 1645." [60] A solar eclipse was ex-pected on September 1, 1644. On July 25, Schall presented a report, illustrated with sketches, in which he calculated the time of the eclipse for all the principal cities of the empire. A month later he submitted an outline of the calendar for the next year. The court promoted a contest between Schall and the local schools of astronomy.[61] This resulted in a signal vic-

tory for the Jesuit. The emperor conferred high honor on Schall,
and ordered that all astronomers in the service of the state
should be enrolled in his classes.

The invading Manchus were not scholarly men. The scholars
under the Ming dynasty had refused to support the invaders
and fled. Thus the Ch'ing dynasty was alert to avail itself of
the services of Adam Schall.[62] Before the end of 1644 the emperor had named Schall *Ch'in T'ien Chien-cheng*, director of
the Bureau of Astronomy. Before Schall assumed office there
were nearly two hundred on the staff. The emperor ordered the
staff reduced. Schall weeded out over one hundred and made
for himself an equal number of enemies. The Manchus admired
Schall. Within a year his prestige was reflected in the favor enjoyed by his fellow missionaries. Schall's salary as director was
two thirds that of a minister of state. This enabled him to
strengthen the work of the mission.

Adam Schall was the first Jesuit to meet an emperor. The
Manchu emperor often summoned him to his palace at night
to converse with him. Whenever he was kept there late, the
emperor would send him back with several Manchu princes as
a courteous escort. In utter disregard of tradition, the young
emperor frequently visited Schall's house. The official gazette
kept the whole empire informed of the friendship of the emperor for Schall. In the same year members of the Dutch diplomatic mission which visited Pe-king were greatly impressed
with the influential position of the Jesuits. One of the embassy wrote Holland: " He is from Cologne . . . named Adam
Schall, . . . forty-six years in Pe-king, enjoying great esteem
with the emperor of China." [63] Another member of the embassy described the unique position of the Jesuit at the imperial
court: " Father Adam Schall is in such great favor with the
prince that he has access to him at any time." [64] Verbiest wrote
home in 1661: " Schall has more influence upon the emperor
than any viceroy or than the most respected prince, and the
name of Father Adam is better known in China than the name
of any famous man in Europe." [65] Vath adds: " I do not believe

that since the foundation of the Chinese Empire any foreigner has received so many marks of honor and kindly favor." [66] The hierarchy of the mandarinate was divided into nine classes, each with two divisions. As director of the Bureau of Astronomy, Schall automatically was "mandarin of the fifth class," first division. By 1658 he had received eight promotions until he finally, on February 2, was made mandarin of the first class, first division. Only the grand secretaries and the most important princes of the royal blood belonged, ex officio, to this class. As a sign of his rank, Schall, from this time on, wore the red button on his hat and the gold-embroidered crane with open wings on the breast of his tunic.[67] On March 15, 1657, the emperor had ordered an inscription of praise to be erected in front of the church.

Schall undoubtedly had the highest hopes of converting the emperor to Christianity, and the young emperor received instruction in Roman Catholic doctrines, but the demands of the Church requiring monogamy were too exacting for him. Schall's influence rapidly declined after 1658, when the young ruler fell under the influence of the eunuchs, who had regained ascendancy at the court. The eunuchs availed themselves of the old Buddhist trick and enticed the young emperor with concubines, by whom they lured him from Christianity to Buddhism. The eunuchs not only encouraged the emperor to indulge in sexual excesses, but they were engaged in a deep plot to revive Buddhism. They arranged a meeting between the emperor and a Buddhist monk. The monk persuaded the emperor that he had been a Buddhist monk in a former incarnation.[68] On the death of the emperor in 1660, the plot thickened against the privileged position of the Jesuits. When Schall needed every faculty and when the mission most needed his leadership, he was stricken with paralysis, undoubtedly induced by false accusations made against him to the Board of Ceremonies by Yang Kuang-hsien. In November, 1664, the Regent Oboi committed the four Jesuits in Pe-king to prison. Adam Schall was stripped of all his titles and subjected to every indignity. In January, 1665, he was sentenced to death by strangulation. The other three Jesuits were ordered to be flogged and banished from the empire. Seven Christian officials of the Bureau of Astronomy received the same sentence. Execution of these sentences was suspended while the foreign astronomical teachings were subjected to further tests. A solar eclipse was anticipated. In prison Verbiest, assisted by Schall, calculated the exact hour of the eclipse. When the hour approached, the Bureau of Astronomy was crowded with members of the court tensely watching. The men in prison were correct to the minute; the Chinese scholars were again in error. The only result was a series of further hearings before different tribunals. The Jesuits were not really on trial. They were caught in a political conspiracy. In mid-April, the Grand Council, to which they had appealed, acting under pressure of the regent, condemned Schall and his seven Chinese colleagues to decapitation. The regent changed the sentence to the most terrible penalty of the Chinese criminal code — dismemberment of the living body. Before the sentence could be carried out, the empress dowager denounced the unjust persecution of her son's great and good friend. The regent sensed the rising resentment, and after five of the Chinese Christian colleagues of Schall had been executed, the four Jesuits were released from prison. In the meantime all other missionaries in China had been brought to Pe-king. In all, twenty-five Jesuits, four Dominicans, and one Franciscan were assembled, and in 1665 all thirty were banished to Can-ton, where they were kept in detention until 1671. At the same time all churches in China were closed. While the thirty missionaries were being deported to Can-ton, the four Jesuits released from prison were allowed to remain in the capital. Within a year after his release from prison Adam Schall died peacefully on August 15, 1666, closing the most colorful career any foreigner, perhaps, has ever had in China. When he died, his work seemed to lie in ruins.

In 1668 the new emperor ascended the throne after dissolving the regency. One of his first acts was to order the case against Schall and his colleagues reviewed. The Jesuits were vindicated. All Schall's titles were posthumously restored to him and his confiscated properties were given to the mission. His body was honored with an official burial befitting his restored rank. Yang Kuang-hsien was sentenced to exile for having filed false charges.[69] The five Christian astronomers were posthumously restored to their ranks. In 1671 the exiled missionaries were permitted to return to the provinces. The restoration marks the beginning of another period of increasing success for the Church. The next forty years saw Roman Catholic missions reach their highest peak. It was during the reign of Kang Hsi (1662–1722) that the Jesuits made their second attempt to win an emperor to the Christian faith. "The emperor, Kang Hsi, took a great fancy to the Christian religion and would have been baptized if it had not been for the fact that the pope disallowed ancestor worship." [70] The Jesuits defended the ceremonies performed by the Chinese in honor of their ancestors as not being within the category of worship. On this they sought papal approval in the hope that with it the emperor would give his assent and embrace the Christian faith and make it the religion of the country.[71] This was denied in 1705. The Catholics progressively lost favor until the court found it necessary to impose restrictions when the Jesuits began to meddle in civic affairs. An imperial edict was issued against Roman Catholicism in 1724. Severe persecutions then extended all over China. Many missionaries and converts suffered death, imprisonment, or banishment.[72] Thus at the end the Jesuits found themselves in disfavor both with the pope in Europe and with the emperor in China. In 1773 the pope dissolved the Society of Jesus and disillusionment became complete.

Thus the churches that were established in China through matchless devotion and heroism in this period were lost in the dispersion, in which countless numbers perished. They were "lost" indeed, when they discovered that their great leaders, the Jesuits, whose inspiration had led so many into the

Christian faith, were repudiated by the pope who had dissolved the entire Society of Jesus.[73] The tragic fact stands out that Christianity in this period was first compromised by the papal-Portuguese dreams of imperial conquest and later the political struggles within the empire. The Jesuits do not hide the fact that they deliberately linked the cause of the Church with the political aspirations of Portugal and Spain, and with the internal politics of China. Although Ricci was correct in his discernment of the importance of cultural appreciation, and strode out miles in front of the Europeanism of his contemporaries, he erred in identifying his cause with the group of political scholars in the Tung Lin Society. The risks were great, yet, in spite of repeated losses directly related to these political intrigues, the Jesuits adhered to this policy to the end. On the other hand the eunuchs were master politicians who stopped at nothing. Schall held the highest honor that the emperor could bestow, yet it was given him, not for the Christian doctrines he taught, but for the scientific benefits he brought. It was this that shielded the Jesuits in Pe-king from persecution to an extent not always enjoyed in the provinces, but this privileged position incurred the jealousy of other Catholic orders and engendered the rites controversy which embittered the Church and created confusion among Chinese Christians.

The recurring losses of the Church must be seen as a tragedy engulfing in persecutions innocent Chinese Christians who were called to face untimely death because of factors beyond their knowledge and alien to the genius of the Christian faith. The question arises and must be answered: Is the recurring opposition of forces within China against Christianity due to an opposition to the Sermon on the Mount? The answer is, " No." Is it an opposition to Jesus? Again the answer is, " No." Is it an opposition to the dreams of political power and control over human society which the organized Church of this period sought to implement? The answer is, " Yes." Again the Christ had been betrayed by the religious leaders of the day.

V

THE CLASH OF CIVILIZATIONS

IN THIS chapter it will be noted that in the nineteenth century admiration for the Middle Kingdom which had been so strong in Europe in the eighteenth century had disappeared, except on the part of a few savants, who revered China's past. The attitude of the West toward China in the nineteenth century was one of irritation, condescension, and contempt. It was a conflict of civilizations. In each of the spheres, economic, political, racial, intellectual, social, and religious, Chinese and Western cultures collided. In these important arenas Christianity became involved. No one can understand modern revolutionary China without tracing the contributions of the missionary movement to these avenues of thought.

Too many still look upon the Christian movement in China as something that is acted upon by forces beyond its control, rather than as a revolutionary force itself. Christianity has been both a disturber and a contributor. It has shared in breaking down the old China. Not yet, however, had the missionary succeeded in demonstrating to China the unifying spirit of Christ. Missionaries never waved a sword. In these later days, however, the sword overshadowed them. Some of them even defended its use in cleaving China open. The dependence of Christian missions upon foreign military force, and the treaties arising therefrom, in the nineteenth century was responsible for the disastrous losses suffered by the Churches in the Boxer massacre, and for many difficulties since. No one foresaw the inevitable outcome of the leaven implanted in the minds of Chinese students, who in turn became the leaders of revolutionary China, overthrowing the Ch'ing dynasty and setting up the Republic. In spite, however, of the incompleteness of their witness, "the missionary's distinctive achievement was to help determine the character of the impact of the West and the quality of the transformation which follows." [1]

Following the imperial edict of 1724, the Chinese were able to keep all foreigners from entering China for purposes of permanent residence for nearly two centuries, while at the same time they conducted a restricted trade with European ships. The commerce was essential to the nation's livelihood; the dues charged added to the emperor's treasury. By the turn of the eighteenth century the Portuguese had fallen into decrepitude in the Far East and their possessions had largely passed into the hands of the Dutch. In turn the Dutch suffered reverses with the British and were unable to dispute the passage of the British to the coasts of China. Britain was on the rising tide of its fortunes and by 1715 the East India Company, which had long held a monopoly of all British overseas trade with Asia, had firmly established itself as the principal European agency trading in China.[2] Chinese regulations required the ships coming to trade to anchor thirteen miles below the city of Can-ton in the Pearl River. Foreign merchants were allowed to occupy warehouses in the Can-ton suburb during the limited trading season (September to March). All their business had to be conducted through a body of monopolist contractors known as the Hong merchants, through whom all communications had to pass.

During the course of the eighteenth century the trade greatly increased in volume in spite of severe restrictions. The East India Company outdistanced its rivals until it may be said that the China trade developed into an exchange of commodities between Britain and China. The greater the volume of trade, the more tiresome, insulting, and irritating seemed the restrictions imposed by the eight regulations of the Chinese

Government. In 1795 the British Government sent the Macartney Embassy to Pe-king. This was treated in exactly the same way as the Dutch embassies of the previous century had been. It was granted nothing but was obliged to observe the ancient ceremony in which the emperor as " Son of Heaven " received tribute from the outer barbarians who had come from the darkness to worship the light!

It was the expansion of the West in trade contacts that awakened Christians in Europe and America to the vast populations of the world that had been without the Christian gospel. On the crest of this wave, Robert Morrison, the first Protestant missionary to China, arrived off the coast of Can-ton in 1807. Appointed by the London Missionary Society, he had entered the employ of the East India Company that he might live as near as possible to the Chinese and learn their language. The arrangement that existed in the days of Portugal's deal with the pope, whereby the Jesuits were supported by the king, were gone. The East India Company was not disposed to subsidize missionaries. It became necessary for Protestants who were dreaming of carrying out the " Great Commission " to provide the costs of the undertaking.

Morrison succeeded in translating nearly the whole Bible into Chinese. He made the first Chinese-English dictionary and wrote many tracts as a means of disseminating the Christian message. He introduced modern medicine to China. He fostered education. The most valuable source of data regarding these first years of the Protestant movement is to be found in the volumes of the *Chinese Repository,* a quarterly paper published in Macao and Can-ton during the early years of the nineteenth century. Robert Morrison was one of its editors. It is a voluminous work. The early years in China were most discouraging. William Milne wrote in 1820: " Now admit that, with a proportionate increase of labourers, Christianity shall, in every succeeding twenty years, double its accession of numbers; then at the close of the first century from the commencement of the missions the country will have one thousand

Christians."[3] Milne included in his estimate of one thousand Christians all children of Christians. One admires the faith that grew on so slender a stem of hope, yet at the China Centenary Conference in Shang-hai, 1907, a total of 180,000 Protestant communicants was reported. This figure did not include children.[4] This notable achievement was not accomplished without much sacrifice. By no means were all the difficulties created by the Chinese. "The 'heathen heart' is not alone the heart that bows down to idols that abound in temples of India and China; it is the heart which puts its trust in 'reeking tube and iron shard.'"[5]

In the nineteenth century the missionary approach to China was launched by Protestant missionary societies, as though they were the first missionaries ever to enter China. In a marked degree they identified Christianity with the culture patterns of European and American Protestantism. Roman Catholics reopened their missions in the middle of the century and employed aggressive and political means to further their ends. Although Protestants and Roman Catholics found themselves compromised by embarrassments arising out of the impact of Western powers on China, the idea of using political force to secure the rights that Christianity desired in China was employed by both Protestant and Roman Catholic. The idea died hard. This is one of the factors responsible for the Boxer uprising at the close of the century. One of the greatest handicaps the missionary movement had to combat was the traffic in opium in which their fellow nationals of Britain and America were engaged. It is important that a brief review of the scope of the opium trade be given here in order to appreciate the difficulties that Christians in China have ever since encountered because of it.

"A decision was taken at the time of Warren Hastings to decrease home consumption and develop an export trade. It was well known that the Chinese would buy; the Portuguese had been selling them for generations opium they procured at Malwa on the Indian coast. . . . The Company, therefore, resolved to build up an export to China. This was done very methodically; possession being obtained later on the Malwa crop — a move which completed the ruin of the Portuguese at Macao and created a Company monopoly for all India. Though opium was also exported from Turkey to China, chiefly by the Americans, this brand was very inferior and had only a small market, so that the Company had obtained in fact a world monopoly." [6] The East India Company were fully aware that the government of China had forbidden the importation of opium. The Company could not afford the risk of having their own ships carry it. The plot was laid to flood the China coast with opium smugglers who would purchase the opium in India from the Company and sell it to "runners" off the principal ports of the China coast. The Company knew but they were always in a position to affirm their innocence to the Chinese authorities with whom ships of the East India flag conducted legitimate trade at Can-ton. [7] The Company's revenues from these sales of opium at the Calcutta auctions rose steadily. In 1773 they netted a quarter of a million pounds sterling. By 1832 the trade in opium was a million pounds. The extent of the traffic is better seen by the actual number of chests, 150 pounds each, that were shipped to the China trade from India. " At the end of the eighteenth century the figure was in the region of 2,000 chests; in 1820, 4,770 chests; in 1825, 9,621 chests; in 1830, 18,760 chests; and in 1836, 26,018 chests." [8]

This was a period when the conscience of Christendom had not yet sensed the incongruity of slavery and was yet to be aroused over the evils of opium. That the people of England were unaware of the extent of the illegal opium trade being foisted on the Chinese is evidenced in a book written by a visitor to Can-ton at this period. [9]

When the people of England and America first learned of it, they did not realize that the opium trade had operated in direct violation of Chinese law. When the Chinese Government attempted to enforce its laws against opium smuggling, the British merchants besought London for naval protection of British commerce. On the eighteenth of March, 1839, the foreigners at Can-ton were given an edict that took them by surprise:

"I, Lin, Imperial High Commissioner of the Court of Heaven, President of the Board of War, Viceroy of Hu-kuang, issue these my commands to the barbarians of every nation.
"Let the barbarians deliver to me every particle of opium on board their store ships. There must not be the smallest part concealed or withheld. And at the same time let the said barbarians enter into a bond never hereafter to bring opium in their ships and to submit, should any be brought, to the extreme penalty of the law against the parties involved." [10]

This edict recounted the enormous favors bestowed upon the foreign merchants by the emperor and the monstrous ingratitude these same had shown by seducing and deluding the sons of the Middle Kingdom. It reminded the barbarians that if they complied they would receive clemency, but if they refused, the Chinese army would be used against them and all trade would cease. The foreign merchants were given three days in which to comply. A second edict was addressed to the Hong merchants, who were warned that failure to secure the compliance of the barbarians involved penalty of death. The foreign merchants surrendered some 20,000 chests of opium, which was destroyed in 1839 near Can-ton by dissolving the opium in ditches of salt water and sluicing it into the sea. In addition, the merchants at Can-ton were required to sign bonds by which they pledged never to deal in opium again. Collis points out that some of those who signed did so with reservations, for they at once began to operate from a new base at Manila. Commissioner Lin was well aware that as long as it was grown in India efforts would be made to sell it in China. Accordingly he wrote to Queen Victoria, then just beginning her reign:

"Though England is twenty thousand miles from China (three Chinese miles to one English mile), in certain fundamentals she resembles her, there being in both countries the same distinction

between benefit and injury and the same respect for the way of
Heaven. The British have certainly received benefits from China:
rhubarb, tea, raw silk. Are these not the very essentials of life? Nor
did the Court of Heaven begrudge them, for it was acting in ac-
cordance with the immemorial principle that even those in the
farthest confines are human and, so, qualified to benefit by the
Sacred Bounty.

"But how was this incomparable benevolence received? With
ingratitude, with the basest return. A tribe of depraved and bar-
barous pirates had brought for sale a deadly poison, the which
seduced the simple folk, to the destruction of their persons and the
draining of their purse. We have reflected that this noxious article
is the clandestine manufacture of artful schemers under the dominion
of your honourable nation. Doubtless you, the honourable chief-
tainess, have not commanded the growing and sale thereof." [11]

There is no record that Lin's letters ever reached Queen
Victoria. Where they were suppressed is not known. We are
indebted to the missionary editors of the *Chinese Repository*
for the translation and for preserving this attempt of the Chinese Government to bring the opium trade to an end. The
British Government chose to ignore the issue of opium and to
stress the arrogance of the Chinese emperor in masquerading
as "Son of Heaven." Wilberforce had just won his battle for
the abolition of slavery, and had Lin's letter been revealed in
England, there is every reason to believe that humanitarians
would have rallied to fight this evil also. Meantime the merchants on the China coast pressed the British Government for
action to defend British property. The issue of the British flag
was fanned. The debate in the House of Commons in 1840
reveals that the foreign minister, Lord Palmerston, made every
effort to conceal the true state of affairs from the Commons.
The facts began to come to light, but too late, for Palmerston
had already ordered the fleet to sail from India to the China
coast, and there was no telegraphic means at that time by
which to cancel the order. In the effort to force a motion to
suppress the opium trade, Sidney Herbert declared:

"Unless men are blinded by faction they cannot shut their eyes
to the fact that we are engaged in a war without just cause, that we

are endeavouring to maintain a trade resting upon unsound principles, and to justify proceedings which are a disgrace to the British flag."

William Gladstone was then but thirty years of age, but he courageously asked the prime minister:

"I will ask the noble lord a question. Does he know that the opium smuggled into China comes exclusively from British ports, that is, from Bengal and through Bombay? If that is a fact — and I defy the right honourable gentleman to gainsay it — then we require no preventive service to put down this illegal traffic. We have only to stop the sailings of the smuggling vessels; it is a matter of certainty that if we stopped the exportation of opium from Bengal, and broke up the depot at Lin-tin, and checked the cultivation of it in Malwa, and put a moral stigma upon it, that we should greatly cripple, if not extinguish, the trade in it." [12]

Although the motion for censure was defeated by nine votes, Herbert and Gladstone gave voice to the conscience of Britain. This was a period described as " an explosion of vitality, a release of creative energy, an age of intellectual curiosity, moral obliquity, economic anarchy, political wisdom, culture, cruelty, and sensitiveness." [13]

While Parliament debated in England, the opium trade thrived. The price of the drug had doubled after the destruction of the stocks on hand in 1839 by the Chinese. The fleet ordered by Palmerston to proceed from India in the summer of 1839 arrived in China in 1840. It proceeded to the mouth of Pei-ho River about one hundred miles from Pe-king, where the grand secretary met the British officials. He persuaded them to return to Can-ton for further negotiations, assuring them that the emperor was disposed to give full satisfaction. By the beginning of 1841 the British, concluding that they had been deceived, determined to use force. In an engagement at the entrance of the river to Can-ton on January 7, 1841, 500 Chinese were killed and 300 wounded. By January 20 an agreement was signed by plenipotentiaries, providing an indemnity of $6,000,000 for the loss of British property, namely, the 20,000 chests of opium that were destroyed; the cession of the island of Hong-kong to the British crown to be used as a trading base; official intercourse to be thereafter on an equal footing; and trade to be reopened at Can-ton until Hong-kong was ready. The British Government repudiated the agreement, and both rebuked and dismissed their own representative for not demanding larger indemnity and more concessions, and for not using the full strength of the force sent to him to exact his demands.

The Chinese Government repudiated the agreement and condemned to death the grand secretary who signed it. By 1842 the British carried the action north against Nan-king on the Yang-tze River. The Chinese on August 12, after defeat of their forces, signified readiness to meet British demands. There followed the Treaty of Nan-king. It was a dictated peace. The Chinese now had to pay an additional $15,000,000, costs of the expedition against them, and consent to the opening of five treaty ports, Can-ton, A-moy, Foo-chow, Ning-po and Shang-hai.[14] Nothing was mentioned in the Treaty of Nanking about the opium trade! The opium traffic was not stopped until 1908.[15] It stands forever as one of the darkest stains on the history of Western relations with the Orient. It was the greatest single impediment to Christianity in China in the nineteenth century, and a potent weapon in the hands of every anti-Christian agitator ever since.

The cessation of the opium traffic left China with an appetite created for narcotics, which resulted in China's being soon flooded with quantities of morphia, cocaine, and heroin. Figures listed by the advisory Opium Commission of the League of Nations on the seizure of illicit shipments of these drugs during 1928 reveal that two thirds of these seized shipments were bound for China. The cheapness of morphia as compared with opium, and the convenience it afforded for smuggling and consumption, suited both smugglers and addicts. Japan became the worst offender in this regard. According to the League of Nations statistics, the Japanese operated a narcotic factory in

Manchuria. But Japan was not alone in these illegal operations: " The French settlements in Chang-hai Han-kow and Tien-tsin, to mention just a few, were all great centers of the opium and morphine traffic." [16] This fact, combined with other reasons that were equally objectionable to the Chinese, was largely responsible for the student uprisings of 1927 against foreign settlements in China where political refugees as well as smugglers found sanctuary. One of these students asked the author, " Did not the missionary arrive in North America with his Bible at the same time as the trader with his firewater? " Then he pointed out that the Chinese knew that the white race, from which the missionaries came, now occupied the United States and Canada, which once were owned by the red men, who now live on reservations. He added, " The Chinese are determined it shall not happen here." He referred to objectionable signs, which had been for some years at the entrance to the park in one of the foreign concessions in a port city: " Dogs and Chinese not allowed." Such signs have long since been removed, but their utterance of an intolerable racial superiority has rankled in the minds of Chinese students and was among the reasons cited in demands that the foreign concessions in port cities be returned to Chinese sovereignty. " We are determined," he said, " to bring to an end the attitude of superiority that prompts certain foreigners, on seeing a Chinese whose help they wish, to call, ' Boy, come here.' " He added, " To those who treat us as equals we will be loyal friends."

Some years later, in the spring of 1950, at Tien-tsin, the author in conversation with Communist officials noted repeatedly that they referred to the long struggle China was forced to wage against foreign nations over the opium traffic. That the antiforeign and anti-Christian sentiment existing in China today is linked to the days of the opium traffic is due to very adroit propaganda still being employed by those fomenting this sentiment.

The Treaty of Nan-king, 1842, was soon followed by treaties

between China and other European nations and the United States. All these subsequent treaties embodied the "most favored nation" clause, whereby all other nations interested in the China trade were assured of enjoying all rights and privileges of trade given to the British in the Treaty of Nan-king. Thus this treaty became a keystone upon which all China's foreign relations were based for nearly a century. Under the security provided in the treaty, missionary societies began to reinforce their staffs, and several new missions, both Roman Catholic and Protestant, began to work under the privileges of the treaty ports.[17]

Although missionaries were opposed to the opium trade of their fellow nationals, tragedy arises from the fact that millions of unlettered Chinese, subject to mob psychology, were unable to make any distinction between the foreign missionary and the foreign trader. This was true in the first popular antiforeign uprising of 1850–1864, which is known as the T'ai-p'ing (Great Peace) rebellion, led by Hung Hsiu-ch'uan.[18] As a young student of twenty, Hung became interested in Christianity through the tracts of Protestant missionaries. With a meager knowledge of Christianity, his movement rapidly assumed political and military dimensions. The T'ai-p'ings sought to overthrow the Ming dynasty and make Hung emperor. Hostilities began in 1848; they articulated the growing indignation of China's millions against injustices. Although this fever was abated, it was destined to rise again and express itself in three major upheavals in the next hundred years. In 1852, the northward march of the rebels was a swelling horde, capturing city after city from Kuang-si to the Yang-tze. The situation was serious by 1853, when rebels captured the Yang-tze Valley and the southern capital of Nan-king. The unusual character of the T'ai-p'ings lay in the fact that they were a reform group moving from the bottom to the top without adequate leadership. Although they were unintelligent and unsuccessful, they were the first wave of a revolutionary century. Their devastations turned the country against them. One of the greatest disasters was the destruction of the best libraries, including three imperial academies, which were burned and never rebuilt.

Faced with internal rebellion, the Ch'ing court was amenable to further treaty negotiation with Western powers. As a result the Government at Pe-king secured foreign assistance in suppressing the T'ai-p'ing rebellion. However, with foreign assistance came renewed pressure for additional privileges for foreigners.

"In the two wars, 1839–1842 and 1856–1860, China was defeated by Occidental powers and forced to permit the Westerner to reside in several important cities and to travel freely elsewhere, and to grant him certain degrees of exemption from the jurisdiction of Chinese laws and courts. The treaties then exacted from Pe-king were the main framework of the legal basis for the Western penetration of China." [19]

The Chinese Government sought to obtain new agreements that would limit the activity of missionaries and establish more effective control over Chinese Christians. To this the foreign powers, particularly France, would not agree, and the status of missionaries and Chinese Christians remained as it had been fixed by the treaties of Tien-tsin and the French Convention of Pe-king, 1860, with some slight changes of the latter by a second convention, 1865. The treaties of Tien-tsin resulted in the opening of the interior of China to foreign travel and guaranteed protection to the foreigner and his converts. The years between 1860 and 1900 saw the penetration of every province of China by both Roman Catholic and Protestant missionaries.

" By 1897 there were a little over half a million Roman Catholics in China, with more than 750 missionaries. Protestants who before 1860 were confined almost entirely to the five ports and Hong-kong had an even more phenomenal growth. Many new societies began sending missionaries to China. The China Inland Mission had over 600 missionaries by 1895. In 1893 there were about 55,000 Chinese communicants in Protestant Churches, most in coastal provinces, and about 1,300 missionaries, over one half women, from 41 societies. These compared with 189 missionaries in 1864." [20]

The Roman Catholics of the nineteenth century were mainly from France. Over all Roman Catholics France exercised a protectorate which was based on clauses in the French treaties.[21] This was used as a means of heightening French influence, but it also became an increased source of irritation to the Chinese. The larger number of Roman Catholics in China at the close of the nineteenth century as compared with Protestant communicants is due to two factors not present in Protestant experience. First, the Roman Catholic Church includes in its count all baptized infants and children, whereas the Protestants report only baptized and confirmed communicants. The second was the privileged position given to Roman Catholics in the treaty with France. This enabled the Catholic missionaries to offer many inducements, including the protection of the Church, to converts. Indicative of the advantage gained by the Roman Catholics in the nineteenth century was the fact that upon their return to China after two hundred years they re-established themselves in those provinces and cities where Roman Catholics formerly had been located. With the guaranteed protection for converts, which was assured in the French treaties, they made rapid progress in reviving their work. But the last half of the century was repeatedly marked by persecutions, riots, and disturbances which arose out of the activities of Catholic missionaries. This was the result of conflicts arising when certain missionaries relied upon the force of their treaty rights more than upon the winning power of the message they had come to preach. The French Government had to take up the cause of its missionary protégés. There was a marked difference between the British and American treaties, on the one hand, regarding missionaries and their converts, and the French protectorate over Roman Catholics. The American and British missionaries were mostly Protestants, and did not seek more than normal assurances of religious freedom, as incorporated in Article 29 of the American Treaty of 1858.[22] Roman Catholic missionaries assumed rights that challenged the very sovereignty and integrity of China. In so doing, they

were supported by the French Government. One of the most
revealing documents dealing with this vexatious problem is
the memorandum of the Chinese Government through the
Tsung Li Yamen, communicated to the French chargé d'affaires in the year 1871.[23] The memorandum is directed against
Roman Catholic aggressions. The French minister, as well as
other foreign ministers to whom copies of the memorandum
were sent, delayed replying for such a length of time that there
were, unfortunately, no practical results from this effort of the
Chinese Government to gain certain modifications that would
remove grievances. An American who spent many years in
China writes:

" There is no country where the line between the officials and
the people is more sharply drawn than in China. The Roman Catholic Church is a mighty and an ancient hierarchy, and from the point
of view of its representatives it is probably not only natural but inevitable that those who wield powers so absolute should openly
and universally assume them. Thus the bishops, the spiritual rulers
of the whole of a broad province, adopt the rank of a Chinese governor and wear a button on their caps indicative of that fact, traveling in a chair with the number of bearers appropriate to that rank,
with outriders and attendants on foot, an umbrella of honour borne
in front, and a cannon discharged upon their arrival and departure.
. . . All this, and much else, is a part of the settled policy of the
Church, and not an accident of this place or that, and it is a policy
which is in many ways repellent to Chinese pride and repugnant to
their sense of propriety and fitness." [24]

In an edict issued shortly after the treaties of 1858–1860 the
Chinese submitted to the French chargé d'affaires their concern over the unwarranted assumptions of the Roman Catholic
missionaries and accused, to the French Government, the
Roman Catholic missionaries for assuming civil direction over
the acts of their converts, making the convert feel that his primary allegiance was to the Church which saves his soul, rather
than to the State. The words of the edict speak for themselves:

" The foreign missionary is not an official, and cannot interfere
in public affairs. . . . From the information which the prince and
the yamen have gathered (respecting the duties imposed upon them
by their priesthood) these persons found, as it were, among us an
undetermined number of states within the State." [25]

This privileged position guaranteed the Roman Catholic Church by treaty was a contributing factor in the phenomenal accessions to the Roman Catholic faith in the last half of this century. From the special privileges accorded Roman Catholics under the French protectorate arose many abuses.[26] Another serious source of Chinese animosity to the Roman Catholics were the terms of the French treaty of 1860 which provided that extensive properties that had belonged to the Church in the eighteenth century should be restored upon presentation of evidence of previous possession. The memorandum of 1871 of the *Tsung Li Yamen* to the French Government admitted that there was in China a great deal of this property, mentioning that it had changed owners many times and had frequently been greatly improved or in some cases completely rebuilt during more than one hundred years while the Roman Catholics were banished. This memorandum, however, protested: " The missionaries take no account of this; they exact a restitution, and do not even offer the least indemnity. Sometimes they even ask for repairs to be made, or, if not, for a sum of money. Such conduct excites the indignation of the people, who look with no favourable eye upon the missionaries. Such being the case, no friendship can exist." [27] As illustration of how Chinese feelings were aroused, in Can-ton the Roman Catholic missionaries proceeded as though they would establish adequate safeguards to insure that they would never be banished again. They created deep resentment by the erection of a fortresslike cathedral. The site they secured was the former yamen of the governor-general of the province. One of the senior missionaries in Can-ton in 1895 reported having heard a very intelligent Chinese say, while looking at the massive structure: " We Chinese say that that cathedral must come down even if it need be one hundred years." [28]

" The Roman Catholic Church is one of the largest property owners in some settlements of the open ports of China, as in the French concession of Tien-tsin, and in Chin-kiang, often being the principal landlord. The income from these enormous possessions is used for the support of the Church, in default of those annual contributions upon which Protestants rely." [29]

This policy of acquiring vast landholdings by the Roman Church reached such grave dimensions by 1950 that it precipitated serious clashes with the Communist Government. At the end of the nineteenth century the French Government continued to exert steady pressure for privileges for Catholic missionaries through their legation at Pe-king. As a result, on the fifteenth of March, 1899, the Chinese Government issued an edict according political status to the ecclesiastics of the Roman Catholic Church. There was great consternation because of it in the ranks of Protestant missionaries. In retrospect, it would appear that this edict was part of a deliberate plot of the Chinese Government. Pushed by the French in an hour of Chinese weakness, it had no other course but to yield to the incredible demands and allow public indignation to express itself with its own remedy. This soon occurred in the conflagration of the Boxer uprising.

The agreement with France in 1899 according political status to Roman Catholic bishops was simply beyond anything a self-respecting Government could grant. Its only purpose would seem to be a deliberate attempt to add " the last straw " to the list of encroachments of foreign nations upon China. The intensity of China's determination to resist both the future and the foreigner reached white heat at the end of the nineteenth century.[30]

This action coincided with internal tensions in the Chinese Government arising over the reforms that had just been set in motion by the young emperor, which had virtually held China in excitement for a hundred days of that eventful summer. Universities were established by an edict issued on the tenth of July. On the sixteenth of August a further decree authorized the establishment at Shang-hai of a Reform Translating Bureau for " putting into Chinese, Western works on science, arts, and literature, and textbooks for schools and colleges." [31] The reactionary group proceeded to plot with the empress dowager.

If she had not succeeded in seizing the reins of power in overthrowing the young Emperor Kuang Hsu, the Boxer uprising
might never have happened. "A vivid account of China's resistance to the future is recorded by many authors and reached
its pinnacle in the fierce reaction led by the dowager empress
Tz'u Hsi." [32]

Throughout the country there was growing resentment toward the Ch'ing dynasty because of its failure to prevent increasing encroachments by foreign nations. Following the
Sino-Japanese war of 1893, which placed China under heavy
indebtedness to Russia and France for loans to pay the required
indemnities to Japan, France had secured territorial gains in
Annam in 1895, Russia had obtained great concessions in Manchuria in 1896, and Germany had seized the Kiao-chow pen-
insula on the Shan-tung coast, with the port of Tsing-tau in
1897.[33] To add insult to injury, in 1899, France had demanded
and secured political status for Roman Catholic bishops. The
country was in a ferment against the Manchu court for its
capitulation in the face of these national indignities. The empress dowager, in seizing the throne, defended her dynasty by
transferring the accumulated hatred of the people against the
court to all foreigners, who, she declared, had been guilty of
attempting to subjoin her country. Since missionaries were the
only foreigners permitted in the interior of China, they were
accused of being spies for Western powers under the guise of
religion.

Many colorful accounts have been published regarding the
details of the Boxer uprising.[34] Our purpose will be served here
by citing instances in the massacre of missionaries in the province of Shan-si. There are three reasons for the selection of
Shan-si. First, there is the historic reason: Shan-si may be regarded as the cradle of the Chinese nation. Secondly, this is
the area of the earliest beginnings of Christianity in China,
where the Nestorian Church was established and where many
Nestorian relics have been discovered. Thirdly, the reaction
set in motion and fanned into flame by the empress dowager

reached its pinnacle of white heat in Shan-si, where most of the missionaries in China who lost their lives in the Boxer uprising suffered martyrdom, surrounded by mountain ranges which prevented their escape as passes were guarded. Even now there are few who realize that in the one province of Shan-si alone 159 foreigners were massacred — the majority of them at the time the Legations were besieged, but quite a number even after the Allies had taken possession of Pe-king.[35]

The memorial roll includes as martyrs (Protestant):

11 American missionaries and 2 children at Shou-yang.

10 American missionaries and 5 children at Tai-ku and Fen-chow.

13 English missionaries and 3 children at Tai-yuan-fu.

 1 secretary and wife and 3 children of British and Foreign Bible Society at Tai-yuan-fu.

48 missionaries and 15 children of the China Inland Mission.

 3 missionaries and 1 child of Swedish Mongolian Mission.

21 missionaries and 15 children of the Christian and Missionary Alliance.

 5 missionaries of the Scandinavian Alliance-Mongolian Mission.

 2 foreigners visiting in Shan-si at the time.

In most cases faithful Chinese did what they could to preserve property and records of the Church. In almost every mission some of these records are preserved. In Fen-chow an account is told of the return of the first missionary, several years after the massacre. The Chinese banker called on the missionary. With him were two messengers carrying a chest. The banker presented the account book of the mission, showing the balance on deposit with him at the time of the massacre and how it had accumulated with compound interest. In the chest was the total amount in silver bullion. All missionaries there had been massacred, but no Chinese Christian was killed. In many places they too were massacred, and their martyrdom revealed beyond any doubt that the new experience of the Christian faith was more precious to them than life. Protestant missionaries unable to protect themselves were unable to protect their converts. The policy of the Roman Catholic Church of fortifying their missions and making cathedrals that could be used as fortresses in times of civil disorder had been one of the causes of public anger, but it proved the means by which hundreds of their missionaries and converts were saved from massacre. While every Protestant missionary in Shan-si was slain, the Roman Catholics suffered relatively small losses there. The total number of Roman Catholics listed as martyrs in the Boxer uprising reached only 44 in all China, of whom 12 were killed in Shan-si. In contrast a total of 188 Protestant missionaries and children lost their lives, Shan-si missions contributing 159 of the martyrs. Missionaries in other provinces had, in most cases, been able to escape to the coast or to the Legations at Pe-king.

In September, 1900, Pe-king was captured by the allied forces. The imperial court had fled in undignified haste. The foreign powers were determined that China should pay an indemnity for the loss of life and property of their nationals. The Protestant missionaries drew up a list of losses, with a scheme for settlement which won the respect of the Chinese for its fairness.[36]

These claims were most moderate. The cash indemnity sought was not for missionaries but to be used for educational purposes in Shan-si. The final demands made by the foreign powers on China were far more exacting, however, than anything suggested by Protestant missionaries:

" The outline of the terms of settlement with China involved a mission of apology to Germany for the murder of her minister; monuments in desecrated cemeteries; a prohibition of the importation of arms and munitions of war; the destruction of the Taku and other forts; a Legation area in Peking, defended by foreign guards, with provision for other forces elsewhere; a financial indemnity of perhaps 450,000,000 taels of silver, the payment of which is to be distributed through the coming thirty or fifty years; the punishment of specified persons who were most guilty in the late uprising; the suspension for five years of examinations in cities where foreigners were murdered; the universal publication of the fact of these punishments, a strict prohibition under penalty of death of all antiforeign societies, and an imperial edict distinctly recognizing the future responsibility of officials for outrages occurring within their districts." [37]

The Boxer Protocol of 1901 provided the terms of China's indemnity to the foreign powers. The United States did not forget the recommendation of the Shan-si missionaries. It soon made provision for the use of the American part of the indemnity for the education of Chinese students. Some years later the British Government remitted their share of the indemnity, with the provision that it be used in railroad construction in China.

There has been considerable misunderstanding over the term "missionary rights" in China. Many modern missionaries have been embarrassed by the special privileges accorded them by treaty. The bulwark of protection for missionary rights, as distinguished from the general rights of all foreigners in China, is Article 14 of the American Treaty of October 8, 1903.[38] The treaty of 1903 provided that missionary societies could purchase and hold property for missionary work. This rightly avoided the danger of individuals' becoming involved in property questions, with attendant misunderstandings. It may be said in fairness that the American treaty negotiators codified the existing rights and privileges of foreigners in general. The document that they produced gathered together the practices, customs, and privileges exercised by Christian missionaries since 1843 and incorporated them in one clear succinct article. This provided:

"The right to carry on missionary activity, to convert the Chinese, the right to exempt Chinese converts from idol taxes, the right to acquire by rental and by lease in perpetuity — which is technically equal to purchase in fee simple — land and buildings *anywhere* in China, together with the right to erect ' suitable buildings ' on acquired property. These are the acquisitions of the missionary societies as a result of this treaty. These are the rights which are quite independent of the rights of extraterritoriality. If extraterritoriality is abolished *de facto* it does not necessarily mean that these various missionary rights are *ipso facto* abolished at the same time." [39]

The day was not far distant when missionaries were to realize that the control over mission property by "foreign" boards was a barrier to the development of a truly indigenous Church, and particularly as the holdings of certain missions became so extensive as to lay the Christian Church open to the accusation of being foreign-controlled, with its security vested in treaties with foreign nations. By 1907 most of the missionaries were back at their stations in the interior of China, with replacements more than offsetting the numbers killed in the Boxer massacre. The Ch'ing dynasty never recovered; all confidence in the Manchu court was gone. The seeds of revolution sprouted on all sides.

At the Centenary Missionary Conference held in Shang-hai in 1907 a number of resolutions were adopted which were designed to set forth the wholly moral and spiritual aims of Protestant missionaries in China. One of these resolutions especially recommended that all missionaries "be vigilant, lest, in the present national awakening, the Christian Church should in any way be made use of for revolutionary ends, and lest Chinese Christians should, through ignorance, confusion of thought, or misdirected zeal, be led into acts of disobedience against the Government." Another section contained the declaration: "We teach and enjoin on all converts the duty of loyalty to the powers that be, and further staunchly affirm that in fact there are no more loyal subjects of the empire than the Chinese Christians." [40] In 1910 the Edinburgh Conference enjoined all missionaries to "keep clear of all party and faction" and laid down the injunction that "missionaries should have nothing to do with political agitation. This is outside their sphere, and engaging in it can only harm their work. . . . The relation of the missionary as such to the convert is purely religious. He has to him no peculiar relation which in the least entitles him to interfere in the general administration of the country." [41] That these two Protestant conferences felt it necessary to pass these resolutions is indicative of the fact that there were instances of involvement of missionaries in political schemes.

" The Manchu Government, in spite of all its faults and short-
comings, knew a good deal more about the aims and aspirations of
certain sections of its subjects than the missionary societies gave
it credit for, and it certainly far excelled the missionaries in its
knowledge of the Chinese character. . . . It had strong reason to
suspect that many of the Christian converts were by no means
so well disposed towards the reigning dynasty or towards the existing political constitution as the foreign missionary body professed
to believe; and yet it knew only too well from bitter experience that
if it made any serious attempt to bring them to punishment or to
exercise supervision or control over the Christian societies to which
they belonged, the missionary body would immediately accuse it of
persecuting innocent Christians and of breaking its solemn treaties
with the armed powers of the West." [42]

Here is discernible one of the most significant differences
between the Roman Catholic and Protestant missions. We have
noted the tendency of Roman Catholic missionaries to seek
direct political action through their sponsoring " power," to
bolster their cause. Many Protestants disavowed such procedures; but, on the other hand, they brought to China the
major contribution in higher education and these schools and
colleges became the hotbed of new social and political ideas.
Although this was not political action by missionaries, it was
definitely political action by young Chinese intellectuals trained
in mission schools. Protestants must recognize that missionaries shared in planting this ferment.

" China's revolution really began, as a Chinese once remarked,
with the arrival in Can-ton, in 1807, of Robert Morrison, the first
Protestant missionary. . . . That these religious workers were, in
the main, unconscious agents of political, and not merely religious
and social, revolution rendered them none the less potent: new
wine is innocent of ulterior motives as it enters old bottles." [43]

Confronted with rising currents of unrest, the Manchu dynasty as one of its last acts elevated Confucius to the exalted
status of the equal of Heaven. This occurred after the death
of the empress dowager and the ascension of the young Hsuan
T'ung emperor. But it was too late to turn the hands of the
clock back. The action did not meet with any public support.
Discovering that public sentiment was against it, the court

revoked the decree in the hope of averting disaster, but without avail. The Manchu dynasty abdicated. Thus was broken a sacred link, which in the eyes of the people for thousands of years had bound together Heaven and earth.

The Chinese Christians who sprang into political prominence at the outbreak of the revolution were nearly all connected with Protestant denominations. It was natural that, as a result of the formation of the Republic, missionary bodies in China should be quick to take advantage of their enhanced prestige. It was generally interpreted that the Manchus had forfeited the " divine decree " to rule, and Heaven was on the side of the new regime. In 1911, Christians were on the side of the revolutionists. Many Chinese interpreted the change to mean that the Christians had received the favor of Heaven. However, the blind spot of most foreigners in China in the last half of the nineteenth century, namely, the lack of cultural appreciation, persisted even now.

" A great deal can be said for the missionary, but it must also be acknowledged that between 1860 and the close of the nineteenth century, he was often the source of great annoyance to the Chinese population and officialdom. His teaching, intolerant of the customary honors to ancestors, seemed to threaten the Chinese family. Religious practices which formed an integral part of the guild, community, and political life were anathema to him. Christians, therefore, seemed to their neighbours recreant in moral, social, economic, and political obligations and to be attacking the foundations of society and civilization." [44]

In all fairness, most of the pioneer missionaries were in advance of their age, but the Western mind of the nineteenth century revealed a misapprehension of many values in Chinese culture. In the first issue of the *Chinese Repository* Morrison's own editorial shows that all China's religious observances were deemed idolatrous:

" The conduct of the Emperor in praying, fasting and self-examination ought to reprove the sluggish Christian. But we shall do exceedingly wrong if we attempt to excuse such abominable idolatry, and to throw the mantle of charity over that which God abhors." [45]

This criticism was written about the annual ceremonies at the Altar of Heaven when the emperor prayed on behalf of the people. Morrison did not dream that when the Protestant Churches should finally choose the most appropriate term for God, it would be the Confucian term used by the emperor on this occasion. Today it is well recognized that the Altar of Heaven conveyed a very high conception of deism. Ricci had been ready to accept this in the seventeenth century. But the outlook in the nineteenth century was much narrower. As it was shared by the commercial community of foreigners in the port cities, so it was reflected in the attitude of Western nations toward China.

A century after Morrison, another great Protestant missionary, who spent fifty-six years in China, revealed that he was unprepared to admit that the hand of the Eternal had been operating in China before the missionaries entered that land. Arthur H. Smith wrote: "They have the loftiest moral code which the human mind unaided by divine revelation has ever produced, and its crystalline precepts have been the rich inheritance of every successive present from every successive past." [46] One wonders if this author realized that he paid the Chinese the compliment of saying that they had produced all this without the help of God.

There existed a considerable weight of opinion that held that Christianity and Western culture were indissolubly united. One of the most influential missionary writers in Europe of this period maintained that the strength of Christianity was due to its inner vitality and to the powers within Western culture which gave dynamic to the Western world and its religion.[47] Although individual thinkers in the West had protested Western culture in many respects, yet in the mind of the average person in the Occident the supremacy of the white man over other peoples and cultures was due to an inherent superiority of Western culture and religion. Those without racial prejudice would be willing to agree that other races could become their equals, but only by adopting Western religion and culture. That this assumption was too prevalent is beyond question.[48]

" In the early days of the modern Christian movement in China there was a strong current of opinion which held that there was nothing in the religions of China but blind ignorance and super- stitious idolatry. Those holding such views were ready to declare the whole thing worthless and useless and were ready to knock it down with one general condemnation. . . . Christianity was out for conquest. It was a conquest of love, to be sure, but nevertheless it was a conquest." [49]

This was a very kind criticism written by a Chinese Chris- tian. How much greater were the criticisms from those Chinese who had no sympathy for the Christian religion! To the non Christian Chinese in the nineteenth century it was inevitable that Christianity should be confused with Western culture.[50] Because of the antiforeign sentiment stirred up as a result of the incredible encroachments on the sovereignty of China, and on the personal dignity of administrative officials, by the Ro- man Catholic demands through the French Government, the Protestants were destined to suffer in the subsequent uprising even more than the Roman Catholics, who had built for them- selves churches and monasteries that could easily be defended.

It is important to note the fundamental differences which existed in these two simultaneous streams of Protestant and Roman Catholic missions in the nineteenth century and which continues to the present day.

" Protestants believe that a man becomes a Christian not by par- taking of the miraculous power of the seven sacraments but by the confession that the New Testament message of the revelation of God in Jesus is true. The sacraments which the Protestants cele- brate add nothing to the " Word "; they merely bring it, as it were, directly and personally to the believer. . . . The Protestant is con- vinced that *faith* alone, i.e., an absolute reliance upon God and a complete trust in him as he has made himself known through Jesus, is the proper attitude of man toward God. He rejects the Roman Catholic teaching that man possesses power by which he can make himself acceptable to God. . . . In complete reliance upon God and not upon himself, the Protestant proclaims the freedom of the Christian man. Therefrom he derives the doctrine of the *universal priesthood of believers*; through faith in the gospel of Jesus Christ and thereby becomes a free man, subject to God alone, can be a priest who through his words and deeds brings the liberating gospel to his fellow men. Thus the Roman Catholic distinction between priests and laymen is destroyed." [51]

Because of these opposing views there has been no basis whatever for co-operation. From the beginning the two simultaneous missionary streams in China have been distinctly separate movements. But the problem of the Christian Churches in China at this time is by no means a simple division between Roman Catholics and Protestants.

The Protestant missionary movement from the outset has suffered from the multiplicity of its missionary societies and sustaining boards. Latourette mentions that no less than 41 different missions were operating in China in 1893 under the Protestant banner. Following the Boxer massacre, attempts were made early in the twentieth century to remedy this situation, but in the zenith of the Protestant movement, forty years later, when the Laymen's Foreign Missions Inquiry was made, there were 84 societies having membership in the Foreign Missions Conference of North America, and most of these operated missions in China. This figure did not include many faith missions, such as the China Inland Mission, which is the largest Protestant mission in China; nor did it include the Societies of Britain and Europe. To say the least, the total effect of this was tragically confusing to the Chinese, and vitiated the witness of the Christian message.

The river of history sometimes meanders through a plain as the Yellow River wends its way across the wide expanse of Ho-nan and Shan-tung to the sea. At other times history foams and plunges in rapids as the Yang-tze races through its gorges. Thus certain periods are anabolic, when energy is derived from the past or an unconscious momentum is conserved and stored in sufficient reserve to insure a peaceful flow. Other periods are catabolic, when energy is discharged with the expulsive power of revolutionary force. The nineteenth century may be described as an anabolic one for China in contrast to the twentieth century, as shown in the next chapter — the most catabolic in all of its long history. That the impact of the Occidental world upon China has played a large part in this upheaval is widely recognized. That Christianity has had a very significant and revolutionary role in this period of China's history is not so well known. The indignities connected with the infringement of sovereignty resulting from the impact of the West have been a continually bitter experience for the Chinese.

Missionaries are incorrigible optimists. Perhaps unconsciously and not intentionally they have often portrayed only that which was favorable to their cause. A fair understanding of the Boxer uprising demands that consideration be given to the Chinese point of view, and that the Westerner make a diligent effort to sit where they sat (cf. Ezek. 3:15) and try to understand why the Chinese feels and acts as he does in given situations. One of the most persistent sources of irritation between China and the Western powers in the nineteenth century was the Christian missionary, who was often the innocent victim in a clash that stemmed from the foreigner's repeated failure to understand the Chinese.

VI

CHRISTIANITY'S CONTRIBUTION IN THE REPUBLIC

FOR forty years China has been experiencing a revolution that is unparalleled in the history of the world. Though it began slowly, the nation soon found itself in the throes of violent upheavals. What has been taking place in the political and military arena has caught the headlines, but far more significant in its effect upon the future is the deep underlying change in Chinese thought.

The political revolution that swept the Manchus from power in 1911 and inaugurated the Republic was borne on the wave of an ascending nationalism. The Republic was forced to combat the regionalism and provincialism that still held large sections of the country in their grasp. For fifteen years civil war raged in the struggle to weld the vast area of China into a political unity. This was accomplished in the formation of the Nationalist Government in 1926. The enormity of the task embraced a land mass of nearly four million square miles, vaster than Europe. China attempted to crowd what Europe accomplished in seven centuries into the first fifty years of the twentieth century. Europe spent all of the eighteenth century in its industrial revolution. China, on the other hand, has had five simultaneous revolutions raging during the first half of the twentieth century.

The founders of the Republic soon discovered that they had more than a political revolution on their hands. Unlike the small area of the Thirteen Colonies on the Eastern seaboard of

America, when they declared their independence and established the United States of America, or unlike a small island, such as Britain, which had earlier developed its forms of responsible and democratic government, China presented huge difficulties of land mass without modern means of communications. In 1911, the Northeast was removed from the Northwest by over forty days' trail journey by pack animal. The author has covered much of this territory, traveling on one occasion forty-two days by pack saddle in the Ordos area. At close range one obtains a lasting impression of the panorama of arid mountains of loess, gorges, valleys, streams, and the unending but changing scenes of village life.

It was relatively easy to overthrow the Manchu dynasty, which was so corrupt that it crumbled, but the establishment of the Republic was immediately challenged, if not in name certainly in authority, by whoever could seize control in remote areas of the country. In many instances bands of outlaws, who had lived beyond the pale of the Manchu administration, promptly set themselves up as local governments with their leaders as war lords. Thus for fifteen years the Republic struggled to bring the period of the war lords to an end, either by military decision or by negotiation. In spite of these handicaps, the concept of a national government was constantly gaining strength. A sense of nationalism and loyalty for the ideal of the Republic was a burning flame held aloft by students. Thus from the outset of the Republic the contribution of the Christian schools and colleges became an invaluable asset. The good will of the Government toward these institutions was due in large part to the realization that they were rendering an important contribution to the training of leadership which the young Republic so urgently needed. Confronted with overwhelming illiteracy, the difficulties of the new Government were enormous. It was soon apparent that the success of the political revolution rested upon the success of the intellectual revolution. The Protestant translation of the Bible into Chinese was published early in the vernacular, at a time when it was considered a disgrace for any scholar to allow his work to be published in any but the classical style. Thus the dead hand of the past was wrested from the printed page. In 1922 the National Mass Education Movement for adults was launched. The intellectual revolution was in full swing. China was soon experiencing a literary renaissance which in its magnitude exceeded any other in the world's history. Its own ancient classics were translated into the vernacular. Foreign scientific texts were translated into Chinese. Newspapers, magazines, periodicals blossomed. The nation was conscious of being borne on the flood tide of a new day.

Far exceeding the intellectual revolution in its demand for swift change was the social upheaval. The seeds were planted at the beginning of the twentieth century when Protestant missionaries persuaded Christian parents not to bind the feet of their infant daughters and to permit them to attend schools. The impact of young educated women upon the thought of the country has been so tremendous that one of the first acts of the Republic was to enact legislation making foot-binding illegal. Today the girls run, dance, and play on normal and natural feet. Young women have been enrolled in the educational institutions on a par with men. This has happened in the land where forty years ago it was not considered quite proper for a man to look at a woman longer than was necessary to discover that she was not a man. For forty centuries woman had been in bondage. She was owned by her father, sold to her husband, and in her later years, if widowed, subservient to her son. She had no civic status; she could not inherit property, nor was she permitted to be educated. "To amuse men, to bear their children, to bear their burdens" were the functions of women in China for four thousand years. The outstanding contribution of the Christian movement has been the social, intellectual, and civic emancipation of womanhood. In 1931, the new civil code promulgated by the Nationalist Government provided that women should possess equal civic rights with men, and should henceforth be entitled to inherit property from their fathers, brothers, husbands, and sons. They could buy and sell, but no longer could they be bought or sold. For twenty years China has enjoyed the freedom of coeducation. For the first time in four thousand years, young men and women have looked into each others' faces and shared together in discussions regarding the welfare of their country. They have mixed in friendships, athletics, and group discussions as well as in the classroom. This change has not come to pass without sad difficulties, heartaches, and suffering. Parents have stretched their hands toward the past in the effort to restrain their youth. Young China, in revolt, has demanded that it should have the right to make for itself the great decisions affecting its future. Thus, within one generation, China passed through a social revolution that has rocked the foundations of its family system and political structure. The greatest single factor in this social regeneration has been the Christian Church, which gave China a social goal. It presented religion as a creative process tending toward new persons and a new humanity. The new individual was pledged to a new society in which the law of his personal life found expression and embodiment. As self-preservation is the law of nature, self-transcendence became the law of this new society. But the primary emphasis of this social gospel looked for a Kingdom of God which would be expressed in a new social order. In this generation few could be found in China, even among Christians, who would accept Dante's tribute to the Abbot Joachim "who found in the Scriptures that which he longed to find there — the promise of a spiritual renovation, the coming of the Kingdom of God." [1]

Simultaneous with the political, intellectual, and social upheavals, and moving forward relentlessly, has been the industrial or economic revolution. When the construction of the first railroad was started, opposition was so great that the Government ordered the tracks removed. Within a few years the Chinese appreciated the values of more rapid transportation, and railroads began to penetrate in many directions. Yet China has less than ten thousand miles of railroads, or about one mile of track for every fifty thousand inhabitants, compared with one mile of railroad for every five hundred persons in the United States or for every two hundred and fifty persons in Canada. For a long time the wheelbarrow continued to be cheaper than gasoline as a means of transport, but today both the wheelbarrow and the pack animal are giving way to more efficient means of transportation. The old stone gristmill, beside which two women with bound feet labored to crush the grain, providing flour for daily noodles, has given place to steel rolling mills. The home loom finds severe competition in the steam-driven factories. The castor oil lamp, with its dim flicker, has given way to paraffin candle and petroleum lamp. The major cities are now equipped with electricity.

In each of these four revolutions, political, intellectual, social, and industrial, growth can be traced to new concepts from the West. The discovery in the industrial revolution that the use of scientific methods of agriculture, engineering, road construction, river conservation, reclamation dikes, irrigation projects could all contribute to man's control over his environment, have caused radical changes in the religious concepts of the masses. On every hand youth surged forward to conquer the problems of the new age. All four of these revolutions made their direct contribution to the religious crisis, which at the same time was the concomitant and the resultant of them. There has been a tendency in recent years for Chinese to treat the old religions as belonging to the classical past, no longer holding relevance for the new age. The incompatibility of superstition and science led many to renounce all religious beliefs in a sweeping campaign among students. One of the greatest factors in the changing religious concepts has been the work of medical missionaries. Superstitions ran riot around the mystery of life and death. As mission hospitals with Christian physicians and nurses ministered in the name of the Great Physician, doubts were dispersed, fears subsided, and prejudices were cast aside. Mothers who once believed that evil spirits snatched their children from their breasts during the scourge of epidemic diseases learned with relief that vaccination could prevent smallpox, inoculations could prevent diphtheria and typhoid. Preventive medicine shattered prevailing beliefs that a galaxy of evil spirits caused these maladies. The outstanding work of missionary physicians established standards of medicine in China that gave renown to the Christian Church, and often was responsible for the pronounced favor it enjoyed from the authorities. Medical missions in China wrote a saga of heroism, illumined with most loving and sacrificial devotion. Today all Christian hospitals have been taken over by Communists.

To dismiss this loss as a defeat resulting from Russian intrigue, or from the Communist victory alone, is an oversimplification. The Christian Church must recognize that the Church, not Russia, developed the soil in which Communism was planted in China. True, an enemy has sown tares in the field, but the enemy did not plant the tares until the field was well plowed and harrowed by a hundred years of missionary work. Communism simply could not have taken root in China a hundred years ago, because then there was no adequate idea of universal brotherhood. This idea is well stated by George Sokolsky, who spent eighteen years in China:

" Christianity as a religion or a practice of life can only interest me academically — I am a Jew and should, therefore, abhor missions, but I have lived in China during most of my adult life. To the foreigner in China, the Christian mission cannot be a mere question of religious affiliation, for the Christian mission is one of the most vital revolutionary forces in that country. . . . It is the role that Christianity has played in the creating of a distinctive personality that has made missions so attractive to me. What does it matter what the number of converts is? What matters whether there is a large or small number of churches? China will not be saved as a nation by multitudes or by buildings. She requires leadership, and the Christian mission has done more than its share in the reorientation of the Chinese mind from Confucian selfishness, as evidenced by the family system, to the social consciousness as evidenced by the effort of an increasingly large number of Chinese men and women to serve China in a modern manner." [2]

Anyone who would understand the change that has come
over China between 1912 and 1952 must trace the full impact
of Christian missions which contributed the revolutionary and
psychological factors without which there could not have been
any idea of a Republic. The religious crisis is one in which
older religious beliefs have been discredited faster than new
and abiding values were adopted. The critical attitude of
many missionaries toward Confucius, and more particularly
toward Confucianism, stems from misunderstandings surrounding the efforts of the Confucian scholars to make Confucianism a State cult. The underlying motive that sought to
make Confucius the center of a State religion was not due to
any belief or desire to elevate him to the status of a god, but
was rather due to a fear that unless Confucianism were given
the official status of a religion, and placed first among the religions of the Chinese people, it would be handicapped in the
struggle against rival forces. The efforts to make Confucianism
the State religion of China were revived under the Republic,
but failed in 1924, and subsided under the wave of popularity
given the teachings of Sun Yat-sen's *San Min Chu I,* " The
Three Principles of the People's Livelihood." [3] To a large degree the compulsory use of this text in all schools under the
Republic resulted in a marked loss to the prestige of Confucian ethics. The memory and purpose of Sun Yat-sen were preserved in all Chinese schools. Before the Communists gained
ascendancy it was required of all students to repeat his " Last
Will and Testament " and bow three times before his portrait
in a ceremony held on Monday of each week. The first sentences of this " Last Will and Testament " are indicative of the
dominant mood of young China which has existed for the past
twenty years:

" I have served the cause of the People's Revolution for forty
years, during which time my object has consistently been to secure
liberty and equality for my country. From the experience of these
forty years, I have come to realize that, in order to reach this object, it is necessary to awaken the masses of our people and to join

hands with those countries which are prepared to treat us as equals in our fight for the common cause of humanity. At present we have not yet completed the work of the Revolution." [4]

What was expected to happen from the constant repetition of these words by the students of China: " At present we have not yet completed the work of the Revolution " ? It was the Communists who translated this into action.

In the Christian schools missionaries had achieved "success" in supplanting Confucius. The task was made easier as graduates of Christian schools gained ascendancy in the Nationalist Government. It was not unnatural that there were some who hoped that the ground lost by Confucius would be won and occupied by Christianity. Little did they realize that the ground lost by Confucius would be occupied in large measure by the forces of atheism, materialism, and Communism. The Communist regime of the Central People's Republic of China is fully aware of the incompatibility that exists between the totalitarian position of Communism and the respect for personality and individual freedom in the teachings of Confucius. The Communist Government fears that it cannot survive in China without the complete suppression of the teachings of Confucius. This is the reason for the order issued at Pe-king in June, 1949, requiring the collection and burning of all Confucian texts from all libraries and schools, and forbidding teaching of Confucian ethics.[5] This modern attempt to eradicate the ethics of Confucius from China has its counterpart in history. In the third century before Christ, after the Confucian teachings had been lifted into prominence by the devotion and faithful work of Mencius, Chin Shih-hwang ordered the collection and burning of all Confucian manuscripts.[6] If one would understand the cause of fear and consequent destruction of the classics by Chin Shih-hwang, and now by the Communists at Pe-king twenty-two hundred years later, the answer is discernible in the " Doctrine of the Mean " and in the " Analects ":

"Hence the sovereign may not neglect the cultivation of his own character. Wishing to cultivate his character, he may not neglect to serve his parents. In order to serve his parents, he may not neglect to acquire a knowledge of men. In order to know men, he may not dispense with a knowledge of Heaven." [7]

There are those who have taken false comfort at the collapse of Confucian teachings in modern times. Today the whole elaborate system of Confucian ethics is disrupted and the teachings of the sage are discredited. It calls to mind the warning given in the early years of the Republic by two eminent missionaries. Rev. John Ross, of the Church of Scotland Mission, declared: "Those who slight Confucianism appear to have neglected to weigh its influence on the past of China, or its possible place in the future." [8] He was supported by Archdeacon A. C. Moule:

"It is difficult to believe that the attempt recently made by some ardent spirits of Young China to discredit and banish from their curriculum of education the writings of Confucius and Mencius, as out of accord with republican principles, can succeed, save with grave discredit cast upon Chinese intelligence and most justifiable *amour-propre*." [9]

Sir Reginald Johnston counseled that the missionary should claim Confucius as an ally and not oppose him as a foe. He was convinced that there was nothing in the teachings of Confucius that was incompatible with the progress, social, political, or spiritual, of the Chinese people.[10] The Republic dealt Confucianism a heavy blow when it was discovered that Yuan Shih-k'ai was using the Confucian tradition as a ladder by which he would personally ascend the throne. The result was reaction against him and the Confucian scholars. Because of the long history in which Confucianism and the monarchy were so often involved in intrigue, in the public mind these rose and fell together. The eclipse of Confucius in the educational system was so complete that there were those who felt that "less respect was given to Confucius than in any period of China's history since the Chin dynasty." [11]

The official favors which the Republic bestowed on Christianity after the overthrow of the Manchu dynasty were largely the result of political expediency. At the moment of coming to power, the cabinet of the Republic was anxious to gain the good will and support of Western powers. With this in view they adroitly employed the idea of paying respect to the Christian religion, as it was considered the greatest lever in winning support of Western nations. It was not long in making this decision. One of the first actions of the cabinet was to call upon all Christian nations to offer prayer for the new government. This received great attention throughout the world. In China there was exultation in Christian circles over the " Prayer Sunday." One group of Protestants in Pe-king took advantage of the occasion to take temporary possession of the Altar of Heaven, where for centuries the emperor had made his annual prayer to Heaven on behalf of his people. This action of Christians in holding a service on the Altar of Heaven shocked the national and religious sentiment of many non-Christian Chinese. Christians further rejoiced when the Government put in office a Christian as director of education.[12] What was not generally known is that the unexpected action taken by the cabinet in calling upon Christians throughout the world to offer prayer for the new Government synchronized with a serious financial crisis in the political affairs of the nation. " It may be suggested without cynicism that some, at least, of the members of the cabinet who assented to the suggestion of an appeal for a Day of Prayer were actuated by a variety of reasons, among which the spiritual motive was not supreme." [13] The Government issued decrees through the Ministry of Education banishing the Confucian cult. But the tide of reaction soon set in, and within two years the Christian Director of Education was " ordered to vacate his post."

The fact that Sun Yat-sen was a baptized Christian was a source of pride to many Protestant missionaries at the time of the revolution of 1911. He was not in China when the Manchu dynasty was swept from the throne, but Sun Yat-sen was acclaimed by the Chinese as the father of the revolution. He returned at the end of 1911 to accept the position of president of the provisional government, which post he held for only a few weeks until the election of the constituted government. Nothing in the life of Sun Yat-sen revealed his Christian spirit so much as his action in giving up the presidency to Yuan Shih-k'ai in order to save the Republic. Sun spent his life for a "cause" which he would not sacrifice for personal gain. Yuan espoused the "cause" to raise himself. Had it not been for Sun Yat-sen's influence in holding the Republic together, Yuan Shih-k'ai would probably have founded a new dynasty.

When in 1923 the Kuomintang threatened to seize the customs at Can-ton because the revenues were being sent, according to international agreement, to Pe-king, the Western powers sent gunboats to Can-ton. Until the Nationalists could control the customs, they were deprived of revenues. The Western powers gave no support to Sun Yat-sen. For this reason Sun counseled the Kuomintang: "We no longer look to the Western powers. Our faces are turned toward Russia." [14] When the Nationalist forces reached the Yang-tze Valley under the leadership of Chiang Kai-shek in 1926–1927, his Russian advisers included the military genius General Gallen and the political strategist Michael Borodin. When the Communists attempted to seize control over the Nationalist Government, Chiang Kai-shek broke with Soviet Russia.

Because the twentieth century has witnessed the most tragic tensions between China and those Western nations from which most of the missionaries originated, it is of great importance to review here the history of this period. The non-Christian in China naturally expected the Christian missionary to have a connection with the country of his origin. The actions of Western nations toward China caused the greatest embarrassments to missionaries, with complicating losses.

In the first quarter century of the Republic, China was torn by the civil wars among rival war lords who challenged the

authority of the central Government. During these years
the cultural and political struggle between North and South
never ended. The South continually proposed while the North
disposed, but by 1928 the South had disposed of the North
by coalition, and the Nationalist Government under the leadership of Chiang Kai-shek moved the capital of China to Nan-
king, changing the name of Pe-king, " Northern capital," to Pei-
p'ing, " Northern Peace." It was during this period of internal
strife that Japan began its expansion in the mainland of China.
During World War I, Japan seized the area of Shan-tung,
which had been occupied by Germany since 1898, and on May
30, 1915, Japan served China with the " infamous twenty-one
demands." It was largely through the moral influence of America and Britain that the Government of the Republic was able
to resist these demands, which if granted would have given
Japan virtual control over China's ports, customs, and coastal
provinces.[15]

In 1919 the Chinese delegates to the Peace Conference
walked out of the Versailles Assembly when they discovered
that Britain and America had capitulated to the Japanese demand that the former German territory in Shan-tung should
be awarded to Japan as a prize of war. To the Chinese, who
had also been allies in the war against Germany, this was an
unbelievable betrayal. Prior to the outbreak of World War I,
Germany had agreed with China to return the Shan-tung territory by 1921. Therefore, China refused to sign the Versailles
Treaty. In July, 1919, following Versailles, Soviet Russia
received the good will of the Chinese in the hour of their indignation against Western powers. Karakhan, Vice-Com-
missar of Foreign Affairs, proclaimed the readiness of Russia
to renounce all her former special rights and privileges in
Manchuria and to enter into a treaty of equality with China.
This manifesto declared: " All people, no matter whether
their nations are great or small, no matter where they live, no
matter at what time they may have lost their independence,
should have their independence and self-government and not

submit to being bound by other nations." [16] The Soviet Treaty of Friendship (1924) gave China all the civil rights and sovereignty that were denied at Versailles. Chinese opposition to the Versailles Treaty was intensified at the Washington Disarmament Conference in 1922. There the Chinese delegation successfully caused enough disturbance, by refusing to discuss disarmament while Japan occupied Shan-tung, to make it necessary that the Shan-tung question receive priority before any disarmament agreement could be reached. As a result of pressure exerted by America and Britain upon Japan, it was announced by the Japanese Government that the Shan-tung territory would be returned to China. But within six years after returning it the Japanese invaded Shan-tung, to take it back in 1928.

Japan had become alarmed at the victorious march of the Nationalist forces in the Yang-tze Valley in 1927; the coalition of Yen Hsi-shan and Feng Yu-hsiang in North China which drove Chang Tso-lin out of Pe-king and back into Manchuria in 1928–1929; and the possibility of a strong central Government in China. Before this could take place Japan moved into Shan-tung and occupied Tsi-nan in April, 1928. This precipitated matters in China's internal struggle. The Northern leaders quickly made overtures to Chiang Kai-shek, resulting in the acceptance of Chiang's national leadership. Thus from the outset of Chiang Kai-shek's rise to national leadership, he was confronted with Japanese aggression. In 1931 the Japanese had created the "Moukden Incident." By 1933, Japan controlled all of Manchuria under a puppet state. In 1935, Japanese intrigues honeycombed North China. They employed every imaginable device to disrupt the loyalties of the Chinese to Chiang Kai-shek. There were always Chinese who hoped that a change in the Government would bring a revival of Confucianism. The Japanese were quick to play up this divisive element. In 1933, in Moukden, a very significant news item appeared in the Chinese press of September 3: "In view of the fact that the new state of Manchukuo has made the doctrine of Confucianism the standard of national morality, Confucius Day, which fell today, was celebrated with grand fete throughout the country." The Japanese were already planning the invasion of North China and cleverly used this psychological technique in the attempt to upset the Chinese Government by appealing to the Confucian loyalties of the Chinese. That this was realized by the Nationalist Government is evidenced by the publication in the Shang-hai newspapers on June 4, 1934, that "the Nationalist Government had included the birthday of Confucius in the list of national holidays of China."[17] There is no evidence here to indicate that the nationalist Government had any thought of reviving Confucianism, but by appropriately recognizing the birthday of Confucius they effectively offset Japan's strategy in this regard.

On July 7, 1937, Japan created the "China Incident" near Pe-king, demanding more Chinese "Co-operation in Japan's New Asia Coprosperity Sphere." On August 13, 1937, Japan opened attacks at Shang-hai, using the Japanese defense sector of the International Settlement as a base for landing supplies to attack China. The rape of Nan-king followed the fall of Shang-hai. The capital of China fell in December, 1937. Not a single one of the nations that signed the Nine Power Treaty of the Pacific raised an arm to stop Japan. The signatories of that treaty included those nations from which most of the missionaries had been coming to China during the previous century. The treaty pledged the signatories not to take any part of Chinese territory or to allow any other nation to do so, thereby assuring China the freedom to apply all her resources to problems of internal reconstruction without fear of external aggression. By 1938 the Japanese invasion was in full blast. To the consternation of the Chinese, Japanese troops were rolling beyond Nan-king toward Han-kow and other cities of the interior on mechanized military equipment manufactured in the nations which had proposed and signed the Nine Power Treaty of the Pacific and which had sent most of the missionaries to China. Australia was the only signatory nation that placed an arms embargo on shipments of military supplies to Japan.

It was during this crisis that the Christians revealed their kinship with all who suffered. Missionaries elected to remain in China under the perils of the Japanese invasion and shared the privations and sufferings of some forty millions who were uprooted in the ensuing conflict. In this period many misunderstandings existed in the minds of the Chinese because the Christian nations of the West furnished Japan with the military supplies that enabled Japan to wage unprovoked war on China. Missionaries, by staying in China, behind the lines of conflict, in the battle zones, taken prisoners by the Japanese, risking their lives caring for the wounded, did more to dissociate Christianity from the political actions of Western powers than anything they had ever done before. The confidence of the Chinese in the integrity and neutrality of the missionaries who elected to remain with them and share their peril enhanced the prestige of the Church.

Chiang Kai-shek recognized the moral void into which China was settling at this time because of national despair. He sought to establish the New Life Movement to rally the people. In 1934 he declared that the New Life Movement called for a revival of the " cardinal virtues of propriety, loyalty, honesty, and honor, which have constituted the bulwark of our national existence." [18] The history of these eventful years reveals Chiang Kai-shek leading his people to resist the enemy with stubborn, indomitable courage, against insurmountable odds. For ten long years before American and British forces entered the war, China battled alone against Japanese aggression. It was during the height of the struggle that the Nationalist Government issued the proclamation from Chung-king, removing all restrictions that had been placed on the teaching of religion in Government-registered schools. In 1929 the ministry of education had decreed that mission schools, in order to qualify their graduates for entrance to Government universities, must abandon the compulsory teach-

ing in religion. Now the Nationalist Government officially declared that the Christians in the war had demonstrated that
the Christian religion had a constructive contribution to make
to the future of China. Out of disaster the Church had moved to
signal triumph. Never in their history had the Christian
Churches found so large a place as in this hour of China's or-
deal.

In December, 1943, public recognition was given to China
by President Roosevelt and Prime Minister Churchill when
they invited Generalissimo Chiang Kai-shek to meet with them
at Cairo.[19] At the Cairo Conference, Chiang Kai-shek represented the nation that had suffered the most, and which at
that time had inflicted the heaviest military losses upon the
Japanese. Chiang is accused by those who dislike him of being
a stubborn man. Only a stubborn man of indomitable will
could have led a nation so utterly unprepared for war to resist the armed might of Japan with such heroism for fourteen
years. At Cairo a solemn pledge was given to the Christian
generalissimo of the Republic of China by the Christian president of the United States and the Christian prime minister of
Great Britain. The pledge was publicly proclaimed to the
world that all the territories seized from China by any other
nation during the previous fifty years would be returned to
the full sovereignty of China. This included all the areas occupied by Japan, particularly Formosa and Manchuria, which
had been uppermost in the Chinese mind for many years. The
Cairo declaration was the occasion of great rejoicing in China.
This was a major factor in the ability of the Chinese to continue their resistance to Japan throughout the remaining years
of the war. Chiang emerged from World War II as the hero of
China and was acclaimed one of the leaders of the free world.

American foreign policy in China during the period 1944–
1950 stands in marked contrast to the previous century of
American policy in China from 1844 to 1943. Any study of the
loss to the Churches of China must include some understanding
of the factors that contributed to the failure of American for-

eign policy in China, because most of the foreign missionaries in China during this period were from the United States. The severance of diplomatic relations between China and the United States, apart from the Nationalist Government at Formosa, and the withdrawal of all United States consuls from the mainland of China, naturally heightened the tension against America. It became inescapable that these circumstances should involve American missionaries in China in increasing difficulties.

The Chinese possess an intense capacity for hatred. This has often been expressed in patriotic movements, such as the National Humiliation Day, which was observed on May 30 for many years to solidify public sentiment against Japan over the " infamous " twenty-one demands of 1915. But the Chinese also possess an equally marked capacity for forgiveness, once the cause of friction is removed. In all the relationships of Chinese Governments with Western nations there was no nation that developed so favorable a place in the esteem of the Chinese people as the United States. The Chinese had come to look upon America as their great and good friend whom they sought to imitate in many ways. The temporary resentment against America over the Treaty of Versailles was removed and soon forgotten after Shan-tung was restored to China in 1922, following the Washington Disarmament Conference. After 1922, Americans were soon in full ascendancy again and held the preferred place in Chinese esteem until the dark days of Japanese aggression, when the Chinese found it most difficult to reconcile the oft-expressed policy of American friendship for China with the unrestricted sale of war materials by America and other Western nations to Japan. When Japan attacked Pearl Harbor and Hong-kong, followed by the entry of America and the British nations in the war against Japan, the Chinese felt that at last the Western nations were taking their stand on China's side, and a feeling sprang up toward America and Britain that was comparable to forgiveness. The rational Chinese mind felt that there was a certain justice in the bruises inflicted on America at Pearl Harbor and Manila, and on Britain at Hong-kong and Singapore. It was then that China's unusual capacity to forgive sprang forth with a revival of the most cordial relations with both America and Britain. A further reason was the tremendous encouragement derived by the Chinese from the realization that they were no longer alone against the enemy. Allied with them were the Western democracies, which gave them assurance of ultimate victory. This revival of American prestige was augmented by the Lend-Lease program, 1941–1945, and the American military and financial aid to China that immediately followed American entry into the war.[20] At the same time the Chinese achieved the culmination of twenty-year endeavor, the abolition of the unequal treaties and the negotiation of treaties of equality with the United States, Great Britain, and Canada. These were tremendous stimuli to a nation ravaged by wanton war.[21]

It was to be hoped that victory would inaugurate an era of the closest co-operation and resultant prosperity for both the Western democracies and China. Instead, the years following victory have witnessed the collapse of all American influence, in spite of the most unprecedented amount of material aid ever given China by any other nation in all history.[22] The position of other Western nations, such as Great Britain, Canada, or France, has been hardly any better. The rapid deterioration in the Nationalist Government of China, and its removal from the mainland to Formosa as a result of the triumph of the Communist forces, caused increasing difficulties for the Christian Churches.

The names of Mao Tse-tung, Chou En-lai, and Chu Teh have been identified with revolutionary China since the first march of Sun Yat-sen's Kuomintang. By 1924, Chou En-lai was chief of the political department of the Nationalist Whampoa Military Academy and closely associated with the young stalwart known as Chiang Kai-shek. It was in 1925 that Chiang appointed Chou as political commissar of Chiang's first Nationalist Army. In 1927, when Chiang discovered that the Communists intended to seize power for themselves at the expense of the Nationalist cause, he severed all relations with them. When the Communist Government at Han-kow was forced to yield and escaped over the mountains of Northwest China to Ye-nan in Shen-si, they were led by Mao, Chou, and Chu Teh. For the next nine years the Communists were ruthlessly opposed by Chiang Kai-shek and were compelled to seek their survival in the Northwest. In China the sources of revenue for support of the Government have come chiefly from taxes on commerce in transit. The Communists were driven into the least promising area of China in so far as sources of revenue could be expected. In 1936, when the Communist power was at its lowest ebb, they won new support by their demand for all-out resistance against Japanese aggression and by their readiness to join forces with the Nationalists under Chiang Kai-shek in common resistance to the enemy. During the nine years 1936–1945, China's struggle against Japan was continually handicapped by the internal tensions resulting from Chiang Kai-shek's fears of what would happen if the Communists should be given all the arms they demanded to fight the Japanese. These fears were not without foundation and the dangers were ably foretold in 1928 by Chapman:

"Communism is still a grave menace with which the Nationalist Government will have to reckon. If we are to judge by the history of its development in Russia, bloodier and more extensive holocausts than have yet occurred may be expected from it as it ferments and matures in districts where Government authority is weak; and the Nationalists may yet be driven to meet its challenge by a ruthless process of extermination. Though the leading Russian Communists and a number of the subordinate Russian advisers have been expelled, and the rule of the Chinese Communists within the Nationalist Government has been shattered, many of them having been killed, it would be a fundamental mistake to assume that Communist activity in China is at an end and may be disregarded as a factor of importance in the future. No characteristic of the disciples of Communism is more extraordinary than their unwavering faith and their indomitable courage and enthusiasm." [23]

This accurate appraisal has been fully sustained by the events of the past twenty-five years. Those who failed to believe the plain words uttered by the chairman of the Communist Party in China, Mao Tse-tung, deluded themselves. It would have been well for the Western friends of China to give more weight to the proclamation that was issued on July 13, 1927, by the Soviet Comintern executive: " The revolutionary role of the Government at Han-kow is finished. Therefore, Communists must spread an agrarian revolution and arm workers and peasants." [24] The subsequent actions of the Communists in China supported the constant fear of Chiang Kai-shek that the truce in which they united to fight against Japan was only for the period of the national crisis, and that inevitably they would seize the first opportunity to wrest control of the state by supplanting the National Government. Successive attempts were made by American diplomatic representatives to force a coalition of the rival political forces within China, particularly to bring together in one government the Nationalists and Communists.[25] The " White Paper " released by the U.S. Department of State reveals a wistful hope that in some way Communism will be prevented from engulfing China. There is a fundamental error on the part of many Western minds in the tendency to look at China through Western glasses only, by which we seek parallel patterns that will approximate the democratic processes with which we are familiar. The democratic Western mind is accustomed to government that arises out of the interaction of two or more political parties, with the responsible government formed from the majority party, and the minority party comprising the opposition, acting as a restraint upon the government to prevent abuse of power. We are unable to conceive of an effective democracy without this safeguard. It was natural that American diplomatic representatives in China should feel that one of the most important steps to strengthen the Chinese Government was to insist upon recognition of the rival political party as a component factor in the Government. But in this case, the rival

144 The Lost Churches of China

political party was not merely a minority political party, but was, and had been for years, an armed insurgent group, which both defied the central Government of Chiang Kai-shek and claimed sovereign jurisdiction over the areas it controlled. It issued its own currency and postage stamps, made its own laws, and announced that it sought the ultimate domination of the entire country. By their own admission, if the Communists were ever to become the majority or controlling political instrument, they would not tolerate any opposition party. The United States ambassador, Major General Patrick J. Hurley, discerned this in 1945.[26]

At this time, the terms of the Yalta Agreement had not been communicated to the Chinese. It was only upon the eve of Russia's entry into the war, just preceding Japan's surrender, that Generalissimo Chiang Kai-shek was made aware of the decisions of the Yalta Agreement. In the published papers of Harry Hopkins it is disclosed that the Yalta Agreement was secret and not to be divulged to China until Russia was ready to enter the war.

" On June 15, 1945, Ambassador Hurley informed Generalissimo Chiang Kai-shek of the provisions of the Yalta Agreement pursuant to instructions from the president of June 9, 1945. At the same time the ambassador communicated to the generalissimo Marshal Stalin's categorical assurances regarding the Chinese sovereignty in Manchuria and his oral concurrence to the principle of the Open Door in China, both of which Stalin had given to the president via Harry Hopkins, who had been on special mission to Moscow in May-June, 1945." [27]

On the eve of Japan's collapse, Russia entered the war, occupying Manchuria and North Korea. The United States had provided a stock pile of Lend-Lease military supplies at Vladivostok for this purpose. The Russians were simply unable to expend this vast supply of military equipment in five days of conflict. Moreover, the Russian forces in Manchuria and Korea received the surrender of huge stocks of Japanese arms.

The Nationalist Government of China, at the time of the Japanese surrender, was in control only of the southwest section of China. The first obligations of the Government involved the return to the capital at Nan-king, the reoccupation of Shanghai, the other port cities, and the island of Formosa. Following the surrender of Japan, the United States invited the Nationalist Government of China to occupy Formosa in accord with the Cairo Declaration of 1943, since Japan had seized Formosa from China in 1893.[28] Five hundred thousand Japanese in Formosa were repatriated to Japan. But, to the dismay of the Nationalist Government, the Chinese Communists, whose headquarters were in North China, were alerted to the opportunity and streamed across the North China plains to Manchuria before the Nationalists could occupy the area. Observers were surprised to see the Communist troops marching to Manchuria unarmed. It was in Manchuria that the Communists received arms. When the Nationalist Government was able to give attention to Manchuria, they were confronted with a *fait accompli,* which resulted in civil war with a well-armed insurgent force pitted against them. Inasmuch as Russia was the occupying power in Manchuria at the time of the Japanese surrender, it is inconceivable that the Chinese Communists could have been allowed into Manchuria or supplied with military equipment there without the consent and co-operation of Soviet Russia. The key to this riddle is to be found in the Yalta Agreement. " On behalf of the United States, Great Britain, and the U.S.S.R. on February 11, 1945, Roosevelt, Churchill, and Stalin signed at Yalta an agreement containing the political conditions upon which the Soviet Union would enter the war against Japan." [29] This agreement pledged to restore to Russia the former rights held by czarist Russia in Manchuria prior to the Russo-Japanese War in 1903–1904. That Roosevelt and Churchill would have, or could have, consented to Stalin's demand at Yalta is utterly incredible. The demand was base because there was at the time an existing treaty of friendship between the U.S.S.R. and the Republic of China, the Sino-Soviet Treaty of 1924, which recognized Chinese sovereignty in Outer Mongolia and Manchuria, and in which the U.S.S.R. repudiated the unjust czarist claims in Manchuria which had provoked the Russo-Japanese War. The treaty further pledged Russia to respect the sovereignty and territorial integrity of China. In the Yalta Agreement Stalin secretly obtained from Roosevelt and Churchill the pledge to give back to Russia that which the U.S.S.R. had publicly and solemnly renounced. Moreover, the Yalta Agreement was a betrayal of Chiang Kai-shek, inasmuch as it repudiated the public pledge given by the president and the prime minister to the generalissimo at Cairo in 1943. Thus at Yalta was laid the fuse to a delayed-action explosion which was destined to rock China to its very foundations, and to destroy both the Nationalist Government and American and British influence in China in its chain reaction.[30] In the resultant disaster it was inevitable that the work of American and British missions should suffer and that the Chinese churches that had developed from nearly 150 years of modern missionary endeavor should be thrown into a state of utter bewilderment. The atomic bomb that dropped on Hiroshima killed 100,000, but the psychological bomb that exploded on China broke the morale of 450,000,000 who could not believe that it could be possible. The Chinese, led by Chiang Kai-shek, had fought Japan for seventeen years, in a stubborn struggle against insurmountable odds. They had vowed to lay down their lives but never to lay down their arms until Manchuria should be returned to China. In the hour of victory they were asked by their trusted allies to drink the dregs of humiliation and bitterness.

Chiang Kai-shek was China's national hero, almost worshiped as a symbolic figure of patriotism and resistance. On the eve of Russia's entry into the war, Chiang was advised by the President of the United States that he must assent to the Yalta Agreement, the nature of which was disclosed to him for the first time. He was asked to accept the assurance that Russia would negotiate a new treaty of "friendship," and Chiang was asked to send an emissary to Moscow with power to negotiate such a treaty with the Soviet Union, ratifying the Yalta Agreement.[31] The Sino-Soviet Treaty of Friendship and Alliance was signed August 14, 1945, in Moscow. The negotiators on behalf of China were Dr. T. V. Soong and Dr. Wang Shih-chieh. This treaty pledged that the Soviet Union support "will go exclusively to the National Government." [32] In February, 1952, at Paris, the General Assembly of the United Nations, by a vote of 25 to 9, found Russia guilty of flouting this treaty. Chiang Kai-shek had had serious misgivings, but the provisions of the Yalta Agreement positively and unequivocally gave no possible alternative for him to do anything but assent and negotiate the new treaty. His hand was forced.[33] No statement in all the 1,054 pages of the "White Paper" issued by the U.S. Department of State is so accurate or so revealing as: "It was, however, unfortunate that China was not previously consulted." [34]

The news was withheld from the Chinese public by the Nationalist Government in fear of the disfavor with which it would be received. It was not until the Communist forces in North China had become armed with modern equipment and had undertaken open rebellion against the Nationalist Government that the full story of the Yalta Agreement began to filter through to the Chinese people. The first word of it was by the "grapevine," which has always been a most effective method of transmitting important news in China. It was unbelievable, unthinkable, unspeakable, incredible! No, not America! America would not stoop to such betrayal! That both Britain and America would betray China in the hour of victory was simply unbearable! When the Chinese realized the full enormity of what had happened, and that Chiang Kai-shek and his Government had concurred, then the reaction in China, which had first been one of stupefaction, turned to indignation and blind fury. Both Chiang and the foreigners must go, the foreigners because their national leaders had betrayed China, and Chiang for having assented to the betrayal!

The Chinese have always focused their antiforeign agitation against one nation at a time. In this hour the focus is on Amer-

ica. It was inconceivable to the Chinese that the great nation,
so long their good friend, which had helped them so much,
could be a party to such a betrayal. The United States continued to give extensive aid to the Nationalist Government in
the effort to prevent its fall,[35] while it required some considerable time for the full news regarding the Yalta Agreement to
penetrate the consciousness of the mass of China. As this " chain
reaction " developed, the progressive deterioration of the Nationalist Government was accelerated. The question is often
asked, How could the Chinese people assent to the rise of the
Communist regime? The answer is to be found, not in the area
of assent, but because the people were so obsessed that the Nationalist Government must go because of their loss of national
honor and face that they would not tolerate a leader, even
their greatest hero in history, who had capitulated to the dictates of a foreign Government, even a friendly Government,
that had betrayed them. Thus the Communist regime came to
power in China in an hour of great confusion and largely by
default.

It was in this period of confusion that the United States Government turned to an American missionary and besought him
to serve as American ambassador to China. In July, 1946,
Dr. John Leighton Stuart, born in China of Presbyterian missionary parents, himself a Presbyterian minister and the most
noted educational missionary in China, president of Yen-ching
University, was persuaded to accept the ambassadorship.[36]
Dr. Stuart was one of the most beloved and respected Americans in the eyes of the Chinese. In his new capacity he worked
most diligently to save the situation from the impending disaster. Both Ambassador Stuart and General George C. Marshall,
who was in China in 1946, sought to effect a reconciliation between the rival forces of the Nationalists and Communists.[37]
But the very menace that Chiang Kai-shek so accurately foresaw and warned against now lifted its ugly and sinister head.
The Chinese Communists were not just a rival political party
in any democratic sense. They supported the rights of minor-

ities only while they constituted the minority. It had become increasingly clear that whenever the Communists could, by intrigue or conquest, seize control, then the Nationalists would either have to flee or be purged, for no opposition party would be tolerated. There was the deepest misgiving in the minds of many in China as to whether a missionary of many years' service in China could accept the appointment as ambassador of his own country without creating the most grave misunderstandings. This concern needs to be placed against the background of the embarrassing entanglements of Christian missions with the political motives of Western powers in China. Not even the highest integrity and unexcelled reputation of John Leighton Stuart could withstand the revival of the criticism of anti-Christian agitation by antiforeign elements, claiming that *at last* even the American missionaries revealed that their ultimate interests are indissolubly joined with the interests of their national Government. If Dr. Stuart could have remained at Yen-ching University as president, and continued to identify himself with the legitimately national aspirations of Chinese students, possibly joining them in a protest against the Yalta Agreement, the Chinese would have continued to revere him. If Chiang Kai-shek had been able to defy both America and Britain by refusing to assent to the betrayal at Yalta, the Chinese would have been willing to follow him, even on millet alone. All the material aid of food, clothing, tools, weapons, and medical supplies that America sent to China [38] could not erase or counterbalance the resentment of the Chinese because of the loss of face incurred by the infringement on their national sovereignty and honor.

Earlier in the twentieth century the Chinese had found the missionaries their stanch supporters in advocating revision of the unequal treaties between China and the Western powers. The Chinese had been buoyed up since 1943 by the knowledge that the United States and Great Britain had abrogated all pre-existing treaties with China, to be succeeded by treaties of equality and mutual respect, and had guaranteed that all territory taken from China by any foreign nation in the previous fifty years was to be restored to China upon the conclusion of the war with Japan. At the end of the war, when the Chinese discovered that America and Britain had shackled China in the Yalta Agreement with fetters that were controlled by the hands of Russia, the mood of the Chinese was pregnant with uncontrollable portent toward America and Britain.

The great amount of economic aid given to China by America during the war and postwar years created many difficulties in administration. The few Americans who knew the interior of China, and held a grasp of the language, were mostly missionaries. A number of these were released by their Boards to aid in the distribution of relief supplies through UNRRA and other agencies, but the number available was utterly inadequate, so that personnel had to be sent to China for administrative purposes who were lacking both in language and in cultural appreciation of the Chinese. Thus they at times presented to the Chinese the most pronounced attitudes of superiority on the part of the foreigner that modern Chinese had ever seen. This was most unlike the missionaries they had known. This irritation could not be relieved by the superior material benefits that the foreigner brought with him.

" The West has contented itself with pointing out how little Russia can give to China in the way of raw materials, or machinery, or manufactured goods, and likes to contrast what the West can do. We tend to overestimate the appeal of material benefits. We have forgotten that man does not live by bread alone; that he will respond to ideals rather than refrigerators." [39]

The amount of American aid to China after 1945 often bewildered Chinese Christians who had shared with missionaries for many years in rigorous budgeting of mission funds.

Just before the collapse of the Nationalist Government and its withdrawal from Nan-king in the face of Communist successes, Generalissimo and Madame Chiang Kai-shek sought the moral support of the Christian Churches to rally the country behind the Government. The Roman Catholic Church gave its assurance of support by one of its Chinese bishops campaigning publicly for the support of Chiang Kai-shek. In 1947 the Nationalist Government had established diplomatic relations with the Vatican and sent to Rome as envoy a member of the Methodist Church. By 1949 the Chinese ambassador to the Vatican had renounced his Protestant connections and had been accepted into the Roman Catholic Church by confession of faith. In contrast, representatives of the Church of Christ in China and the National Christian Council of China met with Generalissimo and Madame Chiang Kai-shek in an all-day session in which the Protestant leaders stood by the position of strict neutrality on the part of their Churches in the political crisis. They were later to discover that the Communist regime would permit no such neutrality.

Space does not permit us to dwell upon the details of the fast-moving scene which carried the Nationalist Government from the mainland to the island of Formosa. The prominence given to Chiang Kai-shek in all news about China has overshadowed the fact that the only constitutional legislature of China, elected during the postwar years, is also in Formosa. The disintegration of the Nationalist forces proceeded at a faster pace than the onward march of the Communists. In many strategic centers there was no bloodshed. The people of China had decided that Chiang Kai-shek and the Nationalist Government must go. No argument was permitted; none was desired. There was mute universal agreement. The people had not voted for the Communists; indeed they knew not what to expect. Only one thing was clear in their minds: national pride had been affronted by the Western powers, and the affront had been condoned by Chiang Kai-shek and his Government. That was the end. The people were ready to accept any government that offered to redeem their national honor and "face." To any foreign resident of China it was clear that the unrest of 1948 and 1949 was not necessarily the fruit of Soviet intrigue. Long before the Bolshevik revolution, China was stirring, recalling past greatness and nursing resentment of the encroaching foreigner.

"But the urge was there — the urge for justice and integrity within China and an honourable place amongst the nations of the world. This urge persists and has grown stronger in the face of obstacles." [40]

Only the Communists seemed aware of the psychological factors that created the tidal wave that carried them to power. Like a storm sweeping into a low-pressure area, Communism rushed into this vacuum of a helpless and prostrated nation. The conquest by the Communists mystified many Westerners, and even today people are confused as to how the Communists, with their guerrilla armies, with inferior equipment, without air force or navy, without the control of industrial cities like Moukden, Tien-tsin, Han-kow, Wu-sih, Shang-hai, etc., without the large number of Western-trained personnel, cut off from the sources of oil and coal, and scattered in isolated bases throughout the countryside, could conquer the well-trained and American-supported Nationalist armies. How was it possible for the people from desolate Shen-si to organize a nation and defeat the mechanized forces of the Nationalists? The tragedy of these years is a sad story of a nation that had rejected its ancient cultural heritage and was living on a borrowed Western secularism, while at the same time it was betrayed by the same Western nations in whom it had placed its reliance. China had become a nation that had lost its ancient virtue. In its place were vague principles of democracy which were mouthed in platitudinous phrases without being geared to action. The Nationalists had too long talked of democracy and nationalism to survive the shock of Yalta. The Communist leadership was sensitive to the fact that the " victories " of the " Liberation Army " were largely by default. No government could endure unless it could redeem the sense of shame that overwhelmed the people. In the long-drawn-out negotiations at Moscow in January and February, 1950, Mao Tse-tung must have exerted very great pressure upon Stalin, pointing out that Russia could not hope to hold the alliance of the Chinese if it insisted on the terms of the Yalta Agreement, which contradicted the Sino-Soviet Treaty

of Friendship of 1924, in which Russia had renounced forever
the former czarist rights and usurpations in Manchuria. In
signing the Yalta Agreement, Stalin had " forgotten " the Sino-
Soviet Treaty of 1924. When Mao Tse-tung returned to Pe-
king, he brought a new Sino-Soviet Treaty of 1950, in which
Russia agreed to return to China the concessions in Manchuria
that America and Britain had given to Russia in the Yalta Agreement. It is not difficult to imagine how Mao could contend at
Moscow that no government in China could survive the present
temper of the people unless that government could accomplish
the fulfillment of China's nationalistic demands for political
integrity and unimpaired sovereignty. In announcing the Sino-
Soviet Treaty of 1950, the Peking Government declared: "The
Government proved its ability to defend the state, the territorial integrity of the nation, and the national honor and dignity
of the Chinese people." At least the Communists in China knew
what was uppermost in the Chinese mind. Mao Tse-tung returned to Peking immeasurably stronger, to receive the ac-
claim of China. Mao had talked back to Stalin. Whatever Government could articulate the national yearnings into effective
action would have received the support of the people. The people were not concerned with political ideologies so much as
with their national pride. The Government that could both
twist the tail of the British lion and dare to pull a feather
out of the American eagle at the same time received the wildest
adulations of the masses. At last this was a Government for the
Chinese — at least the masses gave it support for this reason.

Christians, Protestant and Roman Catholic, are confronted in
the middle of the twentieth century with cataclysmic losses.
This disaster suddenly engulfed the Churches of China at a
time when they had larger constituencies and apparently
greater influence than ever before. The Christian Churches in
1945 held the highest prestige. Not only Generalissimo Chiang
Kai-shek and Madame Chiang Kai-shek but also many members of the Nationalist Government were either Christians or
sympathetic to the Christian Church. The Chinese had been

confident that with the Christian leadership of Chiang Kai-shek, their Government could expect the " Christian " nations of the West to be fair to China. Thus the disclosure of the betrayal of China at Yalta created such devastating havoc. Communism has capitalized the confusion, presenting itself as a program of realism and action designed to implement the new social order that the Christians had so long talked about.

VII

CHRISTENDOM'S UNWITTING CONTRIBUTION
TO COMMUNISM

THIS chapter reveals the Churches of China in a period of great crisis, rising to inspiring heights, tumbling to bewildering depths, divided in multiple sects, taking the wrong turns, selling out to political masters, making a shambles of the faith. It is heroism and nobility at its best, and degradation at its worst. The Church, which served as the spark plug for five strategic and simultaneous revolutions, loses to the enemy which sowed tares in the night. Atheism, materialism, and Communism have choked the fields so carefully tilled by Christian missions, revealing the fallacy of the materialistic emphasis of the social gospel. The supreme test today does not arise from a conflict between Christianity and the non-Christian religions. The issue is whether there is to be any religion at all in China.

Prior to the outbreak of the Japanese invasion of China, there were, in 1926, 8,200 Protestant missionaries in China. Most of these were from the United States. The annual increase of missionary personnel ranged from 600 to 725 during the years 1916 to 1928. Many of these were short-term workers. The antiforeign uprising in 1927 resulted in the withdrawal of a large number of missionaries. By the spring of 1929 there were about 4,750 Protestant missionaries *in* China. This was approximately 78 per cent of what was considered the "normal number." [1] In 1947, Protestant missionaries included 2,536 from the United States, marking China as the largest mission field of American

Churches. The Protestant Churches reported a communicant membership of 402,539 in 1922, and a gain of an additional 50,000 from 1920 to 1930.[2] By 1935 the Protestants had approached 600,000, and in 1950 reported a membership well over 800,000.[3] The number of Roman Catholics is much larger, due to reasons already given, and is currently estimated at 4,000,000. The number of Roman Catholic missionary nuns and priests in China in 1950 was stated to be about 4,000.[4] The important fact is that when the Communists gained ascendancy in 1949 the Christian Churches exercised an influence in Chinese affairs that reached far beyond their ratio of numerical strength to the whole population. Missionary societies, most of them working through the Chinese Churches which they had helped to bring into being, were operating 13 colleges and universities, 236 middle schools and a much larger number of primary and grade schools, and 260 hospitals. In 1937 there had been 322 mission hospitals in operation, but 62 were closed during the war with Japan, 9 of which are reported to have been destroyed, and 3 had been utterly looted.[5] Some of this destruction was perpetrated by Communists, during the period of civil war. The Communist authorities at the outset of the new regime gave little interference with the operation of these institutions. It was after they had consolidated their political control over the country that they gradually extended their control over all educational and medical institutions. By the summer of 1951, within two years, the essential Christian witness of these institutions was brought to an end.

The majority of graduates from Christian schools and universities have made no profession of the Christian faith. A large factor has been the antiforeign agitation, such as began in 1926–1927 in the anti-British riots in Shang-hai and Pe-king, in which students played a prominent part. At that time the focus of antiforeign feeling was directed against Great Britain, because the student class realized that all the treaties between China and the Western powers hinged upon the treaties with Britain. All other nations claimed, through the most favored nation clause, all benefits that were enjoyed by Britain. If the Chinese could force a revision of the treaties with Britain, it would automatically follow that the revision would affect treaties with all other powers. This factor in the development of atheism, simply as a protest to the connections of Christianity with the Western powers and the objectionable "unequal treaties," was undoubtedly the reason for many intellectuals' being unwilling to become members of the Christian Church. On the other hand, their modern scientific education had disillusioned their minds regarding the animism and superstition of much of China's religious practices. From a religious standpoint the majority of the young intellectuals moved in a vacuum. "Atheism is popular in modern China. This is partly the result of the study of contemporary philosophy of the West by modern scholars and partly due to the atheistic teachings of Communism." [6] It has been estimated that of the quarter million Chinese students at the time of the anti-British agitation of 1927, 75 per cent were atheist or agnostic, and only 25 per cent were religiously inclined, and that of this number only 10 per cent held any personal religious conviction. Of this small number the majority were Christians, a few being Buddhists.[7] Because of Christianity's historic connection with the Western powers, and because of the overemphasis given the social benefits connected with Christianity, what was begun as a message of spiritual power became lost in a materialistic race to outshine Communism.

In 1929 it was announced that one of the provisions of the concordat signed between Mussolini and the Vatican was that the Italian State undertook to subsidize Catholic missions in China. "Likewise the fact that under the direction of Mussolini a subsidy of ten million lire is to come to Italian missions in China is a sign of healthy rivalry in the further spread of Christianity in China." [8] To Roman Catholic minds in the West this was an occasion for rejoicing. But the Chinese met it with increased anti-Christian propaganda. It became just another evidence in their hands by which to charge the connections between Christianity and imperialism.

Christianity has been compromised by its attempts to gain ascendancy in China through political alignments with influential states, powers, or parties. The right of Christianity to exist in China has repeatedly rested on external forces outside itself, which it sought to employ for its protection and thereby to expand its interests. Seldom has the Church dared to trust its cause solely on its innate character and its own spiritual resources and message. This is the chief reason for the accusation by the Communists in China that the Church is allied with Western imperialism. The Nestorians used political alliances to gain their security, only to result in their ultimate destruction. The loss of this historic Church, and the obliteration of the Franciscans at the end of the fourteenth century, confronts Christians with a challenge that can only be ignored with dire peril. Christianity was so completely wiped out in China that when the first Jesuit missionaries reached there two hundred years later they had no knowledge that Christians had been active in China a thousand years before them. Jesuit prestige rose in the seventeenth century to the highest places of honor, only to crash in the aftermath of political intrigues. The imperial edict of the eighteenth century banished the Jesuits and all other missionaries, suppressed Christianity throughout the empire, and closed the doors of China to all foreigners. Protestant missionaries began their work in China at the beginning of the nineteenth century, followed a generation later by Roman Catholics. Both these streams of missionary endeavor became entangled in the political involvements of Western nations with China. At the very dawn of the twentieth century the Boxer massacre attempted to wipe out another century of missionary endeavor. It was China's fourth attempt to purge the land of foreign missionaries. In the twentieth century Western Christendom has sent to China the greatest number of missionaries ever sent to one country in all history, both Protestants and Roman Catholics, together with the greatest outpouring of treasure dedicated to the building of a strong Christian movement in this vast country, which holds nearly a fourth of the world's population. Again the Chinese have arisen to cast out missionaries, accompanied by persecution, imprisonment, and often massacre. The remarkable thing is that Christianity made as much progress in China as it has made under these perilous handicaps.

There is a tendency for Christians in the West to dismiss the losses in China by blaming it on Communism. This is an over-simplification which dodges our responsibility. The appalling fact is that in the middle of the twentieth century the Churches of China, both Protestant and Roman Catholic, are lost in confusion; countless Chinese Christian leaders and missionaries have suffered imprisonment and martyrdom. In spite of many instances where the connections of Christian missions with the Western powers have compromised the Churches of China across the centuries, missionaries have never learned the full folly of this perilous procedure. The glaring lesson of history is that Christianity has been cast out of China five times in thirteen hundred years. Each exodus of missionaries has resulted from the repercussions of political entanglements. This is the most serious charge of the anti-Christian forces. Thus it constitutes the most glaring, although unwitting, contribution of Christianity to the rise of Communism. The Church that seeks to be God's instrument must avail itself of the lessons of history.

The second contributing factor is more particularly the responsibility of Christendom in that Christianity in this generation so often neglected to give priority to the teaching of the "first and great commandment." Too often we have sought popularity and prestige by stressing the material benefits the Church had to offer. Christianity was the success religion. Too large a proportion of all Protestant missionary energies was thus expended. Missionaries who were sent to preach the gospel were too often the ones most encumbered with the multitude of humanitarian responsibilities. Many never had the time to acquire a sufficient command of the Chinese language to be

able to make an effective address in Chinese. They attempted
to compensate for this " labor of thought " with labors of love.
China willingly received every social service expression of Christianity in schools, colleges, hospitals, humanitarian aid, famine
relief, and famine prevention projects. Through these agencies
Christianity became popularly conceived in China as the social
reform religion. While these expressions of the faith of Western
Christians were praiseworthy, the question confronts us today as to whether the Protestant Churches have not placed too
much emphasis upon the social interpretation of the Christian
message and too little emphasis upon the actual teaching of
the message of Jesus. Too often our social gospel has been our
only gospel. Many young Chinese students have spoken of
Jesus Christ with deepest respect, but feel that Christianity,
as they see it, is a barrier to the Christ. What they attack is not
so much the religion of Jesus as it is a caricature of Christianity.

Too many Christians of the West have interpreted the Lord's
Prayer and its phrase, " Give us this day our daily bread," as
a supplication for the sustenance of our physical life. Thus we
have witnessed an increased tempo in the emphasis on meeting
the physical needs of China's millions with food, clothing,
health, and education. The ability of Western Christians to
undertake these missions of mercy has been interpreted by some
as evidence of the superiority of the Christian religion over
China's great teachers, such as Confucius and Lao Tzu.[9] This
overlooks the fact that Jeremiah and other Hebrew contemporaries of Confucius and Lao Tzu were hardly more successful in
Israel than the sages were in China. The social services of Christians have been interpreted as a way by which the Western
Church could serve as the instrument of the living God to answer
the prayers of millions for daily bread. Have we forgotten that
" it is written, Man shall not live by bread alone, but by every
word . . . of God." The tragedy of this hour is to be traced to
the failure of the Churches to impart the full meaning of the
words of Jesus, " I am the bread of life." The question arises
whether the Churches in China are not lost because the

Churches of the West, upon whom they leaned for nurture, have first lost the way? The remarkable success of Protestant missions in the twentieth century has been due to factors very similar to those that first brought success to the Jesuit scholars in the seventeenth century. The Jesuits brought to China a contribution of astronomical science which China needed and for which it gave the Jesuits periods of relative prosperity and favor. The Protestants brought, two centuries later, modern educational institutions and scientific medical services. These contributed greatly to the welcome given Christianity, for the missionaries met China's desperate need for scientific education in its race to overtake the twentieth century. The Jesuits of the seventeenth and the Protestants of the twentieth century have this in common: both movements relied heavily upon their gifts of material benefits that China needed rather than upon the primacy of the message they were sent to proclaim. In many cases the Christian schools have been content to demonstrate the superiority of Western scientific education without accomplishing the primary mission of winning the students to Christ. A significant slogan used by some missionaries, and believed by many, was, " Ministry to the secular needs of men in the spirit of Christ *is* evangelism." This is evident in the following appeal from a prominent Chinese Christian layman:

" China needs scientific and technical men to develop her country in order to solve the problem of livelihood. If Christian missionaries could render service in solving this problem, as they have along medical and educational lines, their preaching will be doubly effective. With the majority of the people facing privation, poverty, disease, and starvation, it seems irrelevant to elaborate upon the necessity and glory of prayer. Confucius said, ' One must be sufficiently clad and fed before he can be expected to learn the virtues of propriety and music.' The instinct of self-preservation always stands first in human calculation, and this was why Jesus Christ fed the thousands before he began preaching to them. If Christianity is to be a national force, it must belong to China and must serve China in practical ways. The so-called Christian nations interpret Christian teachings differently in different places. Only a scientific interpretation of its principles can bear the test of survival." [10]

This is a very plausible and appealing argument. Written by a Cabinet minister in the Nationalist Government, it received wide publicity and exerted considerable influence. But the author overlooked completely that Jesus did not feed the thousands before he taught them. The Gospel account of the feeding of the five thousand clearly says, " He came out, saw much people, and was moved with compassion toward them, because they were as sheep not having a shepherd: and he began to teach them many things " (Mark 6:32–44). It was only when the day was " far spent " that the disciples came to Jesus to express their concern that the people should be sent away to obtain food. It was then that the people were told to sit down, and they were fed. Similarly, in the " Feeding of the Four Thousand " (Mark 8:1–9), it is clear in the Gospel narrative that Jesus gave primacy to preaching and teaching, and that the people who thronged to hear him were so hungry for his words of life that they forgot their physical needs until Jesus remembered them (Mark 8:2, 3).

The demands for maintaining educational standards second to none rested on the theory that Christian education must be demonstrated to be the best. Then, it was believed, it would follow logically that the Christian religion would be accepted as the best. This view, to say the least, was not very different from the Jesuit claim of the seventeenth century, that the test of true religion would be determined by the trueness of the forecast of the solar eclipse. Certainly the middle schools and colleges founded by Protestant missions set the highest academic standards in China.[11] Missionaries in the twentieth century gave China the best scientific education, from the primary schools to universities. Modern scientific medicine was the gift of Christianity through mission hospitals, medical schools, and schools for training nurses. Famine relief and prevention was a notable contribution of Christianity, with the introduction of scientific agriculture, irrigation, and engineering. The impelling needs of China, arising out of the Japanese aggression, evoked the greatest outpouring of gifts for humanitarian relief that has ever been known. The application of the social gospel became, for many in this generation, the measuring rod of success, even in religious circles. This vast undertaking was hailed by the contributing Churches as the greatest social application of Christianity in all history. To a large degree it portrayed Christianity in China with such a materialistic emphasis that it appeared to be attempting thereby to outshine Communism. In the end its colossal failure to stop the onward march of Communism challenges Christians to inquire diligently regarding the validity of popular assumptions in present-day Christian thought.

There is nothing wrong with the social gospel except that it became, too often and in too many places, our only gospel. It gave to the contributors an opportunity to make their religious faith relevant to the Chinese who received the aid, but to the Chinese this dazzling outpouring of gifts from the West made Christianity the most materialistic religion they had ever known. The issue is not one that calls for abandonment of the social gospel, but it impels a recognition that we have left undone that which we ought to have done.

Too often a priority has been placed, in the case of both teachers from abroad and Chinese staff, not upon the teacher's faith in the redemptive power of the gospel of Jesus, but in the teacher's competency in his particular field of knowledge. Thus, in the course of time, it often happened that some of the teachers in Christian schools were not Christians. Their competency has been deemed more important than the integrity of the essential mission of the school. Many of the teachers had little, if any, interest in the conversion of their students. They did not consider that this was their responsibility. Is it sufficient to send physicians, educators, scientists, technicians, and engineers to the mission field? Unless these same technically trained men, through their own faith and example, become witnesses of the transforming power of the Christian gospel, they become a peril to the Christian cause. This has been the folly of the extreme Liberal position in Protestant missions.

The author recalls a visit to the Roman Catholic mission at Ta-tung-fu in Shan-si. In a long conversation with Monsignor Hojers, we discussed the problem of the evangelization of China. His attitude toward Protestants was kindly but anxious. He had spent thirty-four years in China. When I asked about his anxiety, he replied: " The Protestant missionaries are too easily diverted from their main job; they spend most of their time doing good works for which they are noted. You will be interested in a recent letter we have received here from the Holy Father in which he reminded us that the diversion of Protestant missionary effort from its primary objective of converting men to Christ places an added responsibility upon the Roman Catholic Church." Liberals are at fault when allowing the social gospel to monopolize most of their energies, but this does not imply a justification of the Fundamentalist position which has given comparatively little emphasis to the social services. Any theological outlook that lacks cultural or social implications is irrelevant. There should be no abandonment of the social gospel, but a clear affirmation that the social gospel and the individual gospel are not two or separate approaches to the Christian mission. Instead, they are inseparable, in that one cannot succeed without the other. If religion ends with the individual, it ends. If it does not begin with the individual, it never begins.

The extreme emphasis of the Church upon applied Christianity reveals the impatience of the Church with the methods of Jesus. Modern Christians have given priority to practical manifestations of the second commandment of Jesus before teaching observance of the first and greatest commandment. The social application of Christianity has given to the donors the opportunity to give tangible expression to their faith, but the failure to impart to Chinese the spiritual sources of this motivation has left a vacuum into which Communism has entered. The Communist Government of China welcomes the Church as a social agency, but if, and when, the Church claims to speak in the name of God, then it is silenced.

" Christianity has been rent asunder by the unsatisfied and unsatisfiable demand for a social gospel; it has been deflected by humanism; it has become half ashamed of its otherworldliness, without which it can make no creative contribution to the problems of the day in which it lives." [12]

Christians are living in an age when they are called to stand up and be counted. The issue in China is not merely one between Christianity and Communism. " The real enemy is a spiritual interpretation of the universe which gives a place to the supreme values of the spiritual life — beauty, goodness, and truth — but which does not give full value to the fact of Personality." [13] Julian Huxley was one of the first to observe that " we are witnessing the dawn of a struggle, not between science and religion, but between the God-religions and the social-religions." [14] It is supremely important that the Church remember and proclaim that human life derives its purpose and dignity from sources beyond our humanity. Without Jesus, Christianity is just another social agency, as the Communists in China wish it to be.

Jesus held a reverence for the individual. This quality in the teachings of Jesus is its distinctive characteristic and marks it as the true fulfillment of the teachings of Confucius. Jesus did not seek the crowds. He found the individual in the crowd. He began his ministry, not by clamoring at the gates of civil power or by challenging the Temple, but by laying siege to the hearts of obscure men and women. He did not attempt to give millions a whitewash of religion, but to make twelve men alive with it. The disciples of Jesus were summoned from the ordinary walks of life. Peter was impetuous; Thomas was cautious. The fact that Jesus chose Thomas should make the Church forever tolerant of those whose minds are searching for the truth. The very forgiveness of Peter by Jesus should make the Church more merciful to those who have erred. Jesus did not employ political means. He did not take advantage of the murder of John the Baptist and start an underground movement to hurl Herod Antipas from the throne. He grieved when his disciples

were disappointed and unable to understand that the Kingdom
of God had already come in their midst. He placed supreme
emphasis on the witness of the Holy Spirit in the lives of men
as the foundation of the Kingdom of God. We have preached a
social gospel, which we should have proclaimed, but in making
it — too often and in too many places — our only gospel, we
have played havoc with Christianity by failing first of all to
preach the " Word " with the significance of the " cross." What
we have given China may have elements of Christianity in it,
but it has not always been the full religion of Jesus as set forth
in the New Testament. Atheism and agnosticism are widespread in China today, largely resulting from the cultural impact of the West upon China in the twentieth century. It is
supremely important that Christians face this crisis. Our greatest mistake will be to engage in defensive arguments to dis-
prove any accusation of blame that may be due us. The
important thing is to recognize our mistakes and to take the
necessary steps to avoid their recurrence.

Confronted with the rising tide of Communism, the Christian Churches employed the fallacy of attempting to forestall
Communism by offering the Chinese a more attractive materialism than could be given by the Communists. It was in this hour
that the Churches were lost. The popularity of Christianity in
modern China often constituted its peril. It had become soft,
pleasant, and social in its application. In the words of a Chinese pastor, " The trouble with the Christian Church today is
that it neither hurts nor tickles anyone." Storm warnings should
have been read in the fact that for many years the majority of
the graduates of Christian schools were leaving these institutions not only without having become Christians but without
any religion at all. They had lost the anchors that previously
held moorings to their former religious beliefs — the schools
had shown them the inadequacy of their old superstitions; too
often nothing positive or vital had taken grip in their mind,
and they were adrift in a sea of atheism without chart or compass. It was thus that Christian missions produced a talented

but lost generation. Communism appealed to these trained young people by demanding of them greater sacrifices than Christianity, in its day of soft ease, dared demand. The shameful paradox is that Communism said to these students: "If ye come after me, ye must deny yourselves," and, "Whosoever loseth his life shall find it." Thus students found in Communism a realism which they missed in Christianity. At least Communism made every student feel that his contribution was indispensable. In 1927 at Han-kow, a young girl student about to be executed for her Communist affiliations told her weeping relatives and friends not to weep for her, saying, "I would rather die for something than to live for nothing like you." The Christian religion in this generation did not often evoke this kind of courage or sacrifice, simply because it no longer demanded it. Jesus did not make entrance into the Kingdom of God an easy or popular step for men to take. The Church must remember that the Kingdom of God cannot be bound within the limits of a particular social institution or belong exclusively to any political system.

A third most serious factor contributing to losses sustained by the Churches of China has been the lack of unity. Thus, unwittingly, the Churches contributed fuel to critics. Following the establishment of the Republic in 1911, missionary work expanded greatly. But Protestant missions have been handicapped by the pronounced cleavage between the liberal and conservative schools of theology. This confused the non-Christian Chinese in regard to the Christian Church, since the competitive character of different denominations contradicted their protestations of unity. Attempts were made to remedy this situation by co-operative agreements between major mission boards. This early resulted in a division of China into geographical spheres of operations, so that missionaries would not be competing against each other. This approach reached successful development in the All China Congress of 1922 at Shang-hai, and the subsequent formation of the Church of Christ in China, in which the Protestant Churches, founded by the major mission boards of the United States, Canada, and Great Britain, were united. Churches adhering to the Anglican Communion and Churches of the Methodist connection felt it necessary to maintain their separate identity, but worked in close co-operation with other denominations in a more inclusive body, the National Christian Council of China. Unfortunately, there was not unanimity among all Protestants. A large number of missionaries were unwilling to accept the leadership of either of these bodies on the grounds of their more liberal theology, with the result that a League of Christian Churches was formed, which comprised the more conservative groups.

This cleavage in the Protestant missionary ranks was almost as deep as the gulf between Protestants and Roman Catholics. It arose from the "Fundamentalist" conception of faith and theology, which gave little heed to the epoch-making contribution of Luther in the Protestant Reformation. Luther shattered the Roman Catholic conception of faith. He held that mere adherence to a guaranteed doctrine, with the idea that holding that doctrine is a meritorious action which God will reward, is destitute of regenerative power. In its place Luther put a positive, vital, and evangelical faith. Faith meant no less than trust in God, who has revealed himself in Jesus Christ. Unhappily, this central theme of the Reformation has been lost by a large section of the Protestant Church. Many Liberals unwittingly allowed their preoccupation with the social application of Christianity to obscure this central theme. The Conservatives, or "Fundamentalists," having renounced the pope and his authority, sought an authoritative and final arbiter. Their authority was no longer the infallible Church, but the infallible Bible. The Bible was held to be the Word of God, and to some extent this conception of authority of the Bible transcended the distinctive message of the Bible, that the *Word* was Jesus Christ who "was made flesh, and dwelt among us." Heart-searching within the Protestant fellowship in more recent years has sought to re-establish the primacy of

Jesus rather than the primacy of the Book as the Word of God. Extreme Fundamentalists have been guilty of presenting only a partial Christian message by their insistence on the literal use of the Bible as the only source of inspiration and doctrine. Unfortunately, some have employed quotations that, when taken from their context and arranged in a sequence that had no relationship to original purpose, seemed to give an authoritative character to a special theological position. Any doctrine dependent upon a jigsaw arrangement of Bible verses must necessarily be in peril of missing the truth — as if a lawyer should take excerpts at random from the criminal code, without regard to context, in order to prove his case. Such a procedure is utterly inadmissible in law and equally inadmissible in theology. Yet the tragedy remains that a large number of Christians have been nurtured in this utterly erroneous conception of the religion of Jesus. No one could be more sincere than these devoted Christians whose fidelity to their Lord transcends their error in the use of the Bible. But the issue is not one of questioning anyone's sincerity. We are confronted today with a tragedy of the first magnitude. Christian missionaries have been thrown out of China again, in spite of all that has been done for China by missionaries in the twentieth century! Surely this must be a sobering experience, sufficiently sobering to enable this generation to inquire whether we have been fully Christian or less than Christian in our approach to China and in our message. Conservatives buttress their theological position and justify exclusion of all other religious teachings, with denunciations of China's religious past, by the assertion of Paul, " There is none other name under heaven given among men, whereby we must be saved." But all Christians believe this. This is not a peculiar tenet of Fundamentalists. The difference between Liberals and Fundamentalists here arises over what is meant by " saved." It must mean saved from something — from tragedy to triumph, from sin to victory, from death to life, from prejudice and littleness to a vision of the bigness of the Kingdom of God as envisaged by

Jesus, from our fears that make Jesus as small as ourselves to a courage that dares to accept his full message, from idle repetitions of his name to a possession of his Holy Spirit. Not only does the world need to be saved, but the Christians need to be saved from an interpretation of Christianity that is less than that set forth by Jesus in the Gospels.

Those who use the Bible as their authority must not ignore the missionary message of The Book of Jonah, or the all-inclusiveness of The Book of Amos, who declared that God is the God of all peoples. Confucius in his assertion: *T'ien hsia shih i chia* — " All under heaven are one family " — takes his place beside Amos, who declared that God had nurtured and led, not only Israel, but also the Ethiopians, Egyptians, Philistines, and Syrians. It is this universality of both Amos and Confucius that Jesus made real and fulfilled. Those who would claim the name of Jesus as the way of salvation must not be content with his name only, but accept all for which he lived and died. Until this happens, Christianity cannot hope to win an indigenous place in China. The expression of Christianity that has too often been revealed is a purely foreign religion, demanding a renunciation of the former religious heritage. For this reason the Fundamentalist interpretation of the Bible has failed to win the respect of Chinese intellectuals.

The Christian Churches of many labels, dependent on Western mission boards, have been an anachronism. In the resultant obtundity they are lost. Loss has fallen upon the Churches when least expected. The popularity of the social application of the gospel in hospitals, universities, schools, and humanitarian relief projects was widespread. Liberals among Protestants took great pride in the growing popularity of the Church. The most prominent members of the Nationalist Government were Christians. But the lack of unity in the Churches presented a paradoxical reflection upon the gospel they preached. The religious imperative of our time demands that the yearning of Chinese Christians for unity be matched with a readiness on the part of Western Christians to forgo their pride in their own denominational labels. Too small a percentage of mission funds and personnel have been made available in the past for interdenominational causes. The Western Churches through their foreign mission boards have paid lip service to ecumenicity and interdenominational endeavor, while the larger part of their budgets has been allocated to work that would reflect credit to their denominational names. This was the easiest way to raise the money. The present upheaval affords the Christian Churches of the West a priceless chance to rethink their policies in this regard. This is the opportunity to abandon forever old denominational rights and prejudices, so that when it may be possible to resume missionary work in China a new era of Christian unity will be inaugurated. This crying sin of Christians must end. It is sin, because as long as our piddling prides are cherished, just so long do we deny the prayer of Jesus on the night of his betrayal.

Christianity has vitiated its witness by its lack of unity in its multiplicity of societies and denominations. The internal dissensions between Orders within Roman Catholicism wrought havoc in the seventeenth century. The cleavage between Fundamentalists and Liberals in the Protestant missions in the twentieth century has been a tragedy. There are not many denominations willing to admit that they are only a partial expression of Christianity. Not all groups who found it popular to give a halo to ecumenicity were prepared to implement it in the concrete needs of the mission field. The glacial leisureliness with which Christianity has moved to create unity within itself cannot be condoned. It has too long been a cause of confusion and mockery among non-Christians. Fundamentalists must admit the error of their concentration upon the illiterate masses. They have avoided the " scribes and Pharisees." Missionaries who attempt to interpret Jesus must remember that he reasoned with the scholars, " both hearing them, and asking them questions." The Fundamentalist position has not won the respect of Chinese intellectuals, who have long been accorded the first rank in their social order. On the other hand Protestant Liberals have held the good will of Chinese intellectuals because of their emphasis on secondary schools and colleges. But we are confronted with the tragic fact that most of the graduates of Christian schools have entered the stream of Chinese life and thought without any profession of faith in Jesus Christ. This fact has convinced some Fundamentalists that their approach was the more nearly correct, but the inadequacies in both wings of Protestant missions was clearly set forth in the *Laymen's Foreign Missions Inquiry* (1933). This report did not receive the implementation that many of its recommendations deserved. The recent losses to Christian missions in China only emphasize its relevance.

The Communist authorities demand of Christianity more rapid advance toward self-support, with a unity beyond any degree heretofore attained. The Church is confronted with a pressure for organizational unity by the Communist Government, and to achieve this every personal hostility or denominational jealousy is fanned to bring the Church into subservience to the Bureau of Religious Affairs of the Government. But this enforced unity was also employed in both Germany and Japan in World War II, and has been employed by all totalitarian governments. Only the Church itself can establish that spiritual unity which alone can redeem our folly. " The yearning of the world for unity can be satisfied only by a divine self-revelation." [15] So long as Christians fail to strive toward spiritual unity, they remain unworthy of their Lord. Christians need to realize that an attitude of appreciation of truth, wherever it may appear, is essentially the Christian attitude, and the only path that leads to unity and ecumenicity.

The fourth major blunder of this period is a particular responsibility of Christian missions. It is Christendom's greatest unwitting contribution to the rise of Communism in China. A generation has arisen " which knew not Joseph." Confucius has been supplanted in his own domain. The steady attacks from missionaries against the citadel of Confucius resulted from a failure to make valid distinctions between the original teachings of Confucius and the superstitions and idolatrous rites of Confucianism. The overthrow of the Ch'ing dynasty with the abdication of the Manchu emperor was followed by the enforced adoption of the Sun Yat-sen ritual and the compulsory teaching of *San Min Chu I* in all schools under the administration of the Nationalist Government. This, in one generation, virtually erased Confucius from the modern scene. There were missionaries as well as Chinese Christians who rejoiced in the eclipse of Confucius in the hope that this held greater opportunity for the Christian Church, but the ground was lost by Confucian ethics far faster than it was occupied by Christianity. The absence of these ancient virtues and disciplines that were inculcated by the Confucian teachings created the perilous vacuum into which Communism entered into possession. Confucius seems to have been aware that the battle for human freedom is not a dramatic contest against evil but the quiet struggle that goes on within the heart of the individual. This great principle was lost. Modern totalitarianism tempts men with pageantry and with final solutions to all problems. Democracy offers only a simple human dignity and a chance to work unceasingly for human happiness, with no reward save the opportunity to go on working. The last battle of democracy can never be fought. The world simply cannot be made safe for democracy, but in a very real sense democracy alone gives hope of creating the conditions that can save the world. The supreme goal of democracy cannot be a perfect state, for it is an illusion to suppose that things will ever reach perfection and cease to change. Democracy can hope only to produce men and women who are capable of meeting new situations effectively. Toward this objective Confucius contributed much. Like Jesus, he put his trust in men. He trusted the human race. History reveals that true and effective democracy is a political ideal difficult of accomplishment. In seeking this goal, the greatest asset that Christians can add is a true appreciation of the ethical teachings of Confucius with his respect for the Supreme Being and the rights of the individual human personality. In being a party to the overthrow of Confucius, the Christian Churches have dug the pit into which they themselves have fallen.

The Communists were quick to discern that the Christian Churches were a moral force that must be captured if the Communists were to succeed. The new regime early turned its attention to this matter. At the People's Political Consultative Conference in Pe-king, September, 1949, which constituted the People's Republic of China, five of the delegates were styled "representatives of the Protestant Christian Churches." No organization of the Churches was given any opportunity of electing these or any other delegates. The "delegates" were selected by the Communist authorities who designated them as the "representatives of the Churches." Their selection was hailed by enthusiasts as evidence of Communist respect for, and good will toward, the Protestant Churches. "Religious freedom is written into the new constitution." [16]

In less than eighteen months after Dr. Frank Price wrote his encouraging report, published in *The Church,* the official organ of the General Assembly of the Church of Christ in China (Shang-hai, 1949), he was accused of espionage and arrested by the Communist authorities under the charge of attempting to undermine China's "National" Christian Movement. Similarly other missionaries who elected to remain in China as long as possible soon found their freedom of movement severely restricted. Gradually limited numbers obtained exit permits. With rare exceptions, no one has been permitted to return. There were, however, among Protestant missionaries those who felt that the Communist Government would ultimately accord the Christian Church an opportunity. Other missionaries, faced with the alternative of expressing sympathy and good will toward the new regime or abandoning their work, unwisely made statements that are not fully supported by subsequent events. Illustrative of such unwarranted optimism is this report:

" Many efforts have been made by the new Govermnent to meet-
these demands, and one of the published statements grants freedom of religion throughout the land. At the beginning of their
regime they opposed the Church and many congregations in North
China were disbanded, but as they gained control and realized
their responsibility they greatly moderated their attitude and today
the Christian Church is comparatively free to carry on its work.
The Church of Christ in China has some strong leaders to whom
the new Government was forced to listen if they hoped to maintain
their position and win the confidence of the people." [17]

This statement is simply too optimistic and contradicted by
subsequent developments. There has been nothing in the relations between the Christian Churches and the Communist
Government of China to indicate that the new Government
had been "forced to listen" to strong leaders of the Church.
But there has been much to indicate in a most ominous way
that the Communists, from the outset of their rise to power,
required the leaders of the Churches to listen to the Government, and to heed its views expressed through these leaders of
the Church, whom the Communist authorities designated to
represent the Church. In October, 1949, a group of nineteen
prominent Christians, whose offices were in the Shang-hai-
Nan-king area, met and issued "The Message from Chinese
Christians to Mission Boards Abroad." This was first published
in Shang-hai in December, 1949. It was published in full in
The Christian Century, March 29, 1950. The opening section
of this "Message" shows an enthusiasm for the new Government of China that is almost ecstatic:

" Out of this will be born a new China, radically different from
the China of old. Compared with the present moment, the changes
of dynasties in the past 4,000 years have little significance; the
revolutions of 1911, of 1927, and the War of Resistance are but
wavelets in the rapids of time. From such a change there is no
turning, and at such time die-hardness has no place.
" A new chapter in the history of China has begun; a new era has
dawned. A new 'People's Government' has been born under the
leadership of the Chinese Communist Party, with the co-operation
of all the revolutionary elements in the country, and with the
avowed common purpose of putting into execution the political,
social, and economic principles of the New Democracy." [18]

One does not often find this word " die-hardness." It is so unusual that its use causes the mind to roam in the quest of where it has been used before. It is an attempt to translate a difficult Chinese expression into an English counterpart. It is the same word used to translate one of Mao Tse-tung's terms in the ninth chapter of his book *New Democracy,* which is entitled " Die-hardism Refuted ": [19]

" The whole world today looks to Communism for salvation and China looks upon Communism as a saviour. . . . Whoever chooses to oppose Communism must be prepared to be mauled and torn to pieces by the people. If you have not yet made up your mind about being mauled and smashed to smithereens, it would be wise of you not to oppose Communism. Let the anti-Communist heroes accept this piece of sincere advice from me, therefore." [20]

No one in China could afford to ignore Mao's warning.

In the common program adopted unanimously by the People's Political Consultative Conference in 1949, are the following statements, which show very plainly the ideological foundation of the new Government:

" The Chinese People's Political Consultative Conference agrees that the ' New Democracy ' shall be the political foundation of the People's Republic of China. The People's Republic of China is a State of New Democracy. This Republic carries out the People's Democratic Dictatorship." [21]

The People's Democratic Dictatorship is outlined in an address by Mao Tse-tung. This is Chinese Communism:

" The Communist party of the U.S.S.R. is our best teacher from whom we must learn. The international and domestic situation is favorable to us. . . . The forty years of Sun Yat-sen's revolutionary work were a failure. . . . Our twenty-eight years are entirely different. We have plenty of invaluable experiences and the following are our three main experiences: a party armed with discipline, armed with the theories of Marx, Engels, Lenin, and Stalin, employing the methods of self-criticism, and linked up closely with the masses; an army led by such a party; a united front of revolutionary strata and groups led by such a party." [22]

The Churches that support this movement are merely included in the " revolutionary strata and groups led by such a party." The representatives of the Protestant Churches chosen by the Communists to be among the "religious personages" to sit on the People's Political Consultative Conference acted as liaison personnel between the Government and the Churches. But not one of these was a Church representative; they were all in institutional work in which the Church of Christ in China was deeply interested, but they were never elected to this office with the new Government by any Church body. Their right as citizens to accept responsibility in their own Government is beyond question, but whether they can truly be called delegates of the Christian Churches is doubtful. However, these five "delegates" not only began to speak within the councils of the Government (one was elected to the Communist Presidium) on behalf of the Church, but soon addressed themselves to the Church on behalf of the Government. Whether willingly or unwittingly, they have served as an effective Communist fifth column within the Church itself. This has sharpened the crisis. Not in all history have there been such divergence of thought, such sharp differences in earnest convictions, both among missionaries and Chinese Christians, as have resulted from the rise of Communism in China. Several thousand missionaries have withdrawn, many through the inability to carry on their work, but a significant number from the conviction that no useful purpose could be served by their remaining longer. As early as 1947, missionaries were deciding to withdraw because of inability to reconcile their personal convictions with the impending shadow, such as:

"But the day of indecision is over, for me. 'There is death in the pot.' If the Communists win in North China it will be a disastrous defeat for everything you and I can hope for this country. Its consequences may eventually be disastrous for our own country as well. Communist control here can only mean a vast expansion of the darkness and gloom already enshrouding so much of our world. A struggle between darkness and light is on, and we are near the heart of one of the hottest spots in that struggle. Not that it is a clean-cut choice between black and white — far from it. In many respects it is a difficult selection between two shades of gray. But the choice is before us, the option is a forced one, and the issue is determinative." [23]

That this clear foresight of Dr. Earl H. Ballou, of Pe-king, was not shared by all missionaries is apparent from many published views of missionaries.[24]

Twenty years ago Moukden Medical College had a visit from Principal D. S. Cairns, of Scotland, who then observed: " The Christian Church in China is too closely associated with the Kuomintang. One day it may pay dearly for this."

" It is now very clear that the Christian movement is indeed paying very dearly for its political associations. It has certainly lost a great deal by being tied to the Nan-king regime. Perhaps in this association it lost some of its vision. Now it must work under a heavy cloud of suspicion for years. If the educated leaders of the Church are to go hand in glove with the new political programme without a very clear statement of the very different motive which activated them, the day may come, as it has come to this generation, when again a heavy price will have to be paid for the present possible political association." [25]

It is important to remember that those missionaries who elected to remain in China under the Communist regime or who sought opportunities of continuing missionary work under the new administration were not thereby expressing their approbation of the new authority or its ideology. They simply acknowledged the respect due the new Government. Although there have been missionary enthusiasts who have waxed eloquent in extravagant adulations of the " Liberation of Christianity " by the Communists,[26] these did not represent the majority. Any missionary movement must be expected to have within its ranks those who make extravagant claims. This human tendency was an embarrassment to the Jesuits in the seventeenth century. It has repeatedly been an embarrassment to Protestants in the twentieth century. This tendency on the part of some missionaries to champion one or another political party in China, or to pick " the winning horse," suggests that something is wrong in their emphasis or primary conception of their task. The missionary should not be the protagonist or the antagonist of the Government of the country to which he is sent. Surely it is sufficient that he observe the admonition of Him in whose name he has gone forth (Matt. 22:21). All honor is due, therefore, to those missionaries who remained as long as possible in China, in spite of difficulty and peril, rendering the honor properly due the new authority, but claiming for God the things that are God's. That the Churches of China included both missionaries and Chinese leaders, Protestant and Roman Catholic, who made this valid differentiation is established beyond doubt, and to their everlasting credit.[27] Unhappily, however, some who were in positions of great trust seem to have acted primarily in the interests of the Communist regime, or to have deemed it expedient to find a compromise acceptable to the Communists, covering the Church with shame and confusion.[28] Their closest friends cannot understand how they could have subscribed to some statements attributed to them, except under duress. This action has made the position of many Christians untenable, yet the tragedy calls for the sympathetic compassion of fellow Christians. It is difficult and almost impossible for those on the outside to realize the full extent of the threats and ultimatums that made certain Christian leaders feel that they had no alternative but to give lip service to the Communist Government. Examination of the nineteen names signed to the " Message " of October, 1949, reveals that so many changes had occurred before the " Message " was published in America that the changes become the most eloquent commentary on it. Of those holding the title of " general secretary " in national organizations of the Churches, three had resigned before " The Message from Chinese Christians to Mission Boards Abroad " was published in America. These were the general secretaries of the National Christian Council, the Christian Literature Society, and the National Committee of the Y. W. C. A. Why did these three very prominent Christians resign their offices? Very soon after the establishment of the Communist regime all organizations, including Christian organizations, universities, schools, hospitals, etc., had to be reorganized in the method of " New Democracy." This method provided that servants, workmen, messengers,

gatemen, etc., must be represented on the executive committee
of the organizations that employed them. Many of this group
are uneducated and non-Christian. Moreover, every one of this
group belongs to the newly organized " Union of Workers in
Christian Institutions." This Union is a full member of the
newly organized General Workers' Union, which sets the policies and dictates to the general secretaries and other responsible executives. Thus it became impossible for these general
secretaries to continue in their office. Their resignations made
possible the appointment of persons more sympathetic to the
new regime. For illustration, Miss Cora Teng was immediately
elected the new general secretary of the National Committee of
the Y. W. C. A. Cora Teng was one of the five Christians selected by the Communist Party to represent the Churches on
the People's Political Consultative Conference. Under her
chairmanship there was held at Shang-hai, March 1–10, 1950,
an enlarged executive meeting of the National Committee of
the Y. W. C. A. to draw up a statement of their new general
policy. This statement was published in Chinese papers and
expresses the conviction that it is the duty of the Y. W. C. A.
to echo the voice of their great leader Mao Tse-tung.[29]

A small group composed from Y. M. C. A. and Y. W. C. A. and
Christian schools and universities with a few Church leaders,
who regarded themselves as progressive Liberals, threw themselves enthusiastically behind the new regime, believing that
they could make a contribution as Christians.[30] On May 4,
1950, there was published in *T'ien Feng* (*Christian Weekly*)
a manifesto by a group of religious leaders, including the
" religious personages " who were members of the People's
Political Consultative Conference, inviting all others of religious faith to join them as signers. This was published in Pe-
king on May 29, 1950, and in Shang-hai in *Kung Pao* on the
front cover of the June issue as " China's Great Call to
Peace." [31] Its denunciations of America and its admiration of
Soviet Russia are appalling. In May, 1950, a team of Christian leaders, sponsored by the National Christian Council,

the Y. M. C. A., and five other interested organizations, met in Pe-king with the prime minister, Mr. Chou En-lai, hoping to obtain from him a promise to remedy many grievances, such as confiscation of Bibles from churches, occupation of church property by Communist forces, restriction of liberty of Christian preachers, restriction of travel of missionaries. The prime minister had invited the team to a series of conferences with leading officials of the Communist Government to discuss all issues concerning Christianity in China. The prime minister did not promise to right one of the wrongs submitted to him, but took the position that the Christian Church itself was alone to blame, and that all would be well when the Church did the Government's bidding and became an effective instrument of the Government, as fully as, according to the Government, it had been the tool of Western imperialism. Following this meeting, the policy that the Government expected the Church to follow was set forth at a conference of Church leaders in Shanghai, in a document drawn up by the group who had met with the prime minister. The Christian leaders present were advised that this was the attitude the Church must adopt, and all present were urged to sign it. To the astonishment of many, this document had already been submitted to the Communist Government for prior approval before it was presented for the consideration of the Christian leaders and for their signature. There were diverse opinions and many attempts made between June 3 and July 15 to secure agreement. The bishops of the Protestant Episcopal Church of China objected and withdrew from any joint statement by Protestants, and drafted their own pastoral letter. The general statement was first published in August with over forty signatures of known Christian leaders.[32] By the end of August some 1,500 signatures were added, and the manifesto received much prominence in the Chinese press. But the pastoral letter of the Chinese Episcopal bishops remains as being essentially Christian and unequivocal in its witness. No missionaries were involved in these deliberations. The document issued by the larger body of Protestant Christian leaders made a veritable shambles of the faith. It was not published in English but only in the Chinese press. Little did the Western Church dream of the perfidy that was being perpetrated by the indescribable pressures from the Communist authorities. At the very time that this was happening in China, the final decisions were being made by mission boards to withdraw missionaries from China. Expressions of trust and confidence in the leaders of the Chinese Church were made by Western Churches through their mission boards.[33]

In April, 1951, the Communist Government called to Peking delegates of all Christian bodies that had been receiving financial grants and subsidies from American Churches. There they were addressed by several leaders of the Communist administration for two days, April 17 and 18. On April 24, 1951 the *Ta Kung Pao* of Hong-kong carried a telegram from the " New China News Agency," Pe-king, dated April 22:

" Every delegate in the whole body of the Christian Conference accuses agents of imperialistic crimes. Severely blame Frank Price and others for being tools of American imperialistic aggression. Unanimously beg the People's Government to give severe punishment." [34]

Rev. Frank Price, a Presbyterian missionary, had been arrested just before this conference was held. It was his closest colleagues who sought to placate the Communist authorities by attacking this noted American missionary. The report in the Chinese press on April 24 was soon followed by an official statement issued at the conclusion of the conference on April 21 and published in Hong-kong on April 27.[35] On May 8, 1951, the *T'ien Feng* published the full accusations against Dr. Price and those Chinese Christian leaders who had not conformed.[36] The attacks of leading Chinese Christians against their own colleagues at the Pe-king Conference bear all the marks of having been " inspired " by pressure and demands from the Communist authorities. This certainly was not foreseen. During the early months of the Communist regime a branch office of the Church of Christ in China was maintained at Hong-kong to serve as liaison with the Western Churches. A bulletin, *The Church*, was published in English every few months with information regarding conditions in China. Just a year earlier the situation had seemed hopeful:

" As is well known, religious liberty has been definitely proclaimed as part of the new order, and there seems to be a sincere attempt on the part of the authorities to implement that principle and to stand behind it where it has been transgressed by minor officials." [37]

The sorry spectacle of the general secretary of the Church of Christ in China, which had published these expressions of confidence, later standing before the conference of Christian leaders in Pe-king and denouncing his missionary colleague on his own staff, is a tragic commentary on the state of affairs in the Churches of China in 1951.[38]

Tragedies were not confined to the Protestant Churches. Similar attempts were made to promote an independent movement among Roman Catholics. A Chinese Communist official news dispatch from Chung-king, reported by Reuters from Hong-kong on January 6, 1951, told how the acting bishop of the Catholic diocese of Chung-king headed a list of 695 Chinese Catholic priests and lay leaders who signed a manifesto supporting " the new reform movement in Chinese religious circles." The news dispatch said that the manifesto urged Chinese Catholics to " sever relations with the imperialists " and carry out a program aimed at independence, self-support, and propagation of the faith by Chinese instead of foreign missionaries. Subsequently it was disclosed that extreme pressure had been used and that the name of the Catholic priest, who was acting bishop, had been used to head this list without his consent. In June, 1951, a news dispatch from Szechwan Province reported:

" Father Wang Liang-tso, an obscure parish priest in Szechwan Province, skyrocketed to fame last December on a Chinese Communist propaganda campaign. The Red Press published a manifesto signed by 500 Catholics, proclaiming their support of the

Communist ' independent church ' movement. Father Wang's name led all the rest. Today it was reported Father Wang had been executed for protesting the unauthorized use of his name on the manifesto." [39]

Thus a caution must be held against unjust condemnation of those Chinese Christians whose names are appended to certain incredible documents that have been published in the Chinese press. On June 3, 1951, the Associated Press reported:

" Communist pressure on Chinese Christians reached new intensity today with demands that churches ' completely sever ' all relations with American and European Catholic missionaries inside Red China. Furthermore, a Peiping broadcast said that the followers of Christianity were specifically ordered to: Take an active part in the campaign against America; support the Red Peiping government's policies of land ' reform '; suppress ' counter revolutionaries ' — the Red label for all guerrillas and sympathizers with China's former Nationalist Government." [40]

On July 16, 1951, the Pe-king radio announced that

" the Salvation Army had been banned in Tien-tsin, Northern China, on the ground that it was a reactionary organization directed by imperialists. The Tien-tsin military control commission reported the Salvation Army was one of the international counter-revolutionary organizations set up by imperialists to carry out terrorist activities in Red lands. The radio said that the local Salvation Army deceived the masses, spread counter-revolutionary rumors in the course of preaching Christianity, distributed reactionary propaganda, disrupted the campaign to oppose the United States and aid Korea, and prevented Chinese Catholics from taking part in their reform drive." [41]

The efforts of the Communist Government to control the Roman Catholic Church resulted in the forcible closing in June, 1951, of the Catholic Central Bureau in Shang-hai, and the arrest of Catholic missionaries, with the padlocking of Catholic churches in Pe-king, in August, 1951. The execution of Father Wang Liang-tso in Szechwan was undoubtedly part of a design to intimidate other Christians. A Roman Catholic missionary writes:

" It's not so hard to write a success story tolerably well, but it is another matter to write a downright failure successfully. The glowing success of this story, however, lies in the fact that Christ foresaw and foretold in minute detail just such a failure.

"It's all written in the book for us. It is the failure of the grain of wheat which must go underground and rot to increase its kind a hundredfold. It is the failure of Good Friday, mankind's greatest hour.

"So if we can take this inactivity now I would say that we are successful missionaries. Even St. Paul's hardest hours were not those of his weary travels, shipwrecks included, but rather his restraint under bonds." [42]

A realistic report tells what actually happened in the classrooms of Christian schools:

"The teaching of materialism had become obligatory for all schools. We too are forced to allow the teachers to proclaim from their rostrums that there is no God, that man has no soul, and that the afterlife is only a myth foisted on mankind. These doctrines are propounded to the teachers of primary and middle schools in special training classes conducted for them. The determinative presentation and forced allegiance to these doctrines is the antithesis of scientific inquiry. No room is left for the freedom and dignity of the student's conscience." [43]

In the early months of the Communist victory, permission was granted by the authorities for the holding of the Church of Christ Synod at Tsing-tao in Shan-tung Province. This was the first time this synod had been able to get a full attendance of its eighty representatives in eleven years, because of the long war with Japan. The local Government sent their representative to open the conference. He spoke for two hours. He told the conference that Christianity was on its "last legs," but they were free to carry on, if they wished, until they knew better. But it was not long before prominent Chinese Christians were finding that their support of the Government had placed them in very embarrassing positions. On Sunday, June 17, 1951, the Methodist bishop who baptized Chiang Kai-shek in 1929, Bishop Kiang Chang-chuan, announced in Shang-hai that he had made a "grave mistake" in so doing, and the Methodist Church of Shang-hai proceeded to purge its membership roll of the names of Chiang Kai-shek and his wife!

On July 28, 1951, *The New York Times* published the decree

of the Pe-king Government that all American and American-supported missionary activity in China must close. "A final blow has fallen upon American missionary activity in China." [44] That the Churches of China are "lost" in this hour is beyond doubt. One or other of the four definitions of "lost" used in this volume is applicable to most of the Churches of China. Their lostness must weigh upon the hearts and prayers of all Christendom. Only a new and deeper humility, which will enable us to accept the discipline of this chastening hour, can give to the Christian Churches of the West the grace to rediscover the Way we have lost. Then we shall discern that the present crisis has a divine function to perform. It can serve to cleanse the Church from many activities and attitudes that have been inconsistent with its primary purpose and that have unwittingly contributed to the rise of Communism. In this period of heart-searching, both in China and abroad, the very "lostness" that stirs the mind can become the most fruitful experience in the history of Christianity. To those who are humbly and painfully aware that the Churches of China have lost the Way in this crucial hour, there is no sense of finality, such as the "final blow" mentioned in *The New York Times.* Without doubt it is a "final blow" as far as the intent of the Communists has been declared. But the history of China, if it tells anything at all, is full of inflexible, inexorable, unalterable decrees, which last only during the tenure of the Government that issued them. The Chinese people have again and again risen to overthrow the tyranny of whatever Government affronted their innate sense of human rights and respect for human personality. The full story of the agony and travail of the present hour has not been and cannot be told, even now by those who know. In the past year each day has brought its news of difficulties and tragedy for Christians in China, such as "five Canadian Roman Catholic nuns, who have devoted their lives to caring for Chinese orphans, are under arrest awaiting trial by Communist authorities in Can-ton." [45]

A few days later a Catholic bishop and four priests reached

Hong-kong after three years in a Manchuria Communist prison. With them were two nuns, until recently imprisoned in Shan-tung Province. Their story is told with caution because " others are still imprisoned." The nuns would not discuss their imprisonment because other nuns were still in jail in Shan-tung.[46]

" History's chapters are apt to end while nobody is looking but today, in China, everybody can see a page turning. Every afternoon in the week over the little railroad bridge that spans the river at Lowu, on the border of Hong-kong, the Christian missionaries come plodding out of Communist China. Sometimes only one or two at a time, sometimes in groups as large as 40 or more, fagged and haggard from their long trek out of the interior, women as well as men, Protestants and Catholics, French, Belgians, Germans, Italians, and Americans.

" For a while the Christian Churches were hopeful that they could carry on in China. The incoming Communists said they were all for freedom of religion. Then the climate of tolerance changed: church property was confiscated, more and more missionaries were ' tried ' for espionage. The Communists had dropped their pretense of tolerance; they were out to shut down every Christian Church in China." [47]

Into this holy companionship both Protestants and Roman Catholics have entered. In both branches of the Christian Church the martyrs to the faith are found. The heroic dead will ever speak to the living. It is in the hour of suffering that Christians of all communions have entered into a close unity and fellowship, " and others were tortured, not accepting deliverance " (Heb. 11:35). In May, 1952, there were 193 American missionaries — 153 Roman Catholic and 40 Protestant — held in Communist China. All of them were reported under various restrictions, charges, and punishments, including 32 in prison.[48]

" Vatican reports reveal 23 archbishops and bishops with 300 priests, lay brothers, and nuns, mostly foreigners, in jail on Dec. 31, 1951. German-born Archbishop Cyril Jarre, 74, of Tsi-nan, died in April, 1952, after nine months' imprisonment. More than 1,200 missionaries had been expelled, including 12 prelates, 530 priests, 40 lay brothers, and 650 nuns." [49]

The Christian faith rests squarely on man's experience of God (John 14:23). In Christianity, God is never far away, but always in every experience the God of history is there, whether we know it or not. Those who ignore him can do so only at their peril.[50] It will be a tragedy if Christians seek comfort from the idea that our losses in China arise from the Communists who have ruined our work. Communism is a social philosophy in which society is organized into passionate action to bring about the millennium without God. Christians must face the bald fact that there has been something woefully inadequate in our interpretation of God, that left China with such a religious vacuum that Communism could enter like a rushing wind. Missions may have cast out the " unclean spirit," but in failing to give China something better than it had before, have we not created a situation in which the last state is worse than the first? (Matt. 12:43–45.) This has been the unwitting contribution of Christendom to the rise of Communism. Five times in thirteen hundred years Christians have been ejected. Is God speaking to us? The hope of the future lies in an overwhelming sense of our having lost the Way. This very experience of being lost has a divine function to perform. If history has any lesson at all to give us, it is that to the Churches that penitently seek him God will restore " the years that the locust hath eaten " (Joel 2:25).

VIII

CONCLUSION

THE Church that fails to heed the warning of the lost Churches of China will itself meet a similar fate in time. Christians must not treat the present crisis as merely the work of evil forces. This tumultuous upheaval of China's millions is the struggle of the human spirit for a more abundant life. The tragedy of the lost Churches of China is much greater than is yet realized. The widespread judgment of condemnation upon Communism has within it the danger of explaining the reasons for losses as due solely to the rise of Communism. If this view should prevail, Christendom will be deprived of the chastening lessons which this hour holds. Communism in China is but a temporary phase of a resurgent nationalism. Those who advocate aggressive military action to overthrow the Communist regime in China seem to imagine that when this has been accomplished they will be able to return as before to their missionary tasks. These minds fail to discern that if it were not Communism, it would have been some other expression of Chinese nationalism that would have met the demand for the recovery of their national honor and sovereignty. The Chinese Church became lost because it was so largely dependent upon the Western Church which first lost its way. It is the Western Churches that first developed such concern for externals that they have made it difficult, if not impossible, for Christianity to live. The damaging indictment of Christianity in China across thirteen centuries is that it repeatedly employed political forces to gain its ends. Christianity must take its stand that the Kingdom of God cannot be bound within the limits of any particular social institution, nor can it belong exclusively to any political system, for it has a higher calling to which it must adhere. It can and does, however, inspire the men and women who in their respective civic capacities take sides in the economic and political arenas. Through the lives that are influenced by the Church, the spirit of Christianity makes its effective impact upon the world. Christianity must be more than content with this leavening process; it must believe in its supremacy.

Is it fair to criticize Christian schools and universities in China for not producing a majority of Christians among their graduates when no one in America, Canada, or Britain any longer expects the universities founded by the Churches to produce a majority of Christians among their graduates? If our universities in the West do not conceive it to be their function to produce Christians, why should it be expected of universities founded by the West in the Orient? Chinese students have been coming to the West in great numbers during the twentieth century to study in our universities. Most of these students were not Christians. How many of them became Christians while in our Western universities? The influence of these students on their return to China has been far greater than that of missionaries. Has our liberalism been too liberal? Such liberal scholars as John Dewey and Bertrand Russell lectured in China's national universities and were idealized by young China as the Western paragons of the new age. Their philosophy swayed Chinese students in the agnostic movement. How many Chinese students in America imbibed deeply of a materialistic philosophy, like Hu Shih? Is his agnosticism solely a product of his Chinese heritage, or did his education in America contribute to his convictions? Hu Shih has suggested that the highest form of religion for man is to " live for the sake of the species and for posterity," but he holds that there is no need for the concept of a supernatural ruler or creator.[1]

The present crisis has been widely interpreted as an economic one, in which the advocates of Marxian materialism have triumphed, but the real crisis in China goes far deeper than economics or politics. It is essentially a religious crisis. Its roots are profoundly theological, for theology is concerned with the study of God, and Communism denies the existence of God. Never before has the missionary movement faced such difficulties as are involved in the rise of Communism. The sudden closing of the largest missionary field in the world, with the expulsion of missionaries, is a sobering experience.

" The Communist influence in another sense is a closed system. It has, it is convinced, a complete answer to all the problems. It needs NOTHING. It will not accept guidance easily. And the economic mess which it has inherited from the Kuomintang does not make it doubtful about its own methods. There is no room in its system for a spiritual interpretation. There is no room for God. There is no room for individuality, no room for criticism. There is no real freedom for individuals in speech; there is no freedom of press, no freedom of assembly. There is rigid control of the means of propaganda and of the information provided to the common man. Ultimately it is a completely sterilizing influence. What is to happen when it goes morally bankrupt, as is inevitable if its sources are entirely human? " [2]

Christians must prepare now for that day. Christianity in China has been too busily engaged doing God's work in the ways the Church has thought best, trying to hurry the kind of Kingdom that Jesus did not advocate. Too many have been impatient in wanting to see the Kingdom of God established as a corporate entity of social righteousness, here and now. In its stead we witness the dialectic materialism of Karl Marx, with its repudiation of religion and denial of God, rising to the place of dominance in China. The greatest upheaval since the French Revolution is being enacted with scenes of tragedy and mob verdicts preceding the execution of prisoners. Such procedures make a mockery of justice, yet it is utterly lacking in realism to dismiss the present crisis as a result of purely Communist intrigue.

The spectacle Christians present in standing on the rim of the world, wringing their hands at the China scene and blaming it all on the modern scapegoat of Communism, is far from reassuring. The remedy can only be found in acknowledging our own responsibility and admitting our own mistakes. In this process the Church must recapture the consciousness of being the voice of the living God and demand of men that they return to the truths of God. Communism has perverted the terms long used in democratic processes and has employed them with diabolical cunning. Under the banner of "Liberation" the Communist armies marched to victory. The people were constantly called to express gratitude for their "Liberation," even though it enslaved them. "Co-operation" was the term used to denote compliance and capitulation. The staff of a school or hospital were "co-operative" when they had capitulated. Landowners were "co-operative" when they surrendered. In a similar way "democracy" had been twisted. Committee action was hailed as "democratic," although the group being acted for, or upon, have had no choice in electing the committee. For these reasons the Church must reaffirm its own position. Christianity is concerned, or should be concerned, with people rather than with systems. It is "the Kingdom of God which is not in time . . . but in a different spiritual dimension . . . just by virtue of this difference is able to penetrate our mundane life and transfigure it." [3] The new earth is to be the old earth with a changed spirit. Christianity is essentially a historical religion. It is both a vigorous appeal to history as well as a witness of faith of certain particular events.[4]

The Church may for a period win popular favor by supporting the revolutionary theories of Communism, as some have attempted to do recently in China, but in so doing it vitiates Christianity's claims, which are in themselves revolutionary, in that Christ claims sovereignty over the souls of men. In contrast, Communism is the kingdom of this world and holds that man's destiny is a this-worldly affair, capable of being completed within the process of human history and achievable by purely human powers. It is at this level that the real nature of the Marxist challenge to Christianity is disclosed.

This is the belief that the Christian must regard as blasphe-
mous.

Communist officials have made it clear to Chinese Christians that they have nothing against the Christian Church,
provided that the Church ceases to proclaim that Jesus Christ
is the Son of God. They welcome all Christian leaders who
are willing to abandon the term " ordained minister of the
Word of God " and accept the Communist modification " teacher
of the Christian Church." Those Christians whose moorings
are adrift, whose faith is not Christ-centered, or who feel
it expedient to compromise, are thus persuaded to support the
new regime. The Communists have attempted to " scoop " the
Christian Churches behind their movement to establish Utopia,
here and now. They offer heaven without any hell. It is an
attempt to steal the Christian Church away from its Christ
and the living God. " The Christian must distinguish between
the social revolution which seeks justice and the totalitarian
ideology with its militant atheism which perverts it." [5]

The Churches of China, both Protestant and Roman Catholic, must be recognized as again lost, lost in the sense that
they have been suppressed, closed, or destroyed, or so " controlled " that many of their chosen leaders have lost the significance of the term " Christian " or have lost their freedom of
action to speak as Christians.[6] In the manifesto " China's Great
Call to Peace " the Chinese Christians who signed this document described themselves as representing those who have
religious faith and faith in humanity. There is no reference to
faith in God. The statement had been submitted to the Communist authorities for approval before publication in the Chinese press.[7]

" One of the most fundamental of the differences between
people must be the question whether they believe in God or
not; for on that depends their whole interpretation of the universe and of history." [8] The sooner the Church makes it clear
to the world that it adores and obeys its Lord and will not
hawk him to the highest bidder, the sooner Christianity will

exert its influence in fulfilling Origen's assertion: "The Christians are they which hold the world together." The conflict in China is no longer between Christianity and the non-Christian religions. It is one in which the issue is whether there is to be any religion at all. Communism is the kingdom of this world, which demands that men fall down and worship it and have no other gods before it. Christianity must remember that "religion is sound and true to its nature only as long as it has no aim or purpose except the worship of God." [9] Communism claims the loyalties that God has demanded of men. Regardless of whether these loyalties, which have been accepted for ages as belonging to the Eternal, arise from the Ten Commandments of Moses or from the ethical teachings of Confucius or from the great and first commandment of Jesus or from man's own sense of dependence upon the Unseen, Communism tolerates no loyalty to any God that transcends the Communist State. Thus Communism must be deemed to be a religion. It is the religion of this world, with which Christianity must forever be in conflict. Communism as a faith and system of thought confronts the world with a compound of half-truths and positive error. The half-truths are appealing. The errors arise in a large part from the failure of Christians to be true to the revolutionary nature of their own faith. Modern revolutionary China was really born out of the Christian impact upon Chinese life and thought. It is idle talk that seeks to lay all the blame for the present crisis upon Soviet Russia. The first wave of this revolutionary century began in the T'ai-p'ing rebellion (1850–1864); the second wave was the destructive Boxer uprising (1900); the third wave overthrew the empire and set up the Republic (1911); the present tidal wave derives its momentum from a hundred years' awakening. The word "Communist" was not current before the Bolshevik revolution of 1922. It was not Russia that plowed the fields of China for more than a hundred years. Christian missionaries came to China from almost every country except Russia. Russia has merely capitalized the present crisis to its distinct advantage.

In this present crisis some outstanding Chinese Christians have placed the Church in great bewilderment.[10] One cannot escape from the thought that sincere and consecrated Christians have been either coerced or deprived of their freedom of action. No one can understand their difficulties or their Gethsemanes unless he has been through an experience that denied him all freedom of choice. Just as the laws of democratic nations in the West provide that a man is not morally or legally responsible for signed statements or "confessions" resulting from coercion, even so Christians should suspend judgment against those Chinese Christians who have recently signed statements that their friends find incredible.

Communism has become the most widespread term used in this generation by Westerners to denounce any person or system that is disliked. But if there were no Communists left in China tomorrow, the Churches would still be faced with the atheism that has brought this present chaos to pass. Communism was not seeded by Russia alone. It is a condemnation of the transgression of the primary law of God. Communism is much more than a philosophy of economics which we reject. Communism is a criticism of anemic Christianity. Communism proposes a new definition of God. Wu Yao-tsung, of the Chinese Y. M. C. A., editor of the Association Press and one of the most ardent supporters of the Communist regime among China's Christians,[11] has declared that the attitude of the Communist Government of Pe-king on religion is: "God is truth, truth is found in Communism; therefore, in joining Communism, a man is worshiping God." [12]

Communism in China has early recognized the force of Christianity in China's revolutions. From the outset Communism has sought to communize Christianity in China. The very thought causes many to shudder, but this is taking place today and will succeed unless Christians can Christianize Communism. This challenge is especially well presented in an editorial in *The Christian Century* (August 15, 1951).[13]

Communism is the kingdom of this world to which the Christian Church must address itself fearlessly, demanding recognition of man's inalienable right to worship God, which alone gives dignity to man as a child of God and preserves man's freedom and integrity. "Inherent in all religious experience is an *imperative* urging the believer to *act* — to act according to the will of the Deity or the nature of the universe as revealed to him." [14]

Social radicalism should have no terror for Christians, otherwise child labor and slavery could never have been abolished. The social gospel is not un-Christian. Indeed, our Christian duty is to do not less but more in seeking to make the conditions under which men live consonant with Christian brotherhood. But this must never be undertaken as a substitute for the nurture of man's soul, or for the replenishment of the poverty of his spirit. This is the primary function of the Church. When it is neglected, the Church is lost. Some years ago the author met Chow Kwo-hsien, son-in-law of the great Confucian scholar Liang Chi-chao. For eight years Mr. Chow had represented the Government of China abroad. He knew the United States and Canada from long associations in Washington and Ottawa. In North China he gave me this penetrating analysis of the religious needs of his people:

"I am a Christian, but I have a quarrel with missionaries. Men like you have come to China, impelled by the most wonderful thing in the world. You find here a country of stupendous needs which all make their dynamic appeal. As Christians, you have stepped forward and have accomplished wonders in helping China find a solution to her problems. For this we are grateful, but you have failed to give China the dynamic power that enables your own country to rise to our need. We do not need your money as much as we need this same spirit, which has made your own country great. There is no hope of China's emerging from her chaos and tragedy until there shall be sufficiently large numbers of men and women who have been brought into the experience of the life that is in Jesus Christ, so as to change the whole substance of our national life. This is the priceless message you have for China; without it we are lost. But you missionaries lean over backward in being willing to hide your Christian gospel if it is not welcome, in being content to share in social reforms and economic uplift at every point. This you have done and done well. But it is not enough. Until through the efforts of Christians the thought of China shall be permeated by the personality of Jesus, China will not be able to accomplish social reforms for herself. In terms of the centuries to come that is your greatest task." [15]

The great illusion of our time has been that Western civilization could conquer sin and tragedy and that democracy could achieve security in our own existence. The catastrophe in China teaches us that no life, no nation, is able to overcome the finiteness of sin and tragedy.

The first duty of Christians, as they face the stupendous losses in China, requires humility in order to undertake the most searching self-scrutiny, to discover, if possible, wherein lies the misplaced emphasis that has contributed to these losses. Christians must accept responsibility for sowing the seeds that germinated in the struggle for political freedom, the cultural renaissance, the social revolution, the industrial upheaval, and the religious crisis. We have been proud of our part in the first four, but it is the last of these five that is the most important and for which the Church has found itself the least prepared. The emphasis on the social and cultural contributions of Western Churches to China, in which the West found cause for pride as a concrete application of Christianity, had by 1949 absorbed the major part of all missionary energies. In some of the missions only a small part of the total expenditure was devoted to evangelistic work. A generation of graduates from Christian schools arose in China who were heartily in favor of the social application of Christianity without knowing its Founder as their Saviour.

The dominant aspiration of the Chinese is, not Communism, but nationalism, in which national sovereignty and self-respect demand an end of encroachments of foreign powers. It was on the crest of this wave that the Communists came to power. Whenever Communism fails to give the Chinese the fulfillment of the nationalism for which they have struggled so long, then Communism will be rejected. The Communists already imperil their position by leaning so heavily on Russia. Before the Western democracies can expect to be heeded again in China they must show sufficient humility to renounce their betrayal of China at Yalta. This was the greatest loss of "face" in the history of the Republic. A Chinese cannot survive without his self-respect or "face." Only admission of error on the part of the West can restore this to the Chinese mind. There is much to indicate that deep down the Chinese would prefer to be friends with the democracies of the West, if only the West could restore the loss of face suffered by the Chinese in the Yalta Agreement.

The Christian Church can lead the way to this reconciliation. At the same time the Church must hold eternal hostility against every form of tyranny over the mind of man. While it thus must be on guard, it must at the same time recognize that the greatest need of our time is for humility. Humility is a mark of strength, not weakness. The weak person is likely to be on the defensive. He is afraid to admit that he is in the wrong. Missionaries need to be on guard lest they become unconsciously proud of a false humility. There is a valid distinction between humility and gentleness. One thinks of the loving gentleness that has characterized the unselfish devotion of so many missionaries. This won the admiration of the Chinese. But humility is much more than gentleness. Humility reveals the strong person who is not afraid. He can admit his mistakes without losing stature or "face." He is able to discern truth wherever it appears; he is respectful. The missionary movement has often mistaken gentleness of spirit for humility, and many whose unselfish devotion and kindness deserve only the highest tribute have at the same time held a pride in their work that prevented them seeing the full expanse of the Kingdom of God. Proud of their "humility," they unconsciously buttressed their own superiority in their interpretation of God.

Our generation of missionaries has been the product of the greatest era of "success" slogans that the world has ever known. We have come from a civilization and culture of salesmen. We have made Christianity the "success" religion. Thus we have too often attempted to be salesmen of the Christian religion and found ourselves a part of a highly organized sales force, with the demands of sending agencies and supporting boards for statistical reports that would ever reveal encouraging success curves, similar to the most modern methods of business salesmanship. The pressure of salesmanship to concentrate only on the salesman's product or brand has its counterpart in the multiplicity of sects in the modern missionary approach to China. Too many missionaries have had little more humility than an ardent salesman. Jesus did not bid us to go and sell, but to go and tell.

We have been trying to sell a conception of God that is not big enough. The solution to the problem that confronts us is not to be found by simply throwing Communism out of China, in the hope that then missionaries can return and pick up their work again. This hour demands that Christians seek for that spirit of humility which will recognize that God does not need the protection of the Christians, but that God does demand that Christians shall humble themselves before him (Matt. 6:13).

We must not mistake travail for death, instead of looking for the birth that is impending in the convulsions of the expiring order. Noiselessly the leaven lightens the lump of human clay, in spite of the prophets of doom. The daylight will not fail to return after the night is done. The only important question is whether the Christian Church will become sufficiently chastened to lay hold of all truth wherever God has revealed it to all peoples.

The skepticism and materialism of this age can be defeated only by a positive affirmation of the Christian faith. This will require of many that we go back to where we lost it. Those of us who have been missionaries in China must think of this hour as a judgment upon our work and upon ourselves. The challenge to all belief in God confronting the Christian Church in China at the middle of the twentieth century is a deeper and more sinister challenge than that of the older paganism that opposed earlier missionaries. This new challenge arises from an atheism that is flanked by a powerful social philosophy, and swept forward on a wave of passion that at times reaches uncontrollable action. If the Church is to meet this crisis in a way that captures the opportunity within it, it must lay hold of truth at its very foundations and proclaim it fearlessly. Those who are willing to accept this chastening hour must test the validity of their own position by examining the historical evidence.

Christianity has each time come to China as a foreign religion, and has, with rare exceptions, failed to recognize the fact that there was a contradiction in its message. Christianity proclaims that there is only one God, and that he has made himself known to all peoples, but missionaries in China have too often insisted that Western interpretations of Christianity possessed the only true and definitive knowledge of God. Consequently, again with rare exceptions, few missionaries entered into a sympathetic appreciation and understanding of the men who had walked with God in China's historic past. Western Christians seem to forget that Jesus Christ was born in Asia.

In each period, within each branch of the missionary movement, there have been the tidy little minds who came to China sure and certain that they carried the faith once and for all delivered to the saints. They buttressed their faith with walls of prejudice against any possible concession that there was any truth of God in China before their arrival. Fortunately, however, there have been those who were inspired to seek for evidences of the living God moving in the hearts of men. These sensitive spirits have kept a light burning in the window to show the way home. With rare exceptions, missionaries have not appreciated the spiritual values in China's religious heritage, nor has there been adequate effort to relate the Christian faith to the highest aspirations of China's religious thought. Too many missionaries, together with the boards of the Churches that sent them to China, have dismissed China's religious past as completely pagan and idolatrous. Yet even those who have held this position have nevertheless employed in the Chinese translation of the Bible the noblest terms used by Confucius regarding the Supreme Being to denote God. Likewise the loftiest concept of Lao Tzu is used by Christians to make real to the Chinese the first chapter of John. If these two sages of ancient China, who lived in the sixth century before Christ, could have expressed such sublime spiritual conceptions of the Supreme Being and of the Holy as to warrant Christians' adopting their terms in the translation of the Bible, then Christians must be honest enough to recognize that these men have walked with God as surely as the Hebrew prophets of their contemporary period. Otherwise Christianity cannot escape from the accusation of plagiarism. It is not a matter of strategy or expediency that we should recognize the presence of the living God in China's historic past. This must be recognized as the primal duty of Christian humility and integrity. The opposition engendered by a lack of humility, too often manifested by missionaries and other foreigners in their attitude toward the Chinese and their cultural past, is responsible for much antagonism. This arrogant attitude has often been responsible for the subconscious barriers that have existed between the Christ whom missionaries came to reveal and the Chinese whom they came to convert. Karl Barth gives this position a vehement expression: "The missionary is servant not of men but of the Word of God. The divine grace is to be announced as a miracle, not as a bridge that one may build, not as a sublimation of the natural; hence the missionary is not to 'fraternize,' nor accept the fellowship of fallen faiths." [16]

It is very doubtful if Jesus would ever have referred to China's religious heritage as "fallen faiths" (John 10:16). Unhappily the position expressed by Barth has been too frequently shown in the attitude of many missionaries. In spite of all the superstitions and animistic idolatries that crisscross China's religions, the Chinese have kept a light burning in Asia for thousands of years.

Christians are often as guilty as the ancient Israelites in attempting to monopolize God. This generation needs to learn anew the lesson taught the prophet Jonah when he rebelled against the thought of going to preach to Israel's enemy, the Assyrians, in the great city of Nineveh. His actions indicate that he thought the God of Israel had lost his head by including the ancient enemy in his concern. Jonah sought to hide himself until God should come to his senses. Likewise, the voice of the prophet Amos proclaiming the universality of God was a voice crying in the wilderness (Amos 9:7).

Christians who are afraid to let God loose lest he manifest himself to the non-Christian world in a manner far from their domesticated ideas of what God should be like, need to read The Book of Amos. Christian missionaries have been thrown out of China five times in thirteen hundred years. Before Christianity can hope to be worthy of a permanent place in Chinese life it must believe that the awareness of the Holy, which we describe as God, and ascribe to God, was possessed by such great souls as Confucius and Lao Tzu. This must not be adopted as a strategy or concession to win a re-entry to China. Such procedure would violate Christian integrity. But this approach must arise from an imperative conviction that it is Christian so to do, and that this is a part of the revelation of God which Jesus Christ came to fulfill. First century Christians showed a willingness and readiness to abandon historic patterns of culture in order to preserve the Christian spirit which was originally expressed within the form they discarded. Thus they strategically made early Christianity not a Hebrew religion, but one grafted upon Greek and Roman cultures.

We must see the hand of God in this dark hour. " Either all occurrences are in some degree the revelation of God, or else there is no such revelation at all. . . . Only if God be revealed in the rising of the sun in the sky can he be revealed in the rising of a Son of man from the dead; only if he be revealed in the history of the Syrians and Philistines (and Chinese) can he be revealed in the history of Israel." [17] Only when Christians approach China and its cultural past with the same reverence and appreciation of Confucius and Lao Tzu as we have toward Moses and the Hebrew prophets shall we be able to discover the full revelation of God in Jesus. Repeated failure to understand this is responsible for attitudes of superiority which have been resented by the Chinese throughout the history of Christianity in China.

The worst things in Chinese life — the failure of the people to think of each other in compassionate terms, or to emulate more fully the precepts of their sages — must not be compared only with the best things in Christian history. There were many idolatrous practices among the ancient Israelites, and the Law and the Prophets had not enough influence to prevent the crucifixion. The modern idolatries of Christians in the West should make many hang their heads in shame. Christians cannot escape responsibility for their share in the two devastating world wars of the twentieth century, in which millions of Christians were killed by Christians. This fact alone has had a staggering repercussion on the non-Christian peoples of Asia. Unfortunately, " the Church is limited by conventional people with strong convictions on little matters." [18] Christians must humbly recognize that the Western world shares Communism's materialistic dreams and that Christians have attempted to outshine it. Only the methods are different. Similarly the real crisis in China is not different from the real crisis in the West, except in degree. In China the Communists attempt to force the people to renounce or ignore God. In the West our people have already become largely indifferent to God. Only the spirit of humility can save our generation. True humility must acknowledge that God whom Jesus knew and with whom he lived in communion and oneness is the only God of the ages, the God of Abraham, Moses, Elijah, Isaiah, Amos, Confucius, Lao Tzu, and all who have sought him. As Christians, we affirm that the fullness of God is revealed in Jesus as nowhere else in man's experience. But this affirmation must not be made with an exclusiveness never to be found in the words of Jesus. Christians recognize their debt to the Jews and cherish the Old Testament. " The incomparability and unity of God are the fundamental doctrines of Judaism." [19] In their doctrine of the imitation of God, the Jews did not transfer to man the holiest attributes and qualities of God, but the Hebrew prophets proclaimed that these attributes and qualities are what God demands of man. Confucius and Lao Tzu postulated very similar attributes with this same idea of the incomparability and unity of God. Jesus summed it all up in his great and first commandment. The tragedy of our generation lies in the priority we have given to his second commandment over the first.

The second duty of Christians is to serve the cause of truth fully. The Church must uphold and conserve the truths in the ethical teachings of Confucius and Lao Tzu as constituting the religious patrimony of the Chinese. Failure to do this contributed greatly to the creation of the vacuum into which Communism so swiftly entered. The fact that Protestant Christianity had dislodged the Confucian ethics from a central place in Chinese thought did not satisfy the Communists, for the principles of Confucius presented a particular challenge to Communist ideology. The Communist State could not run the risks involved in permitting such dangerous thoughts to gain sway among the people.

In this century the Roman Catholic Church departed far from the scholarly position of Ricci in the seventeenth century. In spite of the splendid work done in this field three centuries ago by the Jesuits, the views of modern Roman Catholics have been far less appreciative of Chinese religious thought than their earlier missionaries. In the twentieth century accessions to the Roman Catholic Church in China have been more numerous from Buddhism than from Confucianism.[20] Thus the great truths enunciated by China's sages have been choked by both branches of the Christian Church through lack of appreciation.

History repeatedly reveals the presentness of the past. Chinese history is marked with uprisings of the Confucian school against those Governments which denied the validity of perennial truths. China will not long tolerate any system of government that completely repudiates the ethics of Confucius. By comparison Communism and other totalitarian systems are a hardy growth. Communism cannot survive in China unless it succeeds in completely suppressing the Confucian ethics, and prevents the Christian Church from teaching the relation of man to God as well as to his fellow man. That the Communists sense this is evident in their attempts to suppress the classics and control the Churches.

" Liberation " is the new name for sham which has been foisted upon the Chinese. Freedom of conscience, man's most sacred heritage, has been denied the Chinese in their " liberation." The Communists further alienate popular support by their repudiation of China's ancient heritage in the destruction of the Confucian teachings.

" In the pressures of the modern world the freedom of man in his human right alone cannot stand; nor does it deserve to stand. It is a sham and a usurpation. It is a sham because it poses as real freedom when, in fact, it is nothing of the kind." [21]

In this crisis Christians must uphold the Confucian respect for human personality and affirm man's ultimate dependence on the Supreme Being as found in the Confucian ethics, and align these with the full interpretation of the brotherhood of man and the Fatherhood of God as revealed in Jesus. This is the heritage of our democratic tradition, for which men have given their lives. It lives subconsciously on its underlying faith in God. If man is a product of material processes alone, as Communism affirms, then both democracy and Christianity are absurd. Democracy is not a system to be believed in just because it produces desirable things for mankind. Democracy is one of the desirable things in itself; it uses the status given men by Christianity. If it is to survive, it must become more conscious of its source of vitality. Its real menace is from within and not from without. It does not exist in the world today save in those countries where the Christian Church is strong and free. Conscious of this fact, the Church cannot escape from a sense of the divine imperative voiced by Jesus when he placed upon his disciples the missionary task, "Go ye therefore, and teach all nations" (Matt. 28:19). This is the logical imperative of the Christian faith. "Whatever the Kingdom of God may mean in the complete significance of the great phrase, it at least means the spiritual unity of all men and races." [22] There are no limits to be set in history for the achievement of a more universal brotherhood in the Kingdom of God.

Warning should be taken from the fact that national pride and "face," with reverence for the historic past, are so great that failure of Christians to show due appreciation of the truths in China's religious heritage may bring to pass a revival of Confucianism, with persecution and opposition to all foreign religions. It would be disastrous if the pendulum should be allowed to swing into a revival of Confucianism on a wave of reaction, as has happened before. Therefore it is the duty of Christians to meet this momentous opportunity to champion truth wherever it appears in the Chinese classics. It is one thing to repudiate the idolatrous paganism, superstition, and animism which have so long been woven with and condoned in Confucianism. All this was rebuked by Confucius. The positive course of action is to lift into prominence the imperishable truths that have been obscured by these superstitions. Thus the present seeming catastrophe can become a divine instrument. The closed doors in this hour only seem to close. The greatest opportunity of the centuries beckons a new missionary approach to China. If mission boards will continue to support their missionaries who have been compelled to withdraw from China, and permit them to enter schools for the more complete study of the Chinese language, with particular emphasis on the truths in China's religious heritage, then this seeming defeat can be consolidated and turned into a spiritual victory. This may be the greatest opportunity ever given to the Christian Church. If we believe that truth wherever found is nonetheless truth, then we must recognize that in China as well as in other lands God reveals himself to all who seek him. The universality of the Christian message rests on the declaration of Christ that he had come, not to destroy, but to fulfill. "The idea of God when firmly held does, as a matter of fact, arm us with courage and strength for the moral battle by the assurance which this gives us of the ultimate victory of the good." [23]

The Chinese equivalent of "indigenous" is a phrase meaning literally "local grass roots." Thus the indigenous Church must mean more than a Western form of Christianity under the leadership of Chinese whose minds have been emptied, or kept unaware, of their own religious heritage in order to have only a Western form of Christianity. The indigenous Church must grow upon the roots of the idea of God that God has implanted in Chinese thought. "Religion grows out of the basal mood of man in his struggle for life, out of the resolution to hold fast under all circumstances to the validity of that which he has learned from experience to be of the highest value." [24] This thought must be firmly held in all periods of perplexity. The Christian's faith must not rest on authority or on dogmatic assertions, but must arise from an appreciation of the supreme values in man's experience. "Religion has its natural basis in the consciousness of an infinite, eternal, and mysterious reality on which we are in the last resort absolutely dependent. And spiritual religion begins with the interpretation of that reality in terms of the highest we know." [25]

"Christianity has always had a way of turning water into wine, of bringing prodigals home, . . . of bringing life out of death, of turning sunsets to sunrises. It is always, whenever it comes into vital contact with its Founder, a religion of surprise and wonder. It does the unexpected. It makes the lame man walk and the blind man see, . . . but it always goes dead and static as soon as it becomes absorbed in its own self-preservation. As soon as it lives unto itself and is concerned only with problems of organization and self-promotion its pulse slows down and its miracles of life cease. Christianity is essentially apostolic, that is, missionary. It is a religion 'sent out' to bless and heal and save. It cannot 'find itself' any other way." [26]

Hope is to be found in the heart-searching that is going on among Christians. The Churches of China, Nestorian, Roman Catholic, and Protestant, have been a part of the whole movement of Christendom, forever falling, forever rising, magnificent at its best, petty at its worst; forever saved by the greatly illumined, the greatly daring, and the greatly dedicated. History reveals that God is never so near as in the hour of man's extremity (cf. I Kings 19:10 ff.).

The missionary task stands in need of an infusion of a new sense of urgency, which can be derived only from an awareness of the immanence of God not less than that manifested by Jesus. One of the difficulties is to make a valid distinction between urgency and anxiety. It is the anxiety in missions that has resulted in competitive pressure for speed and numbers of converts. The Church needs to gird itself with the patience that was always present in the urgency of Jesus. He conceived of a slow leavening process in which his followers would, in hidden ways, cure the vast mass of human life. " The lostness of men was about him, as it is about us; yet the gospel he preached was an unhurried gospel; it had the note of infinite urgency without being breathless; it was not animated by panic, because it had its central certainty of the outcome in God's hands." [27]

Some new age, some new racial or national culture, may conceivably place the spirit of Jesus in a new culture pattern. There is a growing sense of urgency that demands of our age the abandonment of old prejudices in order that our conduct may more closely approximate that of the Jesus of the Gospels. But there is still a tendency on the part of each denomination to designate as Christian every procedure that it has itself approved. It is all too easy to pass from the conviction that something is admirable to the assertion that consequently it is a part of Christianity. "We may make not Christianity but ourselves the center, and conclude that everything is obviously wrong when it is different from what we do." [28]

The words of Gandhi to our generation deserve to be heeded by every missionary to Asia: " I want missionaries to complement the faith of the people instead of undermining it." [29] The Christian mission which takes within its grasp the whole world must find its unity in a spiritual interpretation that should be expected to express itself in many differentiations of form and culture while adhering to an essential unity. The quest for this spiritual unity can be accomplished only when we remember how Jesus startled his disciples by telling them that "the field is the world." There must be humble recognition that God, who was in Jesus, has been working in this field long before us, and still works. The missionary of the future must adjust himself sensitively to the change that has come over our modern world through the multiple means of communications. The idea of the foreign missionary going from one country to another, to carry the gospel, must give way to a more inclusive concept of Christians in all lands entering into a spiritual fellowship that transcends national boundaries and international barriers. The responsibility of this Christian fellowship must be to share with one another in the accomplishment of this quest for spiritual unity, while at the same time witnessing to the non-Christian world, which impinges today upon Christians wherever they live, in every land of the earth. Only such a fellowship can extend the right hand to the lost Churches of China and help them to rediscover the Way.

APPENDIXES

APPENDIX 1

In October, 1949, an influential and varied segment of Chinese Christianity, represented by 21 Chinese Christians, sent a message to Mission Boards abroad in an attempt to explain the changing conditions to these organizations. (*Monthly Report*, Shang-hai, December, 1949, p. 7.) This message reads in part:

" Heretofore, the Chinese Church has been keeping itself aloof from the political torrents that surged around it. The new philosophy considers that all phases of life must necessarily come under the influence of politics in contradistinction to the traditional Protestant view of the separation between Church and State. [This sentence is omitted in the article in *The United Church Observer*, May 15, 1950.] In a world where political influences play such an important part and affect our lives and work so extensively, it is a challenge how the Church as an institution and Christians as citizens in society can perform their Christian functions and discharge their duties to society at the same time. In areas of social service and education we shall have to accept the leadership of the Government and conform to the general pattern of service, organization, and administration. Just how these new adjustments are to be made is for the Chinese churches to determine. We have our privileges as Christian believers. We also have our duties to perform as Chinese citizens and Chinese social organizations.

" Specifically, we wish to invite your attention to three fundamental points of future policy:

"1. The authority of policy determination and financial administration must pass over to Chinese leadership wherever it has not yet been done. Definite steps must be taken for its realization. The principle of self-support must be reiterated and steps taken for its final consummation.

"2. As regards the future position of missionaries, we would like to state:

"a. There is nothing in principle which makes the future position of the missionary untenable, or renders his service unnecessary. On the contrary, there is a definite challenge to work and serve under adverse circumstances, and to bear witness to the ecumenical fellowship. Even though circumstances may render active participation difficult, the mere presence of the missionary will give articulate expression to the Christian quality of our fellowship which transcends all differences and defies all obstacles.

"b. The future contribution of the missionary will lie along lines of special service projects, and not along administrative lines. To *be,* to *share,* and to *live* will be a significant contribution in itself.

"c. The missionary, from now on, will be living and working in a setting that is entirely foreign to the newcomer. Difficult physical and mental readjustments will be demanded from him."

APPENDIX 2

The following paragraphs are translated from the *T'ien Feng* (*Christian Weekly*) published in Tien-tsin on March 25, 1950, setting forth the official policy of the Young Women's Christian Association, signed by Cora Teng as the new general secretary of the Y. W. C. A. This platform received editorial commendation.

"Because of the quick recovery and reconstruction of Russia after the war, China's revolution achieved its great victory and democratic Germany was set up and the people of all the world supported peace with the inspiration of the democratic liberation movement and the recent signing of the Sino-Soviet Treaty. The democratic citadel was never so strong! The Y. W. C. A. ought therefore to echo Chairman Mao's slogan, ' Lean to One Side ' and take your stand with the people and strongly oppose the political and war plans of the imperialists and support lasting world peace. Furthermore we must link up with the Y. W. C. A. members in every country who take the same stand and mutually bear the responsibility of struggling for Y. W. C. A.'s who have been hoodwinked and used by the imperialist countries to take their stand on the side of truth.

" Beloved members! This is now the century of the people. Before our eyes there is only one road. In the spirit of Christ we must grasp the very highest principles of the New China and under the leadership of Chairman Mao and the People's Government thoroughly put into practice the ' Common Principles ' [i.e., of the People's Consultative Conference] and establish a New Democratic China and struggle for progress."

APPENDIX 3

This proclamation was published on the front cover of *Ta Kung Pao* (Shang-hai, Church of Christ in China), June, 1950, V. 22, No. 6, from *New China News Agency*, Pe-king, May 29, 1950:

" China's Great Call to Peace "

" We the people of the religious world send out this proclamation:

" *The Great Call of the Society for the Preservation of World Peace.*

" We, the members of the Standing Committee of the Society for the Preservation of World Peace, ardently respond and ask for the outlawing of all atomic weapons unconditionally. Furthermore we proclaim that whoever first uses these weapons is the war criminal.

"Spread out before the eyes of the people of the world are two roads: the road to peace and the road to war. Apart from considering American imperialism as the head of the war-mongers who want to make war, the rest of the people of the whole world have already determined to go the great road of peace. This decision is so strongly fixed that no violence nor rumors of the imperialistic nations can shake it.

"In the movement to oppose the great wave of imperialistic war, China holds a very important place. For more than one hundred years China has suffered from imperialistic aggression. During her eight years of war against Japan and her four years of war of liberation, the calamities which the imperialists have added to China cannot be numbered. The quick results of China's revolution have greatly strengthened the peace movements and changed the face of the world. It has greatly fright-ened the imperialists and they don't know what to do. In this state of confusion they are more crazily preparing every kind of war machine, hoping for the last struggle. Meanwhile, those of us who are struggling for peace cannot slacken a moment or rest. We must link up with the great mass to let them recognize the true face of imperialism and make them a strong branch of the World Peace Camp.

"If we want to struggle for a lasting peace, we must link up with Soviet Russia, the great rampart of peace, and with all the people of the democratic countries (People's Republics). This Peace Camp represents more than one third of the people of the whole world. Besides this, in every imperialistic country there are large numbers of oppressed races who have, in the same way, determined to oppose war and preserve peace. This strength to preserve peace is stronger than anything else.

"We not only oppose the use of atomic weapons but also oppose germ warfare and the war propaganda of the imperial-ists; we oppose those who set free German and Japanese war criminals, and who are oppressing the colonial peoples who are struggling for race independence and the democratic peace movement; we oppose all the Fascist actions of the imperialists who are brutally treating their own people in their own countries who want peace.

"We who are of those who have religious faith ought to be especially aware of the imperialism which is seizing every opportunity to split the revolutionary camp and to cultivate reactionaries within the camp. We should keep a close watch and without sentiment expose and strongly strike at them and leave them no hole to utilize the name of religion and relief work to do their evil deeds.

"We who stand in the place of those who have religious faith and a belief in humanity call all Christians of China, and all Buddhists and all Mohammedans and those of other faiths, to use all practical and effective words and deeds and link up closely with all the peace-loving people of the world, to protect world peace and struggle for nationalism and independence and make a reality of the People's Democracy."

Signed by:

Y. T. WU (Wu Yao-tsung is Editor of the Association Press, Y. M. C. A., Shang-hai, and one of the five "representatives" of religious groups invited by the Communist authorities to be a member of the People's Political Consultative Conference at Pe-king, September, 1949, and there elected to be a member of the Presidium.

LIU LIANG–MO, also one of the five Christians on the PPCC.

T. C. CHAO, Dean of Yen-ching School of Religion and one of the six co-presidents of the World Council of Churches, elected at Amsterdam, resigned April, 1951, and also one of five Christians as "delegates" to the PPCC.

CHAO PU–CHU, a Buddhist, alternative delegate to PPCC.

CHU CHAN, a Buddhist, alternative delegate to PPCC.

MA CHIEN, a Moslem, delegate to PPCC.

TENG YU–CHIH (Miss Cora Teng), General Secretary of the National Committee of the Young Women's Christian Association and one of five Christians on PPCC as "delegates from religious groups."

YU YU–CHING, General Secretary of National Committee of Y. M. C. A.

H. H. TS'UI, General Secretary of Church of Christ in China.

Z. T. KIANG, Methodist Bishop, Pe-king (the minister who baptized Chiang Kai-shek twenty years earlier).

WANG CHIH–CHANG, CHAO SHU–CHIA, CHEN WEN–YEN, KAO SHANG–JEN, HOU FU–JUN, CHAO FU–SHAN and PE HOU–TIEN.

With the exception of two Buddhists and one Moslem who joined in this manifesto, all signatures above were by Christians, and some of them among the most prominent Christians in China.

APPENDIX 4

This statement was issued at the conclusion of the Conference of 151 Christian Delegates held in Pe-king, April 16 to 21, 1951. It is translated from the *Ta Kung Pao,* Hong-kong edition of April 27, 1951, which carried it as a telegram released by the Official Government News Agency in Pe-king:

"We, the representatives of all the Protestant Churches and organizations in China, gathered in the capital city of our country, Pe-king, to attend a conference of Protestant Christian organizations receiving American financial aid, called by the Central Government's Committee on Cultural and Educational Affairs, issue the following statement, to fellow Christians in China and in the whole world:

"At the time when the peace strength is growing among the people of the world, imperialism has already reached its last days. The encroachment of American imperialism in Korea and in Taiwan is a final show of strength before death. American imperialism is now arming Japan and West Germany, preparing to force its objective. In Korea it has already met the force of the people of China and Korea — it will yet experience in the end defeat and death.

"We strongly oppose this American imperialistic aggression, we strongly oppose the use of atomic weapons, we oppose a separate peace treaty with Japan, and oppose rearming Japan, oppose rearming West Germany. We wish to unite with all Christians in the world who love peace and oppose all schemes of American imperialism to break peace programs.

"But most Christians in the world are good. It is the wicked imperialists who use the Church as their tool in aggression. In July, 1950, the Executive Committee of the World Council of Churches met in Toronto, Canada, and passed a resolution concerning the war in Korea, branding the North Koreans as aggressors, and appealing to the United Nations to exhort member nations to take part in 'police action' in Korea, and opposing the signed appeal of 500,000,000 people (Stockholm Peace Appeal) against the use of atomic weapons.

"This resolution distorts truth. It is contrary to the desires of peace-loving people of the world. The resolution of the World Council of Churches echoes the voice of the U.S. State Department. If one examines this truth-distorting resolution one can see that the World Council is the tool of Wall Street and of the instigator of the Korean War (John Foster Dulles). We express our strongest opposition to this resolution of World Council. We also wish to expose U.S. imperialism which during the past period of over one hundred years has made use of the Church's work in evangelism and cultural activities to carry out its sinister policy. In our manifesto of September, 1950, we emphasized the breaking off of relations between the Church in China and imperialism, and purging out from the Church of all imperialistic influences. We feel that the breaking off of all imperialistic connections and the purging out of all imperialistic influences is the direction that should be energetically pursued by the Church in China, and all Christians in the world. We must cleanse the holy Temple of God and preserve the purity of the Church.

"On December 29, 1950, the Legislative Yuan of the Central People's Government announced its decision concerning the 'Plan to control cultural, educational, and relief organizations and religious bodies receiving American financial aid.' At this meeting we have discussed the draft proposed by the Government concerning the plan to be adopted by Protestant religious bodies receiving American financial aid. We have also heard the report of the Government leaders and had detailed discussions. We recognize the plan of the Central People's Government for the protection of the Protestant Church as certainly careful, complete, and very satisfactory. The 5th section of the 'Common Program' guarantees the people's freedom of religion and belief; moreover we have been given freedom of religion and belief and this state of affairs has greatly encouraged and strengthened Protestant Christians in self-government, self-support and self-propagation. In regard to these Government arrangements, we not only gladly accept them, but we also express the gratitude of our hearts. American imperialism wishes to use the method of freezing assets to cause the Protestant Churches and enterprises dependent on foreign funds to fall into despair. But the People's Government helped us to progress towards a bright future. We believe that the Chinese Protestant Church, relying upon God, and under the guidance of Chairman Mao and the encouragement and help of the Government, will be able to make full use of its strength to raise up a more perfect, a more pure, and a fitter Christian enterprise to serve the people.

"We call upon fellow Christians in the whole country:

" (1) To resolutely support and carry out the Central Government Legislative Yuan's 'Plan to control cultural, educational, and relief organizations and religious bodies receiving American financial aid,' and also the regulations concerning registration for cultural, educational, and relief organizations and religious bodies receiving foreign financial aid and having transactions in foreign exchange, together with the resolution received from the Legislative Yuan and passed by this full meeting concerning 'The Method of Control for Protestant Christian Bodies Receiving American Financial Aid.' *And fi-*

nally to thoroughly and permanently, and completely, sever all relations with American missions and all other missions, thus realizing self-government, self-support, and self-propagation in the Chinese Church.

" (2) To enthusiastically take part in the 'Oppose America, Support Korea' movement, strongly supporting the resolution of the Executive of the World Peace Movement concerning the Five Nations Peace Treaty, support all decisions of the 'Oppose America, Support Korea' People's Central Organization, and also make known and carry out definitely the patriotic program. *Every local church body, every Christian publication must implement the 'Oppose America, Aid Korea' propaganda and make this propaganda known to every Christian.*

" (3) To support the 'Common Program,' support the Government's Land Reform policy, and support the Government in the suppression of the antirevolutionaries, obey all Government laws, positively respond to the Government's commands, and exert every effort in the reconstruction of the nation. We want to be more alert, to resolutely reject the blandishments of imperialism, *to assist the Government to discover and punish antirevolutionary and corrupt elements within the Protestant Church;* to resolutely oppose the hidden plans of imperialists and reactionaries who wish to destroy the three 'self' movements and encourage in each Church and Christian organization the spreading of these movements and denounce in them the imperialists and antirevolutionary bad elements.

" (4) To increase patriotic education, greatly enlarge the study movement in order to increase the political consciousness of the Christians. Finally we call upon all Christians to continue to promote and enlarge the campaign to secure signatures to the revolutionary documents and firmly resolve to make effective the three 'self' missions of the Church, and with the highest enthusiasm welcome the unlimited, glorious future of the People's Republic of China."

APPENDIX 5

These accusations were made by Chinese Christians against their fellow Christians at the Conference of Christian Delegates in Pe-king, April, 1951. The following report is translated from *Ta Kung Pao,* Hong-kong, April 24, 1951, quoting telegram of *New China News Agency,* Pe-king, April 22, 1951:

" *Every Delegate in the Whole Body of the Christian Confer-*
ence Accuses Agents of Imperialistic Crimes. Severely Blame
Frank Price and Others for Being Tools of American Imperial-
istic Aggression. Unanimously Beg the People's Government to
Give Severe Punishment

" All delegates of the whole body of Christians who have been receiving American subsidy, and who had been called to Pe-king to settle the matter, heard through Kou Mo-ju, Assistant Premier of the Legislative Yuan; Lu Ting-yi, Vice-Chairman of the Educational Commission; and the Assistant Secretary, Shao Chwan-lin. After having heard their reports, during the two days, April 17 and 18, in small discussion groups, they began to understand more fully. They began to awaken more fully to an understanding of the long period in which American imperialism has used the Church and the rotten Chinese Church members as their aggressive tools. During the full conference meetings, on the 19th and 20th they began angrily to accuse the bad members of the Church for American imperialistic aggression.

" During the two days of the full conference meetings, eighteen delegates went to the platform to speak. They accused the obviously evil-smelling agents of imperialism, Frank Price, Timothy Richards, and the rotten Chinese Christians, W. Y. Chen, S. C. Leung, Ku Jen-en, and Bishop Y. Y. Tsu. The whole body of delegates unanimously requested the People's Government to punish severely these enemies of the People's Government.

" The first mentioned and accused as an agent of American

imperialism was the former rural work secretary of the Church of Christ in China, Frank Price. Those who accused him were H. H. Ts'ui, General Secretary of the Church of Christ in China; Luther Shao, General Secretary of the Nan-king Christian Church; T. Y. Shen, chief editor of the *T'ien Feng* (*Christian Weekly*); Shih Chung-i, Secretary of the Chekiang-Kiangsu Christian Rural Service Union; Shih Ju-chiang, Students' Secretary of the National Committee of the Y. M. C. A.

"They accused Frank Price of cloaking his movements of American aggression with religion. They accused that during the war with Japan Frank Price acted as adviser to the bandit Chiang Kai-shek and adviser to the foreign section of the Military Affairs Commission and in Chung-king assisted in the training class for interpreters. He had close relations with the American Congress. In 1946 he was recommended by Marshall, the special ambassador of the United States to China, to be a member of the tripartite group for three months. He and Shih Ju-fu, 2d. Lt. of the American Army, helped the bandit Chiang to draft a secret 'Social Education Plan.' In this they planned to use American money in China to propagate the doctrine of slavery. In this he said that if the plan could be put into practice, it could break down the faith of the Chinese people in the Communist Party. His plan was corrected by Marshall and given to the bandit Chiang. In 1948 he wrote a book called *Dawn to Dusk in China*. In this book he falsely created rumors of the Communist Party to vilify the Chinese People's Liberation War and energetically praised the bandit Chiang. He also said in this book that the bandit Chiang was the Washington of China.

"Before the liberation he went everywhere spreading rumors saying that when the Communists came there would be no freedom of faith. The fact is that he spread this rumor and, as Luther Shao said, in accusing him in the conference, 'After Liberation the bells of the churches can be heard every day.' Frank Price also wrote a book called *Home* and used religion to oppose Communism. He brought anti-Communist thinking into the homes of Chinese Christians. Before the fall of Nan-

king he wanted all Christians to go to Formosa. After Liberation he continued to go about Shang-hai trying to break up the
activities of the Chinese Church. But now Frank Price has
come upon his last defeat and shame. H. H. Ts'ui, General Secretary of the Church of Christ in China, in accusing him said
angrily: 'Formerly we suffered poisonous harm from imperialism and fell into their trap. But today we Chinese people stand
erect. We will thoroughly cut off forever our relations with imperialism and establish the Chinese people's own Church.'"

This accusation against Frank Price, noted missionary of the
Presbyterian Church, U.S., was made at the conference held
in Pe-king, April, 1951, by H. H. Ts'ui, General Secretary of the
Church of Christ in China. It is translated literally from the
T'ien Feng (*Christian Weekly*), No. 262–263 (Shang-hai, May
8, 1951). The texts of other accusations against Frank Price
and Chinese Christian leaders, all in a similar vein, appeared
in the same issue of the *Christian Weekly* and are available in
translation from the microfilm copy of the author's unpublished
doctoral dissertation at the University of Chicago.

"In order to make a clean sweep of the rubbish within the
Church, and to increase my political awakening and consciousness, I accuse Frank Price. This is the first time in my whole life
that I have ever accused anyone and I do so in order to expose
the crime of Frank Price, agent of American imperialism. I am
determined to smash the bourgeois sense of face.

"Frank Price was born in China — an American known as an
'old China hand.' In 1948 the General Assembly of the Church
of Christ in China engaged him as their Rural Secretary. He
was the kind of man who was good at linking together the military, political, industrial, commercial, and student classes, in
every group of which he had friends. He, therefore, used these
opportunities to promote the invasion of China. During these
days in the small discussion groups here, I have had my politi-

cal understanding improved and I cannot but confess on be-half of the Church of Christ in China the mistakes we made in inviting him to become a Secretary. Today I have clearly recognized the true face of Frank Price; he has come to China in the cloak of religion as an agent of American imperialism for cultural aggression.

"Frank Price's political principle is thoroughly anti-Communist and anti-Russian. More than once he said to his co-worker, Rev. Chu Chen-sheng, 'Russia has no democracy; only America has real democracy.' He called himself a specialist in the study of Communism. He had read more than 200 books on Marxism and Leninism. He said, 'In the New China there couldn't be freedom and the Christian Church would be per-secuted.' The fact is that not only has the Church not suffered but it has enjoyed perfect freedom. Before Nan-king was 'lib-erated' Frank Price said to his colleague W. B. Djang: 'Why don't you go to Formosa? It is safe there. America will never give up Formosa.'

"During the Sino-Japanese war, Frank Price was Chiang Kai-shek's adviser, closely in touch with him, going at least once a week to see him. Once Frank Price said to me with his own lips that Chiang Kai-shek wanted him to move into his official residence to live. I asked him, 'Are you going to move?' and he said, 'No, because if I stay in his house my ears would be deaf.' His meaning was that he wanted at all times and in all places to be with the Chinese people to spy for information to give to Bandit Chiang's clique and to the American imperial-ists. After the Sino-Japanese war Frank Price accepted an ap-pointment as an adviser to the false (i.e., National Government) Foreign Affairs Bureau and to be responsible for training inter-preters for the Chiang Bandit clique and he used going to study in America as bait to win the Chinese youth and build up his own power and influence.

"Frank Price took his orders directly from the State Depart-ment to promote his work against the people. Furthermore, he could send telegrams directly to the U.S. State Department. All these facts speak for themselves that Frank Price was not an ordinary missionary, because an ordinary American citizen cannot find Army chaplains for the American Government and certainly has not the privilege of cabling the State Department. In the spring of 1949, Frank Price selected fifty Chinese young people who were high school graduates to go to study in America. But his method of selecting these students was very special. Every one of them had to be examined by him in person or by his appointee. These Chinese young people, when they arrived in America, did not live in schools, but in private homes. According to what Frank Price said, this was so that the Chinese young people could enjoy the American way of living. As a matter of fact, this was really to poison the minds of the Chinese young people. We cannot imagine the burning poisonous zeal of Frank Price, the agent of American imperialism.

" Another time Frank Price collected many manuscripts of speeches from various places and asked me to use the name of the Church of Christ in China to print them to provide reference material for Chinese evangelists. The concepts in these essays were questionable so I refused. The fact is that these things show how extraordinary was the zeal and treachery of Frank Price. He planned to use the name of the Church of Christ in China to spread out-of-date and even reactionary ideas in the essays.

" Today I want to declare myself before you all. From now on I shall not speak a single word to Frank Price nor write him one letter [applause]. Also I shall not allow him to come to the Church of Christ in China [loud applause]. From now on I certainly will unite with all the workers to effectively promote the 'Three-self Reform Movement.' I shall try my best to get every church member to put his name on the manifesto and to strongly support the five-power peace pact and to oppose the American rearming of Japan. In the past I was poisoned by imperialism and fell into their trap. Today the Chinese people stand erect: the Chinese Church members also stand erect; we must for all time thoroughly sever the relations with imperialism and establish a Chinese People's own Church."

NOTES

INTRODUCTION

1 Slogan of Student Volunteer Movement.
2 Joachim Wach, *Church, Denomination and Sect* (Evanston, Ill.: Seabury-Western Theological Seminary, 1946).
3 Arthur Toynbee, *A Study of History*, abridged by D. C. Somervell (Oxford University Press, 1947).
4 Bernard M. Loomer, " The Aim of Divinity Education." Foreword in *Announcements of the Divinity School, University of Chicago*, Vol. L, No. 12, October 5, 1950.

5 Daniel J. Fleming, *What Would You Do When Christian Ethics Conflict with Standards of Non-Christian Cultures?* (New York: Friendship Press, 1949).
6 Cf. Aldous Huxley in *Vedanta for the Western World*, ed. by Christopher Isherwood (New York: Marcel Rodd Company, 1946).
7 William Ernest Hocking, *Living Religions and a World Faith* (New York: The Macmillan Company, 1940), p. 254. Used by permission.

CHAPTER I

1 *The Chinese Recorder* (Shang-hai: American Presbyterian Mission Press, 1929), Vol. LXI. Cf. C. F. Johannaber, "Chinese Religious Background," p. 23.
2 Herrlee Glessner Creel, *The Birth of China* (New York: Reynal & Hitchcock, 1937); and *Confucius, the Man and the Myth* (New York: John Day Co., Inc., 1949).
3 *Ssu Shu* (Shang-hai: Commercial Press, Ltd.), VIII, 177.
4 William Morgan, *The Nature and Right of Religion* (Edinburgh: T. & T. Clark, 1926).
5 Quoted by Sir Alfred Noyes,

The Unknown God (London: Sheed & Ward, Inc., 1934), p. 123.
6 Hocking, *Living Religions*, p. 76.
7 Dean W. R. Inge, *God and the Astronomers* (London: Longmans, Green & Company, 1933), p. 237.
8 James Legge, *The Sacred Books of China* (Oxford: The Clarendon Press, 1879–1885); also cf. *The Four Books* (Shang-hai: Chinese Books Co., 1930), pp. 51f.
9 Thomas Whitney, *Confucius, the Secret of His Mighty Influence* (Chicago: privately published, 1901). Copy is in

University of Chicago Library.

10 Y. C. Yang, *China's Religious Heritage* (New York: Abingdon-Cokesbury Press, 1943), p. 47.

11 Sir Reginald F. Johnston, *Confucianism and Modern China* (New York: D. Appleton-Century Co., Inc., 1935).

12 Creel, *Confucius, the Man and the Myth.*

13 *Ssu Shu,* XV, 133.

14 Edmund Davison Soper, *The Religions of Mankind* (New York: The Abingdon Press, 1929).

15 *Ssu Shu,* IV, 129.

16 *The Chinese Recorder* (1899). Cf. C. S. Medhurst, "Tao Teh King."

17 Paul Carus, *Lao Tze's Tao Teh King* (Chicago: The Open Court Publishing Company, 1898).

18 Léon Weiger, " Moral Tenets and Customs in China," *Chine moderne,* 10 vols. (Hsienhsien: Mission Catholique, 1920–1932).

19 *The Fenchow* (Fenchow, Shan-si: 1924), Vol. VI, August, " Peaceful Old Age," by Po Chu-I, tr. by Arthur W. Hummel.

20 Paul Carus, *Selections from Lao Tze's Tao Teh King, Canon of Reason and Virtue* (Chicago: The Open Court Publishing Company, 1903). Cf. the Preface.

21 Legge, *op. cit.,* p. 39.

22 Johnston, *Confucianism and Modern China.*

23 Adolf Harnack, *Die Mission und Ausbreitung des Christentums in den ersten drei Jahrhunderten* (Leipzig: J. C. Hinrichs, 1906), I, 1 f.

24 *The Chinese Recorder,* LVII, 697.

25 *Harvard Journal of Asiatic Studies* (April, 1936). Cf. article by W. E. Hocking. Also Hocking, *Living Religions,* p. 76.

26 Richard Wilhelm, *Confucius and Confucianism* (New York: Harcourt, Brace & Company, Inc., 1931), pp. 154, 155.

27 Henry T. Hodgkin, *Living Issues in China* (New York: Friendship Press, 1932), p. 168; and Sheldon Cheney, *Men Who Have Walked with God* (New York: Alfred A. Knopf, Inc., 1946), " The Poet Lao Tse," pp. 1–37.

CHAPTER II

1 *The Chinese Recorder,* LXI (1929), 252.

2 Eusebius, *Ecclesiastical History,* ed. by Cureton (London: 1861), I, 43. Also cf. Abraham Yohannan, *The Death of a Nation* (New York: G. P. Putnam's Sons, 1916), pp. 34–36.

3 Cf. Labourt, *Le Christianisme*

dans l'empire perse (Paris: 1904).

4 John Stewart, *Nestorian Missionary Enterprise* (Edinburgh: T. & T. Clark); Badger, *The Nestorians and Their Rituals,* 2 vols. (New York: 1852), I, 179; Payne Smith, *Thesaurus Syriacus* (London: 1879); and Layard, *Nineveh*

and Its Remains (New York: 1852).

5 Eusebius, *op. cit.,* I, 43.

6 Gibbon, *Decline and Fall of the Roman Empire* (London: 1881).

7 Bishop W. M. Pakenham-Walsh, *Nestorius and the Nestorian Mission in China* (Shang-hai: American Presbyterian Mission Press, 1908), p. 6.

8 *Ibid.,* p. 8. Also Gibbon, *op. cit.*

9 Kenneth Scott Latourette, *A History of Christian Missions in China* (New York: The Macmillan Company, 1929).

10 *Journal asiatique* (November-December, 1911). Cf. article by Chavannes and Pelliot.

11 H. Pinard de la Boullaye, S.J., *L'Etude comparée des religions,* 2 vols. (Paris: Gabriel Beauchesne, 1922–1925), Vol. I, Chapter III; and A. V. Williams Jackson, *Researches in Manichaeism* (New York: Columbia University Press, 1932), cf. Chapter III, para. i.

12 Roland H. Bainton, *The Church of Our Fathers* (New York: Charles Scribner's Sons, 1941), p. 59.

13 Gibbon, *op. cit.*

14 B. J. Kidd, *The Churches of Eastern Christendom* (London: Faith Press, Ltd., 1927), p. 18.

15 *The Chinese Recorder,* LXI (1929), "The Long Planting of Christianity in China," 252.

16 P. Y. Saeki, *The Nestorian Documents and Relics in China* (Tokyo: Maruzen Company, Ltd., 1937), p. 85.

17 Pakenham-Walsh, *op. cit.,* p. 9.

18 *Variétés sinologiques,* No. 12, "La Stèle chrétienne de Singan-fou," par Le P. Henri Havret, S.J. (Chang-hai: Imprimerie de la Mission Catholique, 1897).

19 Mrs. C. E. Couling, *The Luminous Religion* (London: Carey Press, 1925).

20 John Foster, *The Church of the T'ang Dynasty* (London: S. P. C. K., 1939), p. 35.

21 Quoted by Pakenham-Walsh, *op. cit.,* p. 11.

22 Henri Havret, *op. cit.*

23 Daniello Bartoli, *History of the Life and Institutions of St. Ignatius de Loyola* (New York: E. Dunigan & Bros., 1855).

24 Saeki, *op. cit.*

25 George H. Dunne, S.J., " Jesuits in China in the Last Days of the Mings " (Unpublished Ph.D. thesis, University of Chicago), p. 342.

26 A. C. Moule, *Christians in China Before the Year 1550* (London: Society for Promoting Christian Knowledge, 1930).

27 Saeki, *op. cit.,* p. 12.

28 Foster, *op. cit.*

29 Saeki, *op. cit.*

30 Moule, *Christians in China.*

31 Saeki, *op. cit.,* p. 85.

32 Yohannan, *op. cit.,* p. 70.

33 Pakenham-Walsh, *op. cit.,* pp. 16 f.

34 Saeki, *op. cit.*

35 W. C. Emhardt and G. M. Lamsa, *The Oldest Christian People* (New York: The Macmillan Company, 1926).

36 Pakenham-Walsh, *op. cit.,* p. 17.

[37] Stewart, *op. cit.*, p. 185. Also *A Church on Fire* (Edinburgh: T. & T. Clark).

[38] Mrs. C. E. Couling, *op. cit.*

[39] Moule, *Christians in China.*

[40] *Bibliothèque Nationale.* Cf. "Collection Pelliot," No. 3847.

[41] Moule, *Christians in China.*

[42] *Journal asiatique* (November-December, 1886). Cf. article by Rubens Duval. Also Devéria, *Notes d'épigraphie mongole-chinoise*, p. 72.

[43] *Revue des missions au Chine et au Congo* (Mars, 1891), No. 26; and *Le Bulletin Catholique de Peking* (1924), pp. 54–56.

[44] A. C. Moule, *Nestorians in China, Some Corrections and Additions* (London: The China Society, 1940), p. 28; *Le Bulletin Catholique de Peking* (Mai, 1941), p. 289; *Bulletin of the John Rylands Library* (Manchester: July, 1925), cf. A. Mingana, *The Early Spread of Christianity; New China Review* (July and October, 1919), pp. 321 and 522.

[45] *Toung Pao*, XXVIII (1931), pp. 78 and 81.

[46] Saeki, *op cit.*, pp. 125–141.

[47] *Journal of the North China Branch of the Royal Asiatic Society* (1929). Cf. Hu Shih, "The Establishment of Confucianism as a State Religion During the Han Dynasty," pp. 20, 21.

[48] *Harvard Tercentenary Publications: Independence, Convergence, and Borrowing* (Cambridge: Harvard University Press, 1937). Cf. Hu Shih, "The Indianization of China: A Case Study in Cultural Borrowing," p. 225.

[49] Pakenham-Walsh, *op. cit.*, p. 11.

[50] Foster, *op. cit.*, pp. 67, 68.

[51] J. Percy Bruce, *Chu Hsi and His Masters* (London: Probsthain & Co., 1923).

[52] L. Carrington Goodrich, *A Short History of the Chinese People* (New York and London: Harper & Brothers, 1943), p. 132.

[53] Foster, *op. cit.*, pp. 159–160.

[54] Saeki, *op. cit.*, p. 15.

[55] Goodrich, *op. cit.*, p. 130.

[56] Emhardt and Lamsa, *op. cit.*, p. 71.

[57] Saeki, *op. cit.*, p. 473.

[58] Chavannes and Pelliot, *Un Traité manichéen retrouvé en Chine.*

[59] Foster, *op. cit.*, p. 162.

[60] K. S. Latourette, *The Chinese, Their History and Culture*, 2 vols. (New York: The Macmillan Company, 1942), I, 209.

[61] Karl A. Wittfogel and Feng Chia-sheng, *History of the Chinese Society, Liao (907–1125)* (Philadelphia: American Philosophical Society, 1945).

[62] Cf. Bruce, *op. cit.*

[63] Gabriel Ferrand, *Relations de voyages et textes géographiques, arabes, persians et turks relatifs à l'Extrême-Orient du VIIIe au XVIIIe siècles* (Paris: 1913–1914), p. 129.

[64] Cf. Arthur H. Smith, *China in Convulsion*, 2 vols. (New York: Fleming H. Revell Company, 1901).

CHAPTER III

1 *Monumenta Germaniae Historica* (Hannover: 1868), XX, 83 f.
2 Saeki, *op. cit.*
3 *Ibid.; Sinological Series*, No. 1 (London: The China Society, 1940), Moule, *Nestorians in China, Some Corrections and Additions*, p. 22; *The Chinese Recorder* (1930), pp. 37–40 and 251–252; *Revue des arts asiatiques* (1931), VII, 1, of. artiolo by Pelliot; *Cheeloo University Journal* (Tsinan-fu: 1935), cf. article by J. M. Menzies.
4 F. Mostaert, " Ordosica " (*Bulletin of the Catholic University of Pe-king*, 1934).
5 Saeki, *op. cit.*
6 Moule, *Christians in China*, Chapter VIII.
7 *Ibid.*, p. 659.
8 Bar Hebraeus, *Chronicon Eccles.*, 3 vols., ed. by Abbeloose and Lamy (Lovanii: 1872–1877), pp. 375 f.
9 Cf. P. S. Hsiang, *The Catholic Missions in China During the Middle Ages* (Washington: The Catholic University of America Press, 1949).
10 Layard, *op. cit.*, p. 79.
11 Emhardt and Lamsa, *op. cit.*, p. 77.
12 W. Durant, *The Age of Faith* (New York: Simon & Schuster, Inc., 1950).
13 James A. Montgomery, *History of Yahballaha III* (New York: Columbia University Press, 1927).
14 Hsiang, *op. cit.*
15 Sir Henry H. Howorth, *History of the Mongols* (London:

Longmans, Green & Co., 1876–1888).
16 *Journal asiatique*, Series IX, Vol. 8, 94 f. Cf. article by Devéria; also *The Journey of William of Rubruck*, tr. by W. W. Rockhill (London: Hakluyt Society, 1900).
17 Gustav Schnurer, *Kirche und Kultur im Mittelalter* (Paderborn: Ferdinand Schoningh, 1924), pp. 11 and 407.
18 Saeki, *op. cit.*, p. 41.
19 D. Hcrbclot, *Bibliothòquo orientale* (Paris: 1781), I, 6.
20 Cf. Montgomery, *op. cit.;* Rockhill, *op. cit.;* Moule, *Christians in China*, p. 108; Emhardt and Lamsa, *op. cit.*, p. 67; and W. E. Soothill, *China and the West* (Oxford: 1925).
21 Kidd, *The Churches of Eastern Christendom*, pp. 400 f.
22 Chabot, *Supplement à l'histoire de Mar Jaballaha III* (Paris: E. Leroux, 1895), p. 2; also *Memoires de l'Acad. des Inscr. et Belles-lettres*, 2 e partie, p. 139.
23 Moule, *Christians in China.*
24 Frederick Hirth, *China and the Roman Orient* (Shanghai: Kelly and Walsh, 1885).
25 Pakenham-Walsh, *op. cit.*, p. 20.
26 Quoted by Moule, *Christians in China*, from *Papal Bulls* in Raynaldus, 1307, No. 20.
27 Moule, *ibid.*, p. 207.
28 Cf. Jean-Marie Sédès, *Histoire des missions françaises* (Paris: Presses Universitaires de France, 1950); also H. P. de la Boullaye, *op. cit.*

[29] Goodrich, *op. cit.*

[30] Donald Attwater, *The Christian Churches of the East,* 2 vols. (Milwaukee: Bruce Publishing Company, 1947), II, 187.

[31] *Cambridge Medieval History,* Vol. VII. Cf. " The Suppression of the Order of the Temple." Also *Encyclopædia Britannica,* 11th ed., XXVI, 591 f.

[32] Attwater, *op. cit.,* II, 187.

[33] *United Nations Series, China,* ed. by H. F. MacNair (Berkeley: University of California Press, 1946), cf. article by F. H. Michael, p. 102; also Yohannan, *op. cit.*

[34] Pakenham-Walsh, *op. cit.,* p. 23.

[35] Yohannan, *op. cit.*

[36] Saeki, *op. cit.*

[37] Latourette, *The Chinese,* I, 278.

[38] *Sinica Franciscana.* Cf. " Relationes at Epistolas Fratrum Minorum," II, 180.

[39] Cf. Nathan Söderblom, *Das Werden des Gottesglaubens* (Leipzig: J. C. Hinrichs, 1926).

[40] Cf. Nathan Söderblom, *The Living God* (London: Oxford University Press, 1933), p. 378.

[41] *Ibid.,* p. 379.

CHAPTER IV

[1] Georges Goyau, *Missions et missionaires* (Paris: Librairie Bloud et Gay, 1931). English text tr. by F. M. Dreves (Edinburgh: Sands & Co., Ltd., 1932), p. 45.

[2] Orestes Ferrara, *The Borgia Pope, Alexander the Sixth* (New York: Sheed & Ward, Inc., 1940).

[3] Goyau, *op. cit.,* pp. 43 f.

[4] Levy Maria Jordao, *Bullarium patronatus Portugalliae regum, in ecclesiis Africae, Asiae atque Oceaniae bullas brevia, epistolas, decreta actaque S. Sedis ab Alexandro III, ad hoc usque appectens* (Olisipone: Typographia Nationali, 1868), I, 106 f.

[5] Ludwig von Pastor, *The History of the Popes, from the Close of the Middle Ages,* ed. by Frederick Ignatius Antrobus, 3 vols. (St. Louis: B. Herder, 1898), III, 489.

[6] Alfons Vath, *Das Bild der Weltkirche, Akkomodation und Europäismus in Wandel der Jahrhunderte und in der neuen Zeit* (Hannover: Joseph Giesel, 1932), p. 36.

[7] Louis Bréhier, *L'Eglise et l'Orient au moyen âge: les croisades* (Paris: V. Lecoffre, J. Gabalda et Cie., 1928).

[8] Attwater, *op. cit.,* I, 211, 212.

[9] Vath, *Das Bild,* p. 47.

[10] *Variétés sinologiques,* No. 58 (Shang-hai: Imprimerie de la Mission Catholique, 1932). Cf. Louis Pfister, S.J., " Notices biographiques et bibliographiques sur les Jésuites de l'ancienne Mission Chinoise, 1552–1773."

[11] *Ibid.*

[12] C. A. Montalto de Jesus, *Historic Macao* (Hong-kong: Kelly and Walsh, 1902).

[13] *Chinese Social and Political Review* (1933), Vol. II. Cf.

Chang Teh-ch'ang, "Maritime Trade at Canton During the Ming Dynasty."

14 Matteo Ricci, *Opere Storiche*, ed. by Pietro Tacchi-Venturi (Macerata: Giorgetti, 1911–1913).

15 L. Delplace, *Le Catholicisme au Japon*, 2 vols. (Bruxelles: A. Dewit, 1909–1910).

16 Francisco Javier Montalban, *El Patronato español y la conquista de Filipinas, con documentos del archivo general de Indias* (Burgos: El Siglo de las Missionies, 1930).

17 Henri Bernard, *Aux Portes de la Chine* (Tien-tsin: Hautes Etudes, 1933). Cf. pp. 102 and 113.

18 Latourette, *The Chinese.*

19 Dunne, *op. cit.*, cf. p. 60.

20 Bernard, *op. cit.*, p. 131.

21 *Ibid.*, p. 401.

22 P. Adelhelm Jann, *Die katholischen Missionen in Indien, China und Japan* (Paderborn: P. Schoningh, 1915), p. 183.

23 Cf. Dunne, *op. cit.*

24 Allesandro Valignano, *Monumenta Xaveriana ex autographis vel ex antiquoribus exemplis collecta* (Matriti: typis Augustini Avrial, 1899).

25 Ricci, *op. cit.*, II, 397.

26 *Ibid.*, II, 413.

27 *Ibid.*

28 Alonzo Perez, *Archivum Franciscanum historicum* (Prope Florentiam: Ad Claras Aquas, 1908), XVI, 405 f.

29 Henri Bernard, *Le Père Matthieu Ricci et la société chinoise de son temps 1552–1610*, 2 vols. (Tien-tsin: Hautes Etudes, 1937).

30 Ricci, *op. cit.*, II, 118.

31 *Ibid.*

32 *Ibid.*, II, 207.

33 *Symposium on Chinese Culture*, ed. by Mrs. S. C. Zen (Shang-hai: 1931). Cf. "Religion and Philosophy in Chinese History," article by Hu Shih.

34 *Ibid.*

35 Söderblom, *Das Werden des Gottesglaubens*, VI, 180–235.

36 *Harvard Tercentenary Publications: Independence, Convergence, and Borrowing*, p. 266, "The Royal Tombs of An Yang," by Pelliot.

37 Creel, *The Birth of China*, pp. 182–184.

38 Gaetan Bernonville, *Les Jésuites* (Paris: Bernard Grasset, 1934).

39 Bernard, *Le Père Matthieu Ricci*, I, 337.

40 Arnold H. Rowbotham, *Missionary and Mandarin — The Jesuits at the Court of Peking* (Berkeley: University of California Press, 1942).

41 Ricci, *op. cit.*, I, 85.

42 Quoted by Dunne, *op. cit.*, p. 124.

43 H. B. Morse and H. F. MacNair, *Far Eastern International Relations* (Boston: Houghton Mifflin Company, 1931), pp. 412 f.

44 Hu Shih, *The Chinese Renaissance* (Chicago: University of Chicago Press, 1935), p. 28.

45 Goodrich, *A Short History of the Chinese People*, p. 208.

46 *Chinese Bulletin of the National Library of Peking* (1935), No. 11. Cf. "Tunglin and Fushe, China's Political Parties in the Ming Dynasty," by Chi Tze.

47 S. Wells Williams, *The Mid-*

dle Kingdom, a Survey of the Geography, Government, Literature, Social Life, Arts, and History of the Chinese Empire and Its Inhabitants, 2 vols. (New York: Scribners, 1883), II, 330; René Fulop-Miller, *The Power and Secret of the Jesuits*, tr. by F. S. Flint and D. F. Tait (New York: The Viking Press, Inc., 1930), p. 245; A. Reville, *La Religion chinoise* (Paris: Librairie Fischbacher, 1889), p. 670.

48 Ricci, *op. cit.*, I, 494 and II, 390.

49 Alvarez Semedo, *Histoire universelle de la Chine*. Trad. nouvellement en françois (Lyons: P. Prost, 1667), p. 326.

50 *Eminent Chinese of the Ch'ing Period*, ed. by Arthur W. Hummel, 2 vols. (Washington: Library of Congress, U.S. Government Printing Office, 1943–1944). Cf. Vol. II, " Yang Lien."

51 *Histoire de ce qui s'est passé en royaumes d'Ethiopie, en l'année 1626, jusqu'au mois de mars 1627, et de la Chine, de l'année 1625 jusques en février de 1625. Tirées des lettres addressées au R. Père Général de la Compagnie de Iesus*. Tr. de l'italien en français par un Père de la même Compagnie (Paris: Sebastian Cramoisy, 1679).

52 Dunne, *op. cit.*, p. 599.

53 *Sinica Franciscana* (Collegium S. Bonaventurae, 1929–1936), II, 225 f., " Relación del viaje al Reino de la Gran China."

54 *Ibid.*, III, 90, " Relationes et Epistolas Fratrum Minorum."

55 *Ibid.*, II, 250.

56 Dunne, *op. cit.*, pp. 438 f.

57 *Ibid.*, p. 405.

58 *Variétés sinologiques*, No. 58.

59 Otto Maas, *Die Wiedereröffnung der Franziskanermission in China in der Neuzeit* (Münster in Westfalen: Aschendorff, 1926). Cf. p. 125.

60 *The Tso Shu: Hsi-yang hsinfa li-hsu*. A Collection of Memorials and Petitions to the Emperor with His Responses. 4 vols.

61 Johann Adam Schall von Bell, *Historica relatio de ortu et progressu fidei orthodoxa e in regno Chinensi per missionarios Societatis Jesu ab anno 1581 usque ad annum 1669* (Ratisbonae: August Jenckwitz, 1672), p. 114.

62 Alfons Vath, *Johann Adam Schall von Bell, Missioner in China, kaiserliche Astronom und Rategeber am Hofe von Peking, 1592–1666* (Koln: J. P. Bochem, 1933), p. 159.

63 Jan Nieuhoff, *Le Voyage des ambassadeurs de la Compagnie Hollandoise des Indes Orientales vers le Grand Chan de Tartarie et extrait du voyage des Hollandois envoyez les années 1650 et 1657 en qualité d'ambassadeurs vers l'empereur des Tartares, maintenant maistre de la Chine*. Tr. M. Thevenot (Paris: Moette, 1696).

64 *Ibid.*

65 Vath, *Missioner in China*, p. 159.

66 *Ibid.*

67 Seraphin Convreur, *Choix de documents, lettres officielles, proclamations, édits, memori-*

aux, inscriptions (Ho-kien-fou: Mission Catholique, 1901), p. 635.
68 *Eminent Chinese,* Vol. I.
69 *Ibid.,* Vol. II, " Yang Kuang-hsien."

70 *The Chinese Recorder* (1929), p. 14.
71 *Ibid.*
72 Jean-Marie Sédès, *op. cit.,* pp. 34, 35.
73 Goodrich, *op. cit.,* p. 224.

CHAPTER V

1 *The Chinese Recorder* (1929), pp. 254, 255.
2 Maurice Collis, *Foreign Mud* (London: Faber & Faber, Ltd., 1950; Knopf, N.Y.), intro.
3 William Milne, *Restrospect of the First Ten Years of the Protestant Mission to China* (Malacca: Anglo-Chinese Press, 1820), pp. 334–338.
4 *China Centenary Mission Conference Records* (New York: American Tract Society, 1907).
5 William Ernest Hocking, *Permanence and Change in Church and Mission,* address at conference of Modern Missions Movement, Rochester Theological Seminary, 1935. Privately published (Chicago: Modern Missions Movement, 1935).
6 Collis, *op. cit.*
7 Morse and MacNair, *op. cit.*
8 Collis, *op. cit.,* p. 76.
9 *Ibid.,* pp. 31–33.
10 *Ibid.,* pp. 213, 214.
11 *The Chinese Repository,* ed. by Robert Morrison (Canton: 1839), I, 234.
12 Hansard. Cf. " The Opium Debate," *Parliamentary Debates,* Vols. 52–54.
13 R. J. Cruikshank, *Charles Dickens and Early Victorian England* (New York: Chanticleer Press, Inc., 1949).

14 Latourette, *The Chinese.*
15 *The Chinese Recorder* (July, 1930), LXI, 403–408.
16 *Ibid.,* p. 409.
17 Cf. Morse and MacNair, *op. cit.*
18 *Eminent Chinese,* p. 361.
19 Latourette, *The Chinese.*
20 *United Nations Series, China.* Cf. Chapter XIX.
21 Jean-Marie Sédès, *op. cit.*
22 *The Chinese Recorder* (July, 1930). Cf. " The Negotiations Leading to the Missionary Rights in the Sino-American Treaty," by Padelford, LXI, 443 f.
23 Arthur H. Smith, *China in Convulsion.* Cf. Vol. I, Chapter IV.
24 *Ibid.,* Vol. I, Chapter V.
25 *Ibid.,* I, 49.
26 *The Chinese Recorder* (November, 1899).
27 Memorandum of Tsung Li-yamen to French Government.
28 *The Chinese Recorder* (February, 1895). Cf. article by Noyes, " Five Storms of Wrath."
29 A. H. Smith, *China in Convulsion,* I, 58.
30 S. Wells Williams, *op. cit.,* II, 463 f.
31 A. H. Smith, *China in Convulsion,* I, 133 f.
32 J. C. P. Bland and E. T. Backhouse, *China Under the*

Empress Dowager (Philadelphia: J. B. Lippincott Company, 1910).

33 Morse and MacNair, *op. cit.*

34 Cf. A. H. Smith, *China in Convulsion;* E. H. Edwards, *Fire and Sword in Shansi* (Edinburgh and London: Oliphant Anderson and Ferrier, 1903); Marshall Broomhall, *Martyred Missionaries of the China Inland Mission with a Record of the Perils and Sufferings of Those Who Escaped* (London: China Inland Mission, 1901).

35 Edwards, *op. cit.*

36 A. H. Smith, *China in Convulsion,* II, 729.

37 *Ibid.,* pp. 734, 735.

38 *The Chinese Recorder* (1930), p. 441.

39 *Ibid.,* p. 447.

40 Johnston, *op. cit.*

41 *Edinburgh Reports. Report of the International Missionary Conference, 1910* (London and New York: International Missionary Council), VII, 95 f.

42 Johnston, *op. cit.*

43 *United Nations Series, China,* IX, 129.

44 Latourette, *The Chinese.*

45 *The Chinese Repository,* editorial by Robert Morrison (May, 1832).

46 A. H. Smith, *China in Convulsion.*

47 Cf. Gustav Warneck, *Modern Missions and Culture,* tr. by Thomas Smith (Edinburgh: James Gemmell, 1888).

48 This hymn by Bishop Reginald Heber is found in most hymnals.

49 Y. C. Yang, *op. cit.,* pp. 18 f.

50 William H. P. Faunce, *The Social Aspects of Foreign Missions* (New York: Missionary Education Movement, 1914), p. 103.

51 Wilhelm Pauck, *The Heritage of the Reformation* (Boston: The Beacon Press, 1950), p. 115.

CHAPTER VI

1 *Cambridge Medieval History,* VII, 319 f. and 791.

2 *The Christian Century* (January, 1933).

3 Sun Yat-sen, *San Min Chu I — The Three Principles of the People's Livelihood,* tr. by Frank W. Price (Shang-hai: Institute of Pacific Relations, 1927).

4 Leonard Shih-lien Hsu, *Sun Yat Sen, His Political and Social Ideals,* trans. and annoted by L. S. Hsu (University of Southern California Press, 1933), p. 43.

5 *The New York Times* (June 24, 1949).

6 L. M. Outerbridge, "The Transformation of Religious Concepts in North China" (Unpublished Master's dissertation, Divinity School, University of Chicago, 1933).

7 *Ssu Shu — The Four Classics,* XX, 70.

8 *China* (July, 1913), pp. 662 f.

9 Moule, *The Chinese People* (London: 1914).

10 Johnston, *op. cit.*

11 *Ibid.*

12 *Peking Daily News* (August 27, 1913).

13 Johnston, *op. cit.*

14 T. F. Romig, "The Agony of China," in *World Faith in Action,* ed. by C. T. Leber (New York: Bobbs-Merrill Company, Inc., 1951), p. 182.

15 Morse and MacNair, *op. cit.*

16 *Ibid.,* p. 670.

17 Johnston, *op. cit.*

18 Wen Han-kiang, *The Chinese Student Movement,* p. 104.

19 Department of State, *United States Relations with China* (Washington: U.S. Government Printing Office, 1949). Cf. Annex 33, p. 519.

20 *Ibid.*

21 *United Nations Series, China,* X, 151.

22 *U. S. Relations with China,* Chapter VIII, No. 185, pp. 1042–1054.

23 Herbert Owen Chapman, *The Chinese Revolution, 1926–1927* (London: Constable & Co., 1928).

24 *Ibid.*

25 *U. S. Relations with China.* Cf. "Letter of Transmittal," pp. vii–xii.

26 *U. S. Relations with China,* pp. 99, 100.

27 *Ibid.,* p. 116.

28 *Ibid.* Cf. Annex 33, pp. 518, 519.

29 *Ibid.,* IV, 113.

30 *Ibid.* Cf. pp. 113 and 519.

31 *Ibid.,* IV, 116 f.

32 *Ibid.,* p. 117.

33 *Ibid.,* p. 114; and *Time,* Vol. LIX, No. 6, Feb. 11, 1952, p. 36.

34 *Ibid.,* p. 115.

35 *Ibid.,* Chap. VIII, Annex No. 185, pp. 1042–1054.

36 *Ibid.,* p. 173.

37 *Ibid.,* pp. 132–214.

38 *Ibid.,* pp. 1042 f.

39 *South China Sunday Post* (January 1, 1950).

40 *South China Sunday Post* (January 1, 1950).

CHAPTER VII

1 *The Chinese Recorder* (1929), pp. 276 and 611.

2 "News Release," International al Missionary Council (New York: July 14, 1933).

3 *The Church* (Shang-hai: The Church of Christ in China), February, 1950.

4 *Hongkong Standard* (January 6, 1951), III, 5.

5 *Monthly Report* (Shang-hai: December, 1949).

6 *The Journal of the North China Branch of the Royal Asiatic Society* (1933). Cf. article by M. Freeman, LXIV, 70.

7 *The Chinese Recorder* (1926), p. 292.

8 *Ibid.,* LX, 254, 255.

9 *University of Chicago Round Table* (December 23, 1951), 717:17.

10 *The Chinese Recorder* (1929), LX, 17.

11 *Report of the Fenchow Station, Shansi* (1914).

12 Hocking, *Living Religions.*

13 Temple, *Essays,* p. 173.

14 Johnston, *op. cit.,* p. 235.

15 *The University of Toronto Quarterly* (October, 1934). Cf. article by William Temple, "Back to Unity," p. 19.

16 *The Church* (Shang-hai: December, 1949).

[17] *The United Church Observer* (Toronto: May 15, 1950), p. 14.

[18] *Monthly Report* (Shang-hai: December, 1949); *The Christian Century* (March 29, 1950), p. 398.

[19] Mao Tse-tung, *New Democracy* (Shang-hai: Rapid Current Publishing Company, 1949).

[20] *Ibid.*, p. 52.

[21] *The Church in Red China.* Collection of notes from many missionaries, published in Hong-kong, 1950.

[22] Mao Tse-tung, *On People's Democratic Dictatorship* (Peking: New China News Agency, 1949), pp. 15 f.

[23] Earl H. Ballou, *Peiping Bulletin*, No. 23, privately printed.

[24] Cf. *The Christian Century* (February 25, 1950), p. 242.

[25] Dr. H. S. G. Garven, Glasgow University, in a statement to the author (December, 1949).

[26] *Canadian Far Eastern News Letter.* Cf. Willmott's " News Notes from West China."

[27] Outerbridge, *The Lost Churches of China*, Ph.D. thesis, University of Chicago library, Appendix I.

[28] Appendixes 4 and 5.

[29] Appendix 1.

[30] *The Christian Century* (March 2 and September 14, 1949), Vol. 66, pp. 265 and 1066.

[31] *T'ien Feng* (Tien-tsin: May 4, 1950); *Kung Pao* (Shanghai: June, 1950); *New China News Agency* (Pe-king: May 29, 1950), Appendix 3.

[32] Outerbridge, *The Lost Churches of China*, Ph.D. thesis, University of Chicago library, Appendix H.

[33] *The United Church Observer* (February 15, 1951).

[34] *Ta Kung Pao* (Hong-kong, April 24, 1951).

[35] *Ibid.* (April 27, 1950), and Appendix 4.

[36] *T'ien Feng* (May 8, 1951), and Appendix 5.

[37] Cf. *The Church* (Feb., 1950).

[38] Appendix 5.

[39] Associated Press (Hong-kong, June 21, 1951).

[40] *The Chicago Tribune* (June 4, 1951).

[41] *Ibid.* (July 17, 1951).

[42] *China Missionary Bulletin, cum Approbatione Ecclesiastica* (Hong-kong: 1950), II, iii, 264.

[43] *Ibid.*, p. 258.

[44] *The New York Times* (July 28, 1951).

[45] *The Chicago Tribune* (March 18, 1951).

[46] *Ibid.* (April 13, 1951).

[47] *Time* (Aug. 20, 1951), p. 40.

[48] *Chicago Daily News*, May 8, 1952. Statistics released by China committee of the Foreign Missions Division of the National Council of the Churches of Christ in the U.S.A. Also cf. *Life*, May 19, 1952, pp. 51–55.

[49] *The Sun-Times*, Chicago, June 1, 1952, also cf. *Time*, April 7, 1952.

[50] Cf. *Re-thinking Missions*, ed. by William Ernest Hocking (New York: Harper & Brothers, 1933), Chapter III.

CONCLUSION

1 Wen Han-kiang, *The Chinese Student Movement*, p. 73.
2 Dr. Hugh S. G. Garven, Glasgow University, in letter to author (December, 1949).
3 Toynbee, *op. cit.*, p. 348.
4 *Scottish Journal of Theology* (March, 1951), Vol. IV, No. 1. Cf. article by Florovsky.
5 *Christianity and Crisis* (January 23, 1950).
6 Cf. Appendixes 2, 3, 4, and 5.
7 Appendix 3.
8 H. Butterfield, *Christianity and History* (New York: Charles Scribner's Sons, 1950), p. 113.
9 Joachim Wach, *Sociology of Religion* (Chicago: University of Chicago Press, 1943), pp. 380, 381.
10 Cf. Appendixes 1, 2, 3, 4, 5.
11 Cf. Appendix 3.
12 *Time*, special section on China (June 18, 1951).
13 *The Christian Century* (August 15, 1951), ed., p. 934.
14 Wach, *Sociology of Religion*, p. 378.
15 Related to the author and quoted in *The Missionary Herald*, Vol. CXVII.
16 *The British Weekly* (March 30, 1933).
17 William Temple, *Nature, Man and God* (London: Macmillan and Co., Ltd., 1935).
18 Henry Knox Sherrill, Presiding Bishop of the Protestant Episcopal Church in the United States of America.
19 Arthur Marmorstein, *Studies in Jewish Theology*, ed. by J. Rabbinowitz and M. S. Lew (London: Oxford University Press, 1950), p. 117.
20 Léon Weiger, *Histoire des croyances. Chine moderne*, 10 vols. (Hsien-hsien: Mission Catholique, 1920–1932).
21 William Temple, *The Hope of a New World* (London: Student Christian Movement, 1940), pp. 22 f.
22 *Laymen's Foreign Missions Inquiry. Regional Reports of the Commission of Appraisal. China*, ed. by Orville A. Petty (New York: Harper & Brothers, 1933). Cf. introduction by Rufus M. Jones, "Objectives of Protestant Missions."
23 Hocking, *Permanence and Change.*
24 Harold Hoeffding, *The Philosophy of Religion.* Tr. from German by B. E. Meyer (London: Macmillan & Co. Ltd., 1906).
25 Morgan, *op. cit.*
26 *Laymen's Foreign Missions Inquiry. Regional Reports. China.* Cf. Rufus M. Jones, II, xi.
27 Hocking, *Permanence and Change.*
28 Daniel J. Fleming, *op. cit.*, p. 171.
29 Mohandas K. Gandhi, *The Mahatma and the Missionary*, edited by Clifford Manshardt (Chicago: Henry Regnery Co., 1949).